Love in the Elephant Tent

How Running Away with the Circus Brought Me Home

Kathleen Cremonesi

ECW Press

To anyone who has ever felt like
a square peg in a round world.

For all the girls with turbulent minds
and untamed hearts who danced by
themselves when no one asked.

And with great respect for the animals,
men, and women who sacrificed their
freedom, health, happiness, or lives for
"the show that must go on."

Some names and personal details have been changed to protect privacy. The names of public figures have not been changed, excluding one that would have caused confusion with another person in the book. Individuals who were not instrumental to the story have been left out. On occasion, time has been condensed. While some quotes are verbatim, other portions of dialogue have been recreated to help the reader share my experiences as I remember them.

Memory, in my opinion, is like a sunset. We see it so clearly from our vantage point at the time, and the most striking ones seem to sear themselves into our minds. But view that same sunset from another angle, a few moments later, or through the lenses of our individual lives, and it will likely appear, and be remembered, differently.

I cannot speak for the memory of others; I cannot know their truths. I know only my own, and the following pages represent my truth.

The trouble is,
if you don't risk anything,
you risk even more.

— Erica Jong

PROLOGUE

NOMADS

Spain, 1988

"Come," he said, reaching for my hand as we ducked under the wall of canvas.

Sunlight penetrated the white roof of the elephant tent, illuminating the interior with a warm, peaceful glow. Down the line of swinging trunks and bobbing heads, animals shifted their weight from foot to foot, swaying rhythmically as if dream-marching in place. I inhaled the musky animal scent and felt far away from the chaotic realm of the traveling circus.

The tip of an elephant trunk, pink and moist as a pig's snout, appeared in front of my eyes. With the finger-like protrusion on the end of her trunk, the elephant studied me. She inhaled, and it felt like someone turned a vacuum cleaner on in my face. She exhaled. Wet fermented air whooshed past me. Her trunk brushed over my ear and tickled its way along my neck, leaving a wake of goosebumps. I giggled and stepped into her touch. The elephant sniffed my clothing, paused at my waist, and then continued on to my shoes before swinging her trunk away.

Stefano, the handsome Italian elephant keeper I'd met just hours earlier, towed me along as he worked his way down the line greeting each animal in a deep, gentle voice. "*Ciao*, Raya. Hello, Mary. You been good girl today, Lola? And how about you, Gooli? *Hola*, Bambi. Yes, and hello to you too, Kama. How my beautiful girls are doing?"

A flap of pink-edged ears, a tractor-like grumble, a mousy squeal, the lowering of a knobby head—each of the six animals returned his greeting in her own way. The troupe of Asian elephants loosely filled one long side of the tent; their presence overwhelmed the entire space.

I stood wide-eyed, transfixed by their swaying. "Why do they all move that way," I asked, "rocking back and forth?"

"Elephants are nomads. They supposed to keep moving. To roam free. Get what they need and move on, not be chained to a circus." Stefano's green eyes revealed his distress. "Whether I am here or not, these animals will be, so I do what I can to see they are cared for," he said, stepping toward an elephant.

Mary, her head the size of an armchair, towered eight feet in the air. Her eyes were pools of mahogany, her skin cracked, desert earth. I touched it. Stiff whiskers raked my palm as I stroked her jaw. Next to Mary's ear, coarse gray skin softened to a freckled pink. Stefano watched from over my shoulder as the elephant sniffed my clothing, my hair. Her huge pupil followed me while I caressed her jowl and traced the furrows beneath her eye. When I let my hand fall to my side, Mary looped her trunk under my wrist. I stiffened. Stefano, his hands on my hips, his warm breath on my neck, reassured me from behind.

My bracelets tinkled as Mary raised my arm to her eye. From behind thick-lashed lids, she stared not at my hand, but at my face. I heard her whooshing breath, smelled her animal scent, felt her craggy skin against my own. Mary held onto my wrist, moving with me as I drew my fingertip up past her eye and then down to her mouth. I leaned back against Stefano. His touch aroused me. Hers thrilled me. Between the two, I could barely breathe.

CHAPTER ONE

OUT THE DOOR

I grew up in the wing of an old motel. Rooms five, six, seven, and eight had been lifted from their foundation in Eugene, Oregon, transplanted into the nearby woods, and modified barely enough to be called a house. The previous owners had turned one bathroom into a kitchen, leaving the plastic-curtained shower stall intact to serve as the pantry, and walled over a second bathroom to hide the toilet in the living room. I can still see the little red plaque nailed to my parents' bedroom door. *Checkout time is 12 noon. Please be sure to remove all belongings.*

There are times when I wonder if spending my teenage years within walls that had once rattled with thousands of comings and goings contributed to the transience that consumed my young adult life. In a home with four front doors, how could a family plant roots and allow them to grow?

My father checked out first, in some ways years before he actually packed his cigarettes and his tools and walked out the door.

My siblings didn't last long, either. At seventeen, my sister began her trek up and down the West Coast, seeking stability in a handful of boyfriends and husbands. One of my brothers abandoned college to travel the Midwest, living out of a car, selling Bibles to believers, earning meals by memorizing random excerpts of a book he'd never read. My other brother spread his twenties across the world's military bases. He found home in a helmet and a gun.

Brothers and sister gone, father remarried, mother working—by my senior year in high school, our motel-home felt hollow, and I spent 1983 filling that void. More. Farther. Wilder. Higher. Fast paces and far-flung places. I chased the anticipation of *what comes next?* And each exercise in excess took me another step further away from everything I'd ever known.

College in California saved me from small-town Oregon, but school sufficed only until I discovered Grateful Dead–style emancipation. Hopscotching across the States in my Volkswagen bus, I followed the music, followed the fun. The kaleidoscope of the Dead was as much about becoming one with the music and one with each other as it was about being different from everyone else. Tour after tour, we traveled thousands of miles by bus, car, plane, or thumb until we reached the next concert and let out one big home-again sigh. Home, where everything we needed—meals, tickets to the show, customers to purchase our goods—seemed to be ready and waiting, and a few hours of selling my hand-woven beaded jewelry usually provided enough for me to live on and travel.

Within days, we'd be back on the road, like some psychedelic gumball rally, prodding our jalopies toward the next town.

Seeing the same faces over and over around the country built a sense of community that drew me into the Grateful Dead experience; it is also what pushed me away. After eighteen months, tie-dyed dreadlocks and glow-in-the-dark leggings became predictable and ordinary, satiated became saturated, marvelous became monotonous. I had to move on. So I traded my fringed leather vest and paisley silk gauchos for a button-down blouse and navy linen skirt to earn traveling money working at a bank. These weren't blind costume changes. I was running as if my future depended on it. Underneath that button-down blouse, I was giddy. Intoxicated with possibility, intoxicated with life. And then, in the fall of 1988, I loaded my backpack, bought an open-ended plane ticket to Amsterdam, and lit out in search of destiny and a damn good time.

Strange languages, blue money, ornate buildings, and tight, steep staircases. For two weeks, I explored Amsterdam, the land where prostitutes fill windows and marijuana fills menus. I followed narrow streets and canals through mazes of tall skinny houses, and in the world-famous red light district, where pastel hues spill onto the sidewalk through plate-glass windows, I giggled and grimaced past displays of rubbery sex toys, Long Dong Silver videos, and colorful brothels. The gussied-up, showcased women made me think of Barbie dolls lined up in a toy store display—except these dollies struck lewd poses and had nipples poking through their brassieres.

I felt like Dorothy in Oz. Amsterdam's confluence of long-hairs, skinheads, and everything in between was as close as I could get to being on the road without going anywhere, but I was a weathervane subject to the prevailing wind. By late

October, the prevailing wind was a cold and rainy gale from the north.

The only person I knew on the entire continent was Beth, a woman from home who had a soft spot for musicians. Last I'd heard, she was in Amsterdam—though with no phone and no address. I was lucky enough to learn from some street musicians that she frequented a particular bar. When we finally connected, her freckled cheeks and smiling blue eyes warmed me like a mug of tea. Beth's "home" was a squat called The Island, a cluster of old warehouses and bohemian shelters that housed both temporary and career travelers, as well as the homeless.

It was there at The Island where I met Colin, the street performer who would spur me into my southbound journey when he looked down at me from under the rain-soaked rim of his blue woolen hat and asked in a haughty English accent, "Well, Yankee, can you bang a tambourine and ask for money?"

Studying the juggling clubs that poked through the ripped seam of Colin's rucksack, I realized that nothing about this man ignited a romantic spark or even intrigued me. In fact, his winning quality was that he seemed perfectly harmless. Besides, traveling with him and his fellow buskers could open doors. I knew my $1,200 in savings would never last a year in Europe, and eventually I would have to work. But not any job would do. After four months of strangling myself in respectable clothing in San Francisco's financial district, I'd had enough dress codes and alarm clocks to last a long time. Between baton-twirling, cheerleading, school plays, and community theater, I'd been hauling myself onto stages since I was six, when my siblings and I sang "This Land is My Land" for a school talent show. Joining a performing troupe was right up my alley.

Colin and I, plus his mandolin-playing best friend and an

Irish woman, set our sights on Perpignan, France—the place Salvador Dalí once called the center of the universe. During the weeks the four of us traveled together, we busked only twice and earned but a few dollars each time. Colin ended up $100 in my debt and had no way to repay it. Perhaps that's why his idea of hooking up with a group of English gypsies following the orange harvest through northeastern Spain sounded like a good plan. My father would call trading hard labor for five bucks a day character building. Not me. An entire continent lay in wait, and I wanted to be on the road. But I needed the money Colin had borrowed, so I moved into a converted Bella Vega bus to pick oranges with my fellow buskers, a few English travelers, and the lovely Jennifer.

Jennifer wasn't her real name, and Jennifer wasn't really a her. The morning she found us at a labor cooperative, Jennifer was dressed like a normal Spanish teenage boy—tight jeans, tight shirt, and slicked back hair. I saw him migrating toward our eccentric entourage from the far side of the crowd. Each step Jennifer took became more effeminate, as if he sauntered through a sex-warp. When Jennifer reached us, he was a she. By dusk, she'd moved onto the bus with her few clothes, a makeup bag, and her gaff—the handy little panty that makes clothed male genitalia indistinguishable from female. Jennifer's hot temper, outlandish behavior, and wacky sense of humor kept me laughing, and I admired her sense of self. Together we picked oranges, cooked communal meals, and grew weary of our crowded living conditions.

Things changed when Colin's new girlfriend and his mandolin-playing buddy from our busking crew were arrested for indecent exposure. Though his unpaid debt had alienated Colin from me over the past weeks, I still wished I could have said something to ease his pain, but no such words existed.

His best friend was caught screwing his girl in the middle of town, and that was that.

This cuckolding set Colin and me on a parallel path once more—both determined to get off the bus. One afternoon in early December, he ran into camp with the rest of the money he owed me in his outstretched hand. "Yank. Yank. Couldn't wait—" He bent over, trying to catch his breath as he pushed a wad of *pesetas* at me. "Circus," he finally said. "There's a circus in town, and we're joining up. I'm going to juggle, and you're going to . . . to . . ."

I looked down at the map spread in front of me and tapped my finger on Portugal. I'd been planning my departure for over a week and had no intention of including Colin. "Not a chance."

"But it's such a *brilliant* idea."

Brilliant? Colin had not turned out to be harmless after all. Was this circus idea as brilliant as when he'd stranded me in Belgium with a groping truck driver who mistook himself for Casanova? As brilliant as when we'd joined these bus-living, ragtag misfits to pick oranges in the Catalonian groves? Or as brilliant as when he had deserted me in a Spanish bar after I'd passed out on my birthday?

Colin pleaded, said he couldn't speak the language worth a damn and that if I didn't use what Spanish I knew to translate for him, he'd end up cleaning bathrooms instead of juggling in the ring. Acting as though foreign soil weakened my footing, I had tagged along with others' harebrained plans since I left Amsterdam. Why not peek behind the velvet curtains? As with everything in life, I could always walk—or run—away. I asked Jennifer to come too, but she said her life already felt like a freak show and saw no reason to make it her profession.

And so, on a warm evening in Villarreal, Spain, Colin and I

followed trumpets, whoops, and hollers down a dirt road. Rings of twirling lights and shimmering flags crowned the big top, and the words *Super Circo Magico* radiated garish pink light.

Colin beamed like a man who'd finally found a place worthy of his talents. "It's beautiful, Kathleen, don't you think?"

"*Magico*," I said, observing the burnt out bulbs on the light strands cascading from the tent's peaks to its tethers. "Just *magico*."

"Come on, Yank. Haven't you always wanted to be a part of this?"

I couldn't recall ever seeing a circus before, much less wanting to be a part of one.

A teenager standing at the entrance to the big top greeted us. His ill-fitting red jacket with its rows of tarnished brass buttons reminded me of a high school band uniform—passed down for generations, mistreated by all who'd worn it. When I told him in Spanish that we wanted work, the boy hollered toward the ticket booth. Inside, a slick-looking man cocked his head, smoothed his gelled-in-place ponytail, straightened his black suit, and strolled over. His gaze traveled down my paisley hippie dress, paused on the silver bangles decorating my wrists, paused even longer on the toe rings peeking out of my well-worn Birkenstock sandals. Colin lifted his shoulders until he reached his full six-foot-two while the ticket man took inventory of the worn-through knees of Colin's jeans, his torn and stained T-shirt, and the tattered collection of woven bracelets on his wrists. The show was in progress, and we couldn't talk to the boss until intermission, Slick explained, shooing us into the tent with a promise to find us at the right time.

Inside the big top, four massive steel columns stretched up past the trapeze swings to the peaks of the tent. Odors of perfume, popcorn, and animal mingled in the humid air.

Two clowns pretending to perform acrobatic feats skipped around the ring wearing gigantic shoes, oversized pants, and red suspenders. Comical hats, ten sizes too small, balanced precariously on their bright wigs. The bleachers bounced with laughter as Colin and I climbed to a couple of empty seats.

Eyes fused to the show, Colin clapped and whistled and stomped his feet to the big band music. Images flashed in my mind. *Kathleen in a clown costume.* I wondered if working here might even be fun. *Kathleen on the trapeze.* Be realistic. *Kathleen in an old band uniform.*

The lights dimmed, and a man with sparkling red coattails announced the next number. Exotic flute music floated out of the darkness. Beams of light revealed gyrating girls in Egyptian headdresses, gold brassieres, and miniskirts. Catcalls and whistles sailed through the tent until the girls ran out and the lights rose to show a menagerie of metal crates. To the rhythm of tribal drums, a gray-haired man sporting a stretchy gold jumpsuit opened the cages that filled the ring. Two snakes slithered from one enclosure onto the dirt floor; a small crocodile crawled from another. Young children hid behind mothers. Older ones edged in for closer looks. Don Serpiente prowled the ring, parading his reptiles for the captivated audience and spiraling a snake as thick as his thigh around his body until he nearly disappeared behind its scales.

Kathleen in a boa constrictor?

Workers hauled cages away as the lights faded. A drum rolled in the dark, and the crowd simmered with expectation. Women struggled to keep screeching children seated. Colin was perched so far forward, a nudge would have toppled him. Six girls rushed in for a quick dance until blaring horns drowned out their music. Spotlights swirled, the drapes flew open, and six elephants burst in. The audience exploded. The passive zoo elephants I'd seen in my youth did not prepare me for the raw energy blasting from the ring.

A baton-waving man at the edge of the ring barked commands, his silver suspenders stretched over his belly to hold up sparkling trousers. Another man—young, dark-haired, and handsome in his blue dress shirt—swiveled his broad shoulders between elephants, urging one forward, directing another back. Royal blue flared from the sequined seams of his black pants as he twisted and turned in a fearless dance among the beasts. The elephants, as if oblivious of their own weight, performed headstands and danced a two-step. They balanced on one foot and marched on their hind legs. Trumpeters blew their hearts out, and spectators *oohed* and *aahed* during the fifteen-minute show. I spied on the boy in blue.

Kathleen in the elephant trainer's arms?

"Yank—" Colin pointed to the ticket man who was waving us down from the bleachers.

As the animals exited the ring, Slick led us under the stands and out through a split in the side of the tent. His jutting hand stopped Colin and me in our tracks as the six elephants hurtled toward us. A gust of animal-scented air tickled my cheeks while the creatures surged past.

We wove through a maze of tired trucks and scruffy campers before stopping in front of a shiny white trailer as long as a school bus. When Slick rapped on the door, a window curtain parted, and a chubby-faced man stared out. His gaze wandered past Colin and landed on me. I looked away, down the row of trailers with their racks of drying laundry and clog-cluttered door mats.

"That goon still looking?"

Colin nodded. "Right at your bum."

Chubby Cheeks was still peering from the window when the

older man from the elephant act finally came to the door. Silver suspenders hung at his sides. Flesh-toned greasepaint settled in his wrinkles and stained the towel cloaking his shoulders. His smirk, plastic and practiced, looked drawn onto his face.

He studied me with the same vigilance. When he spoke, Colin interrupted.

"Sí, sí, sí." Colin pointed to himself, repeating one of the few Spanish words he knew. "*Sí, sí, sí,*" he said again before asking, "What's he saying, Yank?"

"You just told him you can dance in high heels on dirt."

Colin gasped. "Did you tell him I juggle?"

"Mi amigo es un . . . un . . ." High school Spanish hadn't taught me the word for juggler. *"Quiere trabajar como un . . ."* I pointed to Colin, who'd launched into miming his juggling act.

"Sí, sí, sí." Colin mimed his act again. "Me good juggler. Me make you lots of money. M-O-N-E-Y."

The man at the window and the few circus people who'd wandered over laughed. Colin laughed too, not realizing, perhaps, that the joke was on him.

The boss's painted face grew stern. "I have a *malabarista.* If he comes back in the morning, your friend will work as all my men do. You," he said, "will be a dancing girl."

A dancing girl? A cleavage-flashing, pelvis-gyrating, miniskirt-wearing dancing girl?

Colin tugged on my arm. "He wants me to juggle, right?"

"Wrong." I translated everything except the part about Colin being welcome only if I came too.

"Wait 'til he sees me perform," Colin said. "So what if they make me work for a few days?"

I shuffled through the tawdry faces of the show folks in bathrobes, cummerbunds, and sequined bustiers that had gathered around us at the camper door, halfway looking for a bearded woman or a serpent-skinned man. Maybe a boy in blue.

What did I know about the circus? Joining would be impulsive. Reckless. Any prudent person would balk at the idea, but at twenty-three, I had no such inhibitions.

When I look at pictures from those times, I see a girl whose gaze pierces the camera from behind an untamed curl. Her eyes say, *Why* wouldn't *I run away with the circus?*

I wonder if running away was the prize or the price of her freedom.

CHAPTER TWO

THE BOY IN BLUE

Men yelled. Engines belched. A truck rumbled past spewing black fumes. The previous evening, this dusty lot in northeastern Spain had exploded with elephants, trumpets, and showgirls. Only a circle of worn dirt marked where the big top had towered, and the circus's allure seemed to have faded with the spotlights. I teetered at the edge of the emptying field, squinting into the morning sun. But I was hungry for adventure and hungry for a new direction, so I took a deep breath and hauled my full-sized backpack into the commotion of machines and men.

The boss inspected Colin and me by the light of day. Speaking to my breasts, he explained how I'd dance at night and work in the cafeteria by day.

"But I don't cook," I told him in Spanish.

"You'll learn," he said and pointed to the far side of the

lot. "Wait in that car. The driver is the only one who speaks English."

Colin and I settled into the tattered seats of a white Citroën and watched workers maneuver great blue rolls of tent onto waiting trucks. A camper bumped and creaked past us, fighting every inch of rough ground. Grit crept into the car and coated my clothes, my eyes, my tongue. I rolled up the windows and baked under the glare of the Spanish sun until Colin choked me out of the car by filling the small space with cigarette smoke.

Beyond some trucks and an acrid pile of manure, three elephants swatted flies, swinging their stiff tails like Chaplin swung his cane. Their droopy rear ends swayed in unison, back and forth, back and forth. The closest elephant observed my approach. Short black hairs covered the knobs on her immense head, and her ears were so pink, webs of blue veins showed through the skin. The elephant seemed docile and gentle and not at all like the animals I'd seen perform, but I kept my distance. She soon looked away, focusing instead on the heavy chain binding her, using her trunk to trace its path from her front foot to an eyebolt on the truck's side.

Hearing a commotion behind me, I turned to see a man tugging on a rope coming around the front of a nearby semi. Dark curls. Hazel eyes. Pink cheeks. A tank top and jeans that were once white. The boy in blue from last night looked like a naughty angel. A sheen of sweat highlighted the contours of his arms as he struggled with whatever pulled the rope in the opposite direction. A couple of curses later, a skittery zebra followed a cloud of dust into view.

I eased closer as he tethered the animal to the truck's bumper. In English, I asked, "Does it bite?"

The young man looked at me. His mouth twitched as if

he wanted to smile, but his cheeks never followed through. "Sometimes yes. Sometimes no," he said, and tromped away.

I wanted to pet the zebra, if only because he'd insinuated that I shouldn't. When I reached out, the zebra squealed, twisted his striped rear toward me, and kicked. I quickly swiped my finger along its side and scooted back to the Citroën.

Half an hour later, the naughty angel stuck his head in the driver's window. "I am Stefano," he announced, lighting a foul-smelling sausage of a cigarette. Thick smoke poured from his mouth.

"You're not bringing that in here, are you, Stefano?" I asked.

"My name is STE-fano," he corrected. "Not Ste-FA-no." He drummed his fingers on the roof of the car. "The cigarette, is a problem?"

"Listen to her once and she'll never give up," Colin called from the back as he tapped the packet of Drum tobacco in his pocket.

"Cigarettes kill, Colin, especially that stuff he's smoking."

"*Ducados*," Stefano said, "I smoke out here."

"Thanks. I'm Kathleen. Nice to meet you Ste—um, how do you say your name again?"

"STE-fano," he said. "STE-fano. Nice to meet you, Kat'leen."

"It's Kathleen," I corrected. "There's an H in the middle, after the T."

"Got it, a T and an H." He pulled on his cigarette and asked, "The zebra, she bites you, Kat'leen?"

I smiled and shook my head.

"Good, good." The corners of his mouth nudged dimples into his cheeks, and I couldn't help but smile back. Stefano pumped his cigarette a few times, tossed it, and climbed in. Maneuvering the car over ruts, around trash piles, and out of the lot, he glanced at me and said, "So you think you want to join the seer-coos." His voice sounded thick—a result, I figured, of the harsh tobacco he smoked. "And you," Stefano continued, twisting his rearview mirror so he could see Colin. "Boss says you're going to work with the *elefanti*. Is hard work, leetle money."

"Colin is me name." His voice sounded insipid compared to Stefano's. "Best of England and Wales right here in your car, mate." Colin leaned forward. "Actually, the elephants are only stepping stones for me."

Stefano looked confused.

"I juggle," Colin explained. "No way they'll have me working with animals once they see what I do with me clubs."

Stefano cleared his throat and swerved into the passing lane to get around two circus trucks, using the oncoming lane as if it were his own. "When you are ready to leave, you go. I keep working with my *elefanti*."

We drove through orange groves and sped past dusty coffee bars and two-building towns. Stefano played the road like a video game, whizzing in and out of traffic as if he could mitigate any mishap by inserting another coin. I averted my eyes and leaned my back against the door. Coastal wind ruffled my hair and morning sun warmed my shoulders. I studied the man beside me, enjoying the way his soft brown mane curled tighter and tighter as it swooped down his neck and the way his shadow of a beard emphasized the flush in his cheeks.

Stefano caught me staring. The playful bow of his lips affected his entire face, stretching his dimples and crinkling his eyes. "Tell me, how it happens that an *Americana* becomes a dancing girl in a Spanish circus?"

That story could have started two weeks earlier when I decided I had to get off the orange-pickers' bus, or two months earlier with my arrival in Amsterdam and the wild road trip that followed. Or maybe it started two years earlier when wanderlust tempted me out of my office job to follow the Grateful Dead. Perhaps the swinging-door façade of my family's motel-home flickered through my mind, but I did not dwell on those long-ago days. Wherever this journey had started, a Spanish circus was not my destination.

"By accident," I told him, rolling my shoulders. "I bought a one-year open-ended ticket to Europe and came looking for adventure. Amsterdam, Paris, Perpignan . . . and here I am."

"And here you are." Stefano grinned. "Sounds like the spirit of Cristoforo Colombo lives on in America. I should tell you—usually the zebra doesn't bite. Take-down is always a problem. Animals get nervous. Too much work, not enough workers. I am always in bad mood until is over."

Between Stefano's facial expressions and body movements, each sentence became a lyrical production. Watching him talk was easy; the difficulty lay in picking words out of his music. Apparently, understanding me was equally tricky for him.

"So where are you from?" I asked.

"What you say? Sewer-yifrum?"

I repeated my sentence, leaving pauses between the words.

"Oh. Where*ah*. Are*ah*. You*ah*. From*ah*. *Italia*," he said. "I am from *Italia*."

"Is that where you learned English?"

"Yes, but not from schoolbooks. Teachers and me do not get along. I have this Beatles book when I am growing up. One page is a song in English. The opposite page is same song in *Italiano*."

"The Beatles taught you English?"

"That and album covers. *Rubber Soul* is one of my favorites. Was born the same year I was, 1965."

"Me too. November '65." I liked that we had something in common, even if it was only our age.

"*Giugno* for me," he said. "You ever been to Italy?"

"Not yet. But a friend of mine will be in Rome next month, and I might meet her there."

"Best food in the world. You have Italian food in America?"

"All kinds. Pizza. Spaghettios."

"What is Spaghettios?"

"Little round things—" I formed my thumbs and forefingers into circles. "They come in a can with tomato sauce."

"Pasta does not come in a can." Stefano accelerated.

"Sure it does."

He glanced at the sky blue cigarette packet he'd tossed on the dash. "Pasta in a can?"

"In England too, mate," Colin said from the back.

The Italian dismissed our words with a flick of his hand. "Maybe your food is in a can, but is not pasta. The day you see Italy, you learn what *real* pasta is."

Twenty-five minutes and two cigarette stops later, we followed a slow train of circus vehicles into Sagunto. Elephants bellowed from inside their trucks. Stallions stomped and snorted, kicking their trailer's metal sides. Local children ran rampant through the field, squealing and peeking into animal carriers. From café tables that lined the surrounding streets, old men sipped drinks, smoked cigarettes, and surveyed the yelling, honking pandemonium. I stared out of the Citroën's windows, speechless.

Stefano tapped a drum roll on the steering wheel and then

climbed out of the car with a cigarette already in his mouth, its shredded leaves, blacker than black, coloring its tip.

"Is best you come with me," he suggested, and he soon had me filling water barrels while he backed six elephants out of their semis and chained them to the sides of their two trucks.

"Three meters," he told me as he rolled a barrel between two elephants. "Never come closer to them than three meters unless I am at your side."

Elephants ripped at the grass with curled trunks, stripping the ground around them. Green froth dribbled from their mouths, and the air smelled as sweet as a freshly mown lawn. From a safe distance, I filled their barrel, laughing each time one flipped up her trunk to intercept the spray. Colin unloaded tent pieces, stakes, poles, and sledgehammers off a truck. As the sun grew hot, sweat circles stained his shirt and droplets hung from the tip of his nose. When he collapsed onto a pile of canvas, Stefano called him to his feet.

"*Alzati*, Colin. Get up. Get up. Animals must be in the tent soon as possible."

Anni-moles. Possi-bowl. I stifled a laugh at Stefano's self-taught pronunciation.

Shoulders slumped and feet dragging, Colin helped Stefano unfold sections of tent until another worker dropped off three ham and cheese sandwiches.

Stefano watched me ease the pork out of my sandwich and dangle it from my thumb and forefinger. He asked, "What you doing with that?"

"Getting rid of it. I'm vegetarian."

Stefano clamped his bread around the meat and gobbled his sandwich as he hurried off. Moments later, he returned with two men. The lanky one with shifty eyes, dark bushy hair, and a strong body odor kept his distance; the other introduced himself as Ernesto. I shook his hand and thought that too many wrinkles lined Ernesto's kind face compared to his body's youthful appearance.

The four men laced tent sections together and pounded stakes. Colin struggled to keep up. The only time I'd seen his oafish body in perfect coordination was busking in Perpignan, when he'd spun his clubs through the air with the grace of a windmill. Here on the circus lot, he looked like a blindfolded kid playing pin the sledgehammer on the stake. Sure enough, the hammer soon ricocheted into his leg. Colin plunged to the ground, clutching his shin.

"Me leg," Colin cried while Ernesto felt for broken bones. *"It hurts."*

I couldn't understand the words Ernesto spoke to Stefano, but I understood the look. Though Colin hadn't done any real damage, he would be useless for the rest of the day. Stefano and Ernesto helped Colin to a straw bale and sent me to the kitchen for ice.

Fifteen minutes later, I pressed an ice pack against the hot red splotch spreading across Colin's calf. He hissed through gritted teeth and then looked at me with pet-store puppy eyes.

"What are we doing here, Yank?"

"You're going to juggle in a circus, and I'm going to dance," I said. "For as long as it's fun, anyway. I won't last long working in a kitchen."

I pressed one of Colin's hands against the ice pack and slipped away. The woman in the kitchen had said she'd been waiting for me all morning and expected me to return right away. Cutting through the center of the circus to get back there, I stepped from between two trucks into a large clearing and collided with a wall of dust and noise. Sledgehammers clanged against metal stakes. Forklifts clamored from one spot to another. Gears squealed and spit oil as they elevated the words *Super Circo Magico*. Fifty workers reassembled the big top so quickly, it reminded me of a child's pop-up book.

The kitchen occupied the rear of a small delivery truck, and an attached trailer functioned as the workers' cafeteria. The cook, Beata, a bleached-blonde Argentinean daughter of Neapolitan immigrants, welcomed me into her domain. Besides a commercial stainless steel sink, a dented white refrigerator, and a four-burner propane stove, the room was mostly countertops and cabinets. Wire shelves held an assortment of canned beans and fish, mismatched plates and cups, blackened pots and pans. From here, she made enough food to serve all the circus peons. Different food—better food—was prepared elsewhere for the owners, their family, and preferred staff.

"You know how to cook tomato sauce?" Beata asked in Spanish as she thunked a huge can of tomatoes onto the Formica.

I shook my head.

"Minestrone?"

I shook my head again.

"You know how to cook anything?" Beata's green eyes peered into mine.

I make a mean chocolate chip cookie, I started to say when a shadow in the doorway interrupted. The same chubby-faced man who had gawked at me from the boss's camper the previous night swaggered in. He walked around the room, slapping his palm on the countertop, picking up food cans and utensils, touching everything as if to mark it like a dog peeing on bushes. Shoulders spread and chin held high as if compensating for his squat stature, the man approached me and didn't stop until his round belly touched my arm. I jerked away. He repositioned himself inches from my side. I fled farther down the counter, keeping my can of tomatoes between us. When

Beata told him to get lost, he spewed a string of words at her that I couldn't understand. She scoffed. He laughed and swatted her on the behind as he strutted out.

"That animal is Guido, the boss's little brother," she told me. "Stay away from him."

"What did he say to upset you?"

"You shouldn't listen to what Guido says."

"What did he say?"

Beata rummaged through a utensil drawer. "That his brother hired you as a favor to him." She handed me a can opener. "He said you are here to warm his bed."

"You can't be serious." Guido gave me the heebie-jeebies. He couldn't have been more than five years older than I was, but he oozed so much slime that he must have been gathering it for years. I doubt Guido intended to come off as a creep—still, how could he think anyone would be attracted by that ridiculous performance? To a man whose haircut made him look goofy in the way only a bowl haircut can? I started to giggle, but Beata's wary look made me stutter to a stop.

On the far side of the lot, where I'd left an Englishman sobbing among tent pieces, I now found a blue and white elephant tent large enough to house a Bedouin tribe. Two main antennas vaulted its roof sixteen feet in the air. Fifty-eight poles were stuck through its perimeter, and taut ropes connecting the tips of the poles to stakes embedded in the ground kept the whole pavilion erect.

"What happened to helping Beata with dinner?" Stefano asked, hopping down from a supply truck. "Won't food make quicker if you are there?"

"She has it under control. Dinner will be ready in a few hours."

"*Cazzo, che fame.* Means *hangry*," he said.

"Angry? You're mad that dinner isn't ready?"

"Not mad. I mean *oongry*." Stefano patted his stomach.

"You mean *hun*-gry?"

"Oongry, hangry, uun-gry. I mean I need food."

"Then you definitely mean *hungry*."

"Yes. Very hungry." He dropped his cigarette and smothered it with his foot. "Come, come. I introduce you to all my girlfriends."

Soon, Mary had her trunk looped under my wrist as I traced the craggy grooves on her face. Steadied against Stefano's strong chest, deep into my heady exchange with the elephant, I didn't notice Colin limp into the tent. Mary's trunk fell away as Colin hobbled toward us.

"Ernesto keeps trying to tell me something about food," he said, "but I can't suss it out."

"Food?" Stefano's eyes lit. "Ahhh—the hay truck is finally here. Colin, come with me. Kat'leen—you stay here. All afternoon I am chasing kids away. They come back when they see me leave. Keep them out," he said as he walked out. "*Do not* go near the elephants. Not even Mary."

I pulled a few straw bales off a stack, pushed them together like a bed, and lay down. Chains shackling the elephants' ankles rattled with each side step they took. Beneath their feet, slabs of lumber bolted to steel joists supported four tons of rocking meat and bone. It was as if each animal had its own personal deck. Every so often, one of them would stretch her elastic trunk straight out toward me until it became long and thin. She'd snort the air, curl her trunk back toward her body, and then return to her swaying groove.

Opposite the elephants, six food buckets, three water drums, two coiled hoses, a box of folded rags, and the straw bales filled one corner of the tent; a broom, a rake, two pitchforks, and a shovel leaned against a wheelbarrow in the other corner. Tools, food, a rack of halogen lights, a battered tape deck, and six elephants—nothing extraneous, nothing out of place.

Soon, a tubby boy led a few kids into the tent. When I yelled, the children scrambled away amid a rush of laughter and squeals. Another kid lifted the side canvas. I jumped to my feet and yelled again. He crawled out as the first boy returned to the front door. These children wanted to play, scattering like pigeons then rushing back as soon as I turned away.

They reappeared at the opposite side—too close to the elephants. I sprinted toward them. An elephant trunk slammed into my head. Rough skin grated my face. I couldn't pull away, couldn't see. I shrieked and fought to free my head from the mass of muscle. The elephant jerked me toward her. Twisting and pulling, I dove out of her reach and landed in the dirt with a thud.

Stefano appeared above me. One hand wriggled under my head, his other brushed a lock of hair from my stinging face.

I pointed to the elephant with wisps of my curls still in her grip. "She tried to kill me!"

"Your cheek is red," he whispered, "and some blood is on your nose. But if an elephant want to kill you, she does. There are no tries."

Stefano helped me to my feet and drew me in her direction. I pulled away.

"Stand up to her now or she will hurt you again." The opposite side of the tent beckoned, yet Stefano held me with his eyes. He said, "Trust me, Kat'leen."

At that point in my life, I didn't trust anyone, especially

not a man I'd just met. But the elephants trusted him. Perhaps that's why I clutched Stefano's hand and stepped toward the animal who had just assaulted me.

"BAMBI," Stefano bellowed. "BAMBI." The elephant squealed and lowered her head. "What you want, international incident? Next thing you know the Americans drop bombs on us.

"She hurts me too," Stefano said, "when I first come to the circus. Beat me so hard she almost breaks my back. Now, she understand I care and she respect me. We respect each other."

Stefano guided my hand toward the elephant's head. Bambi lifted her trunk to my face. I clenched my teeth and steadied myself against Stefano until Bambi dropped her trunk and rejoined the others swaying. Stefano sat me on the straw-bale bed and dabbed blood from my nose with the hem of his tank top. I watched his eyes shift from my nose to my eyes. Felt his hand slip from my shoulder to my waist. His breath on my lips. I leaned in—

"Hey, Yank," Colin called from the doorway. "You have any more ice here?"

"Colin. Hi. Ice? No."

"Where is that kitchen anyway?" Colin mumbled as he limped away.

"What name he calls you?"

"Yank."

I could see Stefano sifting through his English vocabulary. "As in pull?"

"No, as in doodle-dandy."

"What?"

"I should help him find the kitchen."

"Yes," Stefano called after me. "And I'm sure Beata needs you."

Rather than have us dine inside a cafeteria crowded with twenty male coworkers, Beata set up a small table outside for Stefano and me. Colin had refused dinner, preferring the relative solace of the elephant tent to nurse his aching leg. Other workers razzed Stefano when he asked Beata for a candle, but he shrugged off their jeers, explaining that he didn't like to eat without really seeing his food.

Stefano watched me scoop noodles with my fork, fit what I could in my mouth, and bite off the rest. "No wonder they make spaghetti round in America. You will finish with many pieces and no way to pick them up. Watch."

Stefano lifted a few noodles with a single tine and coiled them around his fork. I tried to follow his example, slurping and laughing my way through mouthfuls of spaghetti without biting off any bits while Stefano inhaled his pork chop and then dove into mine.

"What about the way you eat?" I asked. "It's like you haven't seen food for days."

"Is my mother's fault. Whole time I grew up she was in hurry to go to work. All I remember is her saying, 'Come on, come on. Time to get you to Grandma's house. Eat, eat. Faster, faster.'" He stabbed a few chunks of meat and ate them in his strange and noisy way—keeping his lips just far enough apart to breathe through his mouth and still chew.

"Ever tried pausing between mouthfuls to breathe?"

"Waste of time." Stefano polished off the last of my pork chop, exhaled, and leaned back in his chair. "I try to quit the meat once," he told me, "when I first come to this circus. I do it for the animals. I eat so much frozen fish and pork chops the first week I'm here, I thought stopping was going to be easy. Then pasta and lettuce and beans is all I eat for days. I almost die from the hunger." Stefano's eyes paused on my half-full bowl of pasta. "You eating that?"

A yell from within the cafeteria turned our heads. The other worker who'd helped set up the elephant tent stomped down the cafeteria stairs, his gaze stopping on Stefano and me before he disappeared between two trucks. Stefano reeled in my leftovers, eating and breathing and speaking all at once as he told the man's tale.

"Zoltan is the French man who care for the horses. Never washes himself or his clothes. Nobody wants to eat near the stink. Story is he gets into a car accident with his fiancée. She dies. He lives. One day he walks into the circus looking for work, but is wearing expensive clothes and nobody take him seriously." Stefano shrugged. "Crazy Zoltan. His body is here but not his head. Like after his love dies he wants to escape from life, so he come to the circus. Is almost the same thing."

On that first night in the circus, I must have understood that while Zoltan may have come to the circus to escape his pain, I had come to play. And I must have wondered about Stefano's reasons for being there. I doubt I saw a man drenching himself in the circus in an attempt to wash away his past.

Candlelight flickered across Stefano's face as he spoke, highlighting his long, straight nose. Even with the cafeteria ruckus a few feet away, and trailers, trucks, and tents closing in around us, the expanse of sapphire sky above made me feel as if no one else existed. I wanted to crawl right over the table and claim the kiss I'd come so close to earlier.

Instead, pots and pans clattered onto the kitchen floor. Beata screeched, "*Dishes, dishes. Everywhere dishes. Kathleen —*"

Stefano piled his plates on mine. "And I have a show to get ready for."

Halfway through clean up, Guido came to check on me. "You watch out for him," Beata warned after she shooed him away. "I am sure he has plans for you. I am also sure he did not expect you to fall for Stefano."

"How can I fall for anyone?" I shot back at her. "I'm just passing through." But my smile refused to hide.

Beata pinched my arm. When I'd first spotted her petite body in a fuchsia tank top and racy short-shorts earlier that afternoon, I guessed she was in her thirties. That night, huddling together and giggling like schoolgirls as we worked, I noticed the crow's feet her long lashes almost hid and the gray, unbleached roots of her hair. Part mamma, part confidante, Beata nudged me toward the door. "Go to him," she said, and she didn't mean Guido.

The air inside the tent felt warm and moist, and the row of halogen lights draped the back wall in elephantine silhouettes. As the night's last acts wrapped up in the big top, Stefano pitched straw for the elephants' beds.

From the platform of straw bales, I watched Stefano sing to Raya as he piled her deck with straw, noticed how she twisted and turned her trunk around him, playing with his hair and his clothes as he worked. I'd always thought puppies had the unique power to make a guy look cute, but I'd never seen an elephant flirt with a man.

And what a man. Simple. Soulful. One who looks you in the eye when he speaks to you. A man of extremes, either singing or cussing while he works. Brawny and sensitive. Sensual and . . .

I forced myself to look around the tent. Anywhere but at him. "Colin?" I asked, noticing his backpack and mine leaning against the tent's side wall.

"Sleeping in a truck."

Sleep. A bed. The day's excitement had overshadowed the more mundane concerns of life on the road. There's no such thing as dating when you're living out of a backpack. During my years following the Dead around the States, I'd learned that the road accelerates relationships, and getting pulled into or pushed out of someone's life is as easy as flicking through channels on the TV, as risk-free as spouting your problems to a taxi driver. That might have been my excuse, anyway, if asked why I wanted to sleep in the arms of a man I'd met only that morning.

As the noise outside the tent quieted down, Raya lowered herself onto one knee and let her body sink into the fluffy straw until her belly nestled against wood. When she heaved herself onto one side, the planks beneath her creaked until her body stopped rocking. Her side ballooned with each heavy breath. Whhhaaaaaahhh shhhwuuuuuuhhh. Whhhaaaaaahhh shhhwuuuuuuhhh. Bambi and Gooli settled next. The other three stayed on their feet, eating. Stefano cleaned his tools and stowed them in the corner before unplugging the halogens, leaving only the soft light of a low-hanging bulb.

"This is my favorite time in the circus," Stefano said, sitting next to me on the straw bales. "Shut the tent, shut some light, and close the rest of the world outside."

"How did you end up here?" I asked.

"Is nothing too exciting." Stefano's fingers, strong and vibrant, animated his story. "I travel to Spain with a friend, but we have no money." Inviting, perfectly formed lips sculpted his words. "We want to get to Morocco, so we look for work and find the circus." Warmth radiated from his voice, his eyes, his body. "I ask to work with the animals." Stefano moved closer. "My friend is supposed to work on the big top crew, but he hates it. One week, and he is gone." His finger touched one of mine, tracing its outline, over the knuckle, around the nail. "I stay. Now, a year later, I am responsible for the elephants and . . .

"I like your spirit," he said. "Your freedom."

His mouth reached for mine. I couldn't kiss him slowly or quickly enough. My head grew light as I inhaled the earthy smell of animal and straw fusing in the warm air. Stefano's fingers grazed my skin as he eased aside the neckline of my dress to kiss my collarbone. I stopped breathing. Waiting. Wanting.

He whispered, "Ever made love in an elephant tent?"

"What if someone walks in?" I asked, even as I gathered the sleeping bag and blanket from my pack and spread them on the straw.

Stefano laced the tent's entry shut. "No one gets through this closed door unless I choose to open it."

He embraced me from behind. Lips on my skin, dress on the ground—we toppled onto the blanket and tangled together, arching into each other as we held onto the moment. Held onto each other. And when our bodies stilled, I lingered on top of him. Whispers and kisses lasted only until our touching and holding aroused us again.

Finally, we lay still. Our breath grew quiet, easing toward the serene rhythm of sleeping elephants. With the glow from the nightlight illuminating the curves of our nakedness, Stefano turned my face toward his and trailed his thumb across my lower lip. In the shadowy light, I saw him smile. He pulled the sleeping bag over us and drifted to sleep with a leg curled protectively over mine, the weight of his arm across my chest.

All the elephants except Mary were lying down. She seemed to be standing guard, and it filled me with a sense of security, as if this powerful creature had my back. I closed my eyes and listened to elephant lungs inhale monsoons of air. Then quiet. Air rushed from their bodies as they exhaled. Whhhaaaaaahhh shhhwuuuuuuhhh. Whhhaaaaaahhh shhhwuuuuuuhhh. Their breathing nearly drowned out the last sounds of the circus going to sleep outside.

CHAPTER THREE
LETTING GO

December 6, 1988, Sagunto, Spain: Elephants and elephant boys.
Telling myself this enchantment is okay.
It only has to be real for this very second of this very day.

I closed my journal as Stefano crouched in front of the straw bale I sat on. "We're twins," I said, noticing his black tank top and blue jeans. Earlier that morning, he'd been working outside the tent, and I'd unknowingly dressed in the same combination. Dark curls, his short and mine just past my shoulders, completed the picture.

He touched the two ornate silver hoops on one of my ears and said, "You give me one of those and we really be twins. Trade you for mine?"

Stefano unclasped a silver band from his ear, latched it through the newly emptied hole in mine, and then rested his hands on my shoulders. His touch warmed me like the Spanish sun.

I pushed his curls aside and clasped my hoop in his ear. It was a simple exchange, nothing more than a loop of silver, but it left me catching my breath. Something that was part of me for many years was now a part of him.

"I have a plan," he said. "Meet me behind the kitchen after breakfast."

Stefano showed up with two hairy black arms clamped around his neck. Dark eyes peeked over his shoulder. "Careful." Stefano closed his fingers over mine as I reached for the chimp. "Paco bites."

The monkey wrinkled his nose and sniffed my hand, studying my silver bangles before returning his curious gaze to my face. I followed his green collar and chain leash to the strap that looped Stefano's wrist.

Stefano pointed to a rocky hillside behind the circus. "Locals say there are ruins of a *castello* up there, so we go exploring. I will get in trouble for taking Paco, but even a monkey needs to escape the circus sometimes."

Two hours later, a chorus of yelling voices greeted our return. Guido jabbed the air as he bellowed at Stefano. I wondered if his anger stemmed from Stefano taking the monkey or taking me.

Helga, Guido's sister, whisked me toward the costume trailer, explaining that I had to replace an ill dancer. Following her up the stairs into the bright lights of the costume trailer, I said, "But I don't know the dances yet."

"Watch the others. When their hands go up, your hands

go up." She rolled a stool out from under the makeup bench and motioned for me to sit. "When they stop dancing, you stop dancing." Helga unloaded creams and powders from a drawer and began to apply them to my face. "It's simple."

It did not sound simple to me. Sure, I'd tap danced as a child, twirled baton in my teens, and bounced around as a cheerleader in high school, but I'd always been . . . rhythmically challenged. Psychedelic gyrations at 100 or so Grateful Dead shows would not help me here.

In the mirror, I watched Helga press fake lashes onto my lids. I hadn't worn makeup in years, and back when I had, it never looked like this. A wide swash of blue shadow stretched temple to temple, barely skipping the bridge of my nose. Blackened brows arched over obscene lashes. Bright red puddles on my cheeks matched the gooey lipstick that fused my lips and filled my mouth with an awful taste. Half Groucho Marx. Half Gypsy Rose Lee. I didn't know whether to laugh or cry.

Helga flipped through the costume rack, pulling pieces out and holding them against my body before lengthening straps with bits of elastic and shortening hems with safety pins. A few minutes into my fitting, the door flew open. Moments earlier, Guido would have found me bare breasted with a blue spangled miniskirt barely over my bottom. He said a few words to his sister and disappeared. I never acknowledged his presence.

Soon, Helga turned her attention to some wooden boxes stacked in the shadows at the back of the trailer. She brushed the dust from one case and slid its lid off to reveal a rhinestone bikini and feathered headdress. I fingered the scarlet quills. Definitely Gypsy Rose Lee.

Once dressed in the costume, I stared at my reflection, watching the rhinestones sparkle in the lights, looking at the curve of my bare belly. I couldn't wear this in public. I wasn't fat, or even heavy. Maybe thick. But someone had designed this outfit for a skinny woman with no boobs. My 36Cs pooched out of the glittering cups like scoops of ice cream, and the hooks that held the heavy costume onto my body seemed terribly inadequate. Helga fastened the headdress over my tangles and snapped matching cuffs on my wrists. Then she handed me a pair of red-sequined heels. My very own ruby slippers.

"Yes, yes." She stared at my image in the mirror. "Now you are a dancing girl."

A whirlwind of flashing lights, loud music, and revolving costumes whooshed me through the afternoon. I barely kept from twisting my ankles on the ring's soft dirt floor as I scrambled after the other girls in five-minute bosom-and-belly-button interludes. For the opening parade, I clapped my hands, kicked my feet, and hopped on toes jammed into three-inch heels during an improvised rendition of the Tarantella, and then I dashed back out of the ring with the others while dodging an incoming stallion. Ten minutes later, we waited backstage in silver bikinis and capes, ready for the sword-swallower's introduction. One woman attempted to explain the dance, but my limited Spanish did not include such words as *sashay* and *pirouette*.

Before performing in the elephants' introduction, I found a few minutes to pause. From the steps leading out of the dressing room, I watched Stefano weave in and out of the arriving elephants. His commands resonated with authority and tenderness, understanding and respect. The mix of power, courage, and reverence awed me. When I left this circus, and certainly I would leave, I would miss this man.

Moments later, I danced in the sparkly blue miniskirt and top under swirling spotlights. Sweat turned my makeup into paste, and the shoes wore welts into my feet until we rushed out through one curtain and the elephants rushed in through another. The crowd erupted. I grabbed my robe and crept under the grandstand to watch. In his blue dress shirt, Stefano hustled underfoot as the four-ton animals twirled and stomped and careened around the ring.

Intermission began right after the elephants, and Stefano soon reappeared with Bambi in tow. Parents willing to pay for a picture escorted children into the ring so one of the showgirls could take a Polaroid of them on top of the elephant. While stagehands constructed a lion cage behind them, Stefano worked his way through the line, elevating frightened children onto Bambi's back with a father's tenderness. And with Stefano nearby, the elephant that had attacked me the day before—and him a year earlier—was as gentle as her namesake.

The lion number began after intermission, and I returned to the dressing room to prepare for my red-feathered finale. Minutes after the afternoon show ended, we started the whole thing over again for the evening crowd. After the last dance, I finally scrubbed my face, slipped back into the soft cotton paisley of the one dress I'd brought to Europe, and headed for the elephant tent.

Steps from its entryway, I heard Colin scream. He lay crumpled on the dirt floor, his arms wrapped around his legs.

"Look what they've done!" He pulled two flattened plastic juggling clubs from under his body. Another club lay at Kama's feet. "I've got nothing. *Nothing.*" His voice accelerated from self-pity to anger. "Those buggers!" Colin waved a mangled club in the air and charged Kama.

"Colin! No!"

The elephant reared as far as her chains allowed and landed with a great thud. Colin, stopping inches short of her reach, battered the air around her as if swinging at a piñata. Kama lunged at him, snorted, and slapped her trunk against the wood of her deck, which screeched under her shifting weight. Colin hurled one of his clubs, smacking Kama in the forehead. The elephant bellowed and strained to reach him.

Stefano raced into the tent. He tackled Colin and pinned him to the ground. Then Stefano turned his attention to Kama, calming the animal and kicking wrecked clubs out of her reach.

Colin pulled himself up and gathered his things in the vacant way one gathers scorched memories from a home that has gone up in flames. I tried to talk to him, but he had nothing to say. The juggler lumbered away from the circus with his pack in one hand, his useless clubs in the other. I never considered going with him.

The following morning, when Stefano knelt at my side and touched his lips to my cheek, I turned the other cheek. He kissed me again. Giggling, I pointed to my forehead. Stefano made a row of kisses along my hairline. He kissed one eyelid and then the other, the tip of my nose and my chin. I snuggled deeper into the warmth of my sleeping bag and listened to the early morning sounds of the elephant troupe—swishing hay and billowing breaths, the soft clinking of chains as they swayed. If not for Stefano, I imagined I'd be waking up in a tiny worker's bunk. Despite my years living in a VW bus, the thought made me feel as claustrophobic as this thirty-by-fifty-foot tent must have felt for six elephants.

"Wake up, wake up." He brushed a stray curl from my face. "Time to open the tent, and only Kat'leen is still sleeping."

At first I had tried to teach Stefano the correct way to say my name, but his attempts at pronouncing the *th* in Kathleen made him sound like a wheezing asthmatic. Besides, Kat'LEEN sounded purposeful and dedicated. Passionate. I'd already quit correcting him. It had taken me two days, but I had finally managed to pronounce his name properly by reminding myself that Stefano had the same cadence as Stephanie.

All six elephants stood, chomping their breakfasts, swaying like water trapped in a wave pool. I pulled on clothes and lounged against the rolled sleeping bag and blanket to watch the elephants finish their breakfast. Lola reminded me of a curious child. She kept poking her trunk into Gooli's mouth as if checking to see whether the other elephant had eaten anything interesting. Gooli twisted her head and pushed Lola, who then swung around and tried to stick her trunk into Mary's mouth. Paying no attention, Mary continued curling brown hay in her trunk and plunging it between her jaws.

Stefano stopped hauling wheelbarrows of soiled straw and steaming dung to roll a fifty-gallon plastic barrel in front of the first two elephants. As soon as he dropped a hose into it and left the tent, Raya lifted the hose from the barrel and stuck it in her mouth. Water dribbled down her chin when Stefano turned the tap on.

"Raya!" The elephant dropped the hose back in the barrel, but not before spraying her head with the stream of water. "Every time. Raya loves the water even more than the others." Stefano sat next to me on the straw bales. He pinched his bottom lip a few times and then reached out and twirled a lock of my hair around his finger like a corkscrew.

People can often be characterized by their physical attributes—the corpulent man with the strong laugh that lives large, or the hot-tempered redhead who rages through life as if her head were on fire. Perhaps I would be defined by the Shirley Temple ringlets that frame my face. They can be cheeky and fun or breezy and brazen. Sometimes they are loud and get in the way. My curls are unruly and un-ruled; they do not often do as they're told. They are likely to wind around a lover's finger, tickle an elephant's nose, or get under a superior's skin. Attempt to corral them with a good brushing, and they become a halo of Medusa spirals fighting for their freedom, capable of spitting poison or turning onlookers to stone.

If I were to define Stefano by a single physical trait, I would choose his heart. It beats faster than normal. In his teens, Stefano's heart beat so furiously it drove him into tachycardia. His doctors discovered an extra pathway, a shortcut between the atria and ventricles. Fitting for a man who seeks only the most direct route. Mimicking the tempo of his heart, Stefano spins through life with a gyroscopic force that keeps him traveling upright and true and honest. I would come to learn that this honesty is Stefano's defining behavioral trait. I have yet to see him fake an emotion.

When Stefano slipped his finger from my curl, he caught my eyes and said, "I'm glad you didn't leave with Colin."

His declaration surprised me. Not because of what he said—I'd been thinking the same thing. Stefano surprised me because he put his emotions into words and lay them out for all to see. I wouldn't—couldn't—do that.

"I thought Colin was your man," Stefano continued.

"When I saw you standing next to him that first night, asking for work outside the boss's trailer . . ."

"You were there?"

"I heard talk about the gypsy girl. Wanted to see for myself."

I chuckled. "There was never anything between Colin and me."

What I didn't say was that there had never been anything significant between any man and me.

CHAPTER FOUR

HOLDING ON

December 8, 1988, Sagunto, Spain: Morning after next, the circus leaves for another town. Three days ago, I came to the circus. Now, I will be going with it.

And him.

The roof of the elephant tent glowed with bold, midday light. *Songs of Thought,* a compilation a friend had made for me the previous year, one of only two cassette tapes that had earned a place in my backpack, played in the background. "Tupelo Honey" faded and Neil Young's "Long May You Run" filled the tent.

I liked this after-lunch siesta hour, the time of day when everything slowed down, when the whole circus seemed to take a communal breath—unless Helga insisted on dragging me out of the tent for another dance practice. Since I was finally able to keep up with the other girls after four performances, I hoped she wouldn't. Preparations for the shows began at three p.m., and besides a trip or two to the closest bar for coffee, beer, or Moskovskaya, Stefano's favorite vodka, the rest of the day buzzed with activity. Makeup. First show. Dinner prep. Fix makeup. A hurried meal. Half of the second show. Wash dishes. Fix makeup again. Then, at last, the finale. While Stefano put the elephants to bed, I stripped off rhinestones and blue eye shadow. By midnight, we would be back inside our laced-up elephant tent, snuggled in each other's arms.

But on that afternoon, having just begun our after-lunch break, we lay side by side on our straw-bale bed, listening to music. When I stashed the journal I'd been writing in back in my pack, my address book slipped out.

"Can I see that?" Stefano took the green booklet from my hand and picked up my pen. He flipped to the inside back cover and began writing. He asked, "How you spell 'hert'?"

"Hurt? H-U-R—"

"No, 'Hert.'"

"Heart?"

"Herrrrrrrt." Stefano threw his hands in the air.

"Um . . . hearth?"

"HEARRRRRRRTT." Forming his outstretched arms into a circle over his head, he said, "The planet, Kat'leen, the planet. HERT."

I struggled not to laugh. "You mean 'earth.' You're putting an H where it doesn't belong."

"There's no H?"

"Not at the beginning. Try E-A-R-T-H."

Stefano wrote the word in my address book and crinkled his brow. "You sure?" He humphed at my nod and handed the booklet back. I glanced over his name, street, town, country, continent, and planet written in careful block letters. Stefano usually scrawled his name, and he scrawled it everywhere. In the tent, he'd used thick black ink to autograph food buckets, water tubs, and pitchfork handles. I'd seen him scribble it on bar napkins and scratch it in the dirt at the castle, as if here in Spain, in this place of permanence where rock walls last for centuries and heroes forever, Stefano needed proof of his presence.

"Now you won't forget me," he said as I tucked the book away.

"No, I won't forget you. Neither will half of Spain."

"Not quite half." His shoulders rolled forward, following his downward gaze. Stefano scratched at the nubby woolen blanket with a rough-edged fingernail before he focused once more on me. "But everyone up and down the Costa Brava knows I been here—you want to see? Where we been, where we going, everything?"

He led me past the horse tent to the edge of the lot where a row of thirty-five-foot railcars bordered the iron fence surrounding the circus. Five pairs of metal steps and doors lined one side of each wagon. We walked through the door marked "Stefano" and into a seven-by-eight-foot "sleeper." Bunk beds consumed half of the room; a nightstand and the two of us filled the rest. Most workers—called *galoppini,* which seemed fitting since they always had to run—used their lunch break to catch up on sleep. Stefano's roommate snored from the top bunk. In an adjacent room, someone farted.

Stefano kicked discarded shoes and clothes out of our way and pointed to his roommate, suggesting the mess was his. After smoothing the bottom bunk's blanket, Stefano sat down and pulled a small red backpack from underneath the bed. Piece by piece, he emptied his folded things onto the pillow. A sweat-stained suede vest, a felted red beret, one T-shirt, a pair of royal blue shorts, a crimson sweater, and a shabby gray coat; besides the clothing he wore, yesterday's clothing strung up to dry in the elephant tent, and the tattered map he fished out of the bottom of the backpack, these were his worldly possessions.

While Stefano studied his map, I studied the collection of seagull drawings tacked to the pressed-wood paneling. His signature claimed each one.

"Nice seagulls."

He flashed me a homemade seagull tattoo on the back of his left hand. "*Gabbiano* in Italian," he said. "I like seagulls. Their freedom."

"Me too," I said, and repeated the word *gabbiano* under my breath. "I read *Jonathan Livingston Seagull* right before I left the States. It's about this bird who feels different from his flock. He can't accept the limits they conform to, so he flies out on his own to find himself."

"I read that book." Stefano looked up from the map and smiled. "Was good that he find himself."

"Yeah." I squeezed in beside him on the bottom bunk. *Jonathan also discovered that there were others like him.*

"Look," he said, tapping his finger on the map. "There is Villarreal, where we meet. And this dot is Sagunto, where we are now. Maybe two more leetle towns around here and then is Valencia for *Natale*—Chreees-mus."

The holiday would arrive in two and a half weeks. Nineteen-eighty-eight would be the first Christmas since I'd left Oregon at seventeen that I wouldn't return home. While I flitted around Spain in my tank top and cutoffs, my family would trek through our five-acre backyard in parkas and rubber boots for our annual Felling of the Yule, searching out the perfect tree with my grandfather following, ax in hand. All these years later, I can still smell the freshly cut fir boughs . . . Mom's sugar cookies baking in the oven . . .

Sitting beside me on his bunk, Stefano traced his strong fingers over bygone routes he'd traveled through Spain. I leaned closer until I felt the warmth from his skin on mine. Four days. I'd known this man—this tender daredevil of a man, poor in possessions but rich with passion—for only four days. And yet, the simple fact that he sat beside me eased a 6,000-mile longing for my family.

That evening, Stefano prepared to move to the next town, packing little things away first, such as the rags he used to polish the elephants' headdresses and the lights he wouldn't need the next day.

"Any chance you want to go buy me cigarettes?" Stefano asked at one point, tossing his empty packet into a pile of manure.

"That will never happen."

He smiled. Not his usual grin that engaged his entire face, but one that barely lifted the corners of his mouth.

"Don't you hear how they turn your voice all abrasive? Think what they're doing to your lungs. I'll never buy you cigarettes for as long as I know you, so don't bother asking. In fact, why don't you think about quitting?"

His smile flowed into the rest of his face as he said, "That will never happen."

The following morning, pitchforks and straw bales trickled out of the tent. By early afternoon, I locked my sleeping bag and backpack into the semi cab where Stefano and I would spend the night, and he packed food buckets and coiled hoses into trailers. Stefano nestled his girls into their haulers after their first performance, chaining them diagonally into place, three to a truck. Then the real dismantling began. Side walls went first, followed by stakes and poles and guy wires. Piece by piece, Stefano and Zoltan made the tent disappear. By the elephants' second performance, only a urine-soaked trench and a pile of soiled straw remained.

After Stefano watered his elephants, we slipped out of the circus. A block away, in a small courtyard beneath a cluster of apartments, we found a playground. He sat on a swing, and I straddled him, holding onto his shoulders as we swayed back and forth.

"Stefanoooooo," the circus boss beckoned from afar.

Stefano did not get up from the swing. He did not loosen his grip on my hips. He did not even flinch. Instead, he kissed me, a kiss both hard and soft, demanding and questioning. I answered him with all the want and need of a loner on the verge of discovering she'd actually been quite lonely.

"Stefanoooooo!" the boss called as we ducked into a cement play structure. "Stefanoooooo!" he called as we made love in the neighborhood sandbox. "Stefanoooooo!"

Late that night, we snuck back onto the circus grounds and slipped into the semi where we would sleep. The creaking metal and gentle shifting of the cab reminded me that only a few feet away, three elephants swayed in the darkened trailer, awaiting our morning departure. The elephant keeper's warm body spooned against my bare back. One muscular arm looped around my stomach holding me close, the other curled above my head. I reached under my makeshift pillow, found Stefano's fingers, and held on.

CHAPTER FIVE

ALL THAT GLITTERS

The next morning, I prepared the kitchen and cafeteria for travel—filling the sink with dishes and condiments, the oven with pots and pans. I shut gas lines and stashed chairs under tables, latched cupboards and slid window protectors into slots, knocked stabilizing blocks out from under the trailer and pushed two sets of metal steps into their cubbyholes. Dusty and sweaty, I went looking for wash water, only to find that they'd already dismantled the hose bibs that had dotted the circus lot.

En route to the next town, Stefano offered a pension owner a few *pesetas* for a shower. The water was only a dribble, but it was running and hot and private. The last few days, I'd bathed in a bucket of water barely warmed with Stefano's rudimentary plug-in heating element. Shared sponge baths in old cowboy movies ooze romance, but somewhere between the cast iron tub of a spaghetti western and a foot of lukewarm water in the bottom of an elephant's food bucket, the romance leaked out.

Publicity crews had passed through our next town weeks before us to plaster it with images of the famous Spanish clown who headlined the circus, so we paraded into Nules with the same fanfare as we had in Sagunto. Within twenty minutes, I lay under the cafeteria maneuvering stabilizing blocks back into place, just as dirty and sweaty as before my shower.

Stefano, Zoltan, and Ernesto finished raising the elephant tent soon after lunch. They moved on to the horse tent while I spent my siesta with the elephants, sprawled over a bale of straw. A stream of sunlight poured through a tear in the roof of the tent. Dust shimmered like glitter in the shaft of light, and I lay nearby in a dreamy state, watching the elephants pluck blade after blade of grass from the ground. Their great yellow teeth, bigger than hotdog buns and smoothed from years of use, would soon grind it into green mush. I lolled my head from side to side, following the elephants swaying hypnotically to the rhythm of their rattling shackles.

The chains circling one front and one back leg of each animal were bolted to stakes driven deep in the dirt. The elephants were perfectly capable of pulling up the stakes, and on occasion, they did—such as the time Mary had surrendered to the sweet smell of near-ripe fruit and wrenched her stakes from the ground, dragging them along as she feasted her way through a neighboring vineyard. Stefano had recounted how he'd come into the tent that morning to discover her missing. Scanning the nearby hillside, he'd spotted ears and a trunk over the vines one moment, the irate farmer, pitchfork in hand, dashing toward the elephant the next. Stefano never could have reached the two in time to keep either from injury. Fortunately, as if finally realizing the size of the beast, the farmer stopped twenty feet away from the elephant and settled for jabbing the air with the pitchfork and hurling obscenities. Mary, who hadn't seemed to notice the farmer, continued plundering as Stefano led her back to the tent.

One of the dancing girls interrupted my thoughts when she appeared in the tent's doorway saying, "So this is where you waste your time." Previously, the other *ballerine* had spoken to me only when explaining dances or commenting on the mistake I'd made choosing a laborer for a lover, and they made settling into this circus feel like nesting in a sticker bush. That day, the dancer tossed me a plastic sack and said, "You've been here a week. Time to dress like a woman."

Apparently, paisley dresses and worn Levi's made me look like something else.

A fuzzy pink sweater filled most of the sack. Beneath it, I found a pair of denim pants. Embroidered pink hearts decorated the elastic waistline and front pockets. The stretchy blue material would hug every curve as it narrowed to zippered, mid-calf hems. They weren't even *real* blue jeans.

The woman declared that Helga wanted me in the costume trailer and then turned away, her waist-length chestnut tresses spanking the air as she bounced away. I chucked the clothing aside before she made it out the door.

Inside the costume trailer, Helga handed me a bundle of beaded pink spandex to try on. "For the Christmas shows," she notified me. "You're going to ride an elephant."

An elephant? Excitement rippled through me. But at the same time, it needled me that someone had *assigned* me a job without asking my opinion. Ever since I'd quit my desk job two years ago, I'd lived by the motto *My life, my choice.* With someone trying to control what I wore and how I spent my time, working in a circus didn't seem all that different from working in an office. If the assignment were anything besides riding an elephant . . .

On my way back to the tent after the costume sizing, I heard a commotion and followed the noise. I worked my way through the gathering crowd to find Guido with a hose in hand and two men lashing crazy Zoltan to a fence.

"Merdoon!" Zoltan yelled his favorite cuss word (which I figured to be some bastardization of *merde*) and struggled against the ropes. *"Merdoon!"*

Stefano stood off to one side. He hushed my questions and said, "Guido washes Zoltan every few months when the smell gets real bad."

"I've smelled Zoltan," I told him. "That doesn't make it right to tie him up and hose him down."

"No, it doesn't."

"But you're not doing anything to stop it—which makes you a part of it."

"I can't stop Guido, but I can make sure he doesn't hurt Zoltan. At least when is done, Zoltan will sit still enough for me to shave him," Stefano added. "Is too hot that beard. He is always scratching at it, complaining." Turning to me, he said, "I think it makes him crazier, especially in summer."

Someone turned the hose on and the show began. Guido sudsed and scoured Zoltan, making no effort to keep the soap out of his eyes and mouth. He scrubbed the Frenchman's clothes with a horse's brush and then ordered two workers to strip the man to his underwear. "You like this?" Guido yelled at Zoltan. *"Te gusta?"*

Zoltan bellowed. He shrank from the brush as if it burned,

collapsing in on himself and glaring from under eyebrows so wild, they looked like they might fly off his face. Half the circus watched, encouraging Guido and smoking their cigarettes. Unwilling to witness Guido flaunt his power or Zoltan succumb to it, I left for the dressing room. It was early, but at least I'd be alone.

Plastering thick, peachy pancake over my skin as Helga usually did, I recalled Stefano's story about the Frenchman's auto accident and his fiancée's tragic death. I smeared blue above my eyes and applied fake black lashes. What if the acts of abandoning society and then losing himself in the circus had twisted into Zoltan's single strand of sanity?

Makeup finished, I returned to the elephant tent. Inside, Kama fussed with her chains, slapped her trunk on her deck. She eyeballed Zoltan, who slumped against a straw bale. Stefano knelt in front of him, scraping the Frenchman's face with a straight razor, speaking in hushed tones as if calming a frightened animal.

Zoltan glanced my way. Dark eyes contrasted the white shaving cream as starkly as Guido's treatment of this man contrasted Stefano's. I felt like an intruder.

When I returned twenty minutes later, I found Stefano carving his own stubble into a goatee.

"He trusts you," I said. "And he needs help."

"Zoltan doesn't want help." Stefano turned his gaze from his palm-sized mirror. "You seen the way he acts with Kama?"

"No, but I've seen how she acts around him."

"Kama hates Zoltan because he torments her. Doesn't really hurt her, just throws things at her, jabs her with sticks. Taunts her." Stefano sliced the razor through the air with each offense. "And no elephant besides Kama. Is part of Zoltan's insanity," he explained, turning back to the mirror. "He knows what he does is bad. He knows elephants hold grudges. And he knows Kama is meaner than all the elephants. Is why every time she's unchained, she tries to ram him with her trunk, smack him with the tail. Is a constant fight. One day, the elephant will kill him." Stefano looked over his shoulder at me and said, "I think that is what Zoltan wants."

I couldn't get Zoltan off my mind: Guido's bath, Stefano shaving him, Zoltan's death wish. This was business as usual for the circus. Although I found magic in their elephant tent, the ugliness lurking in their shadows churned my stomach like a stunt gone wrong. Waiting for the reptile number, I blocked out the poorly recorded violin screeching from the speakers and pulled against the itchy gold bikini binding my chest. Zoltan hadn't come here to hide or to survive; he'd come here to die. Emotionally? Physically? Twenty years later, I'm still not sure it made a difference to Zoltan. All he wanted was Out. He was bleeding to death, slowly, and neither he nor any one of us attempted to heal his wounds.

When the ring went dark, the other dancers and I piled our robes onto a backstage chair, scurried into the ring, and crouched in position. A single flute called in the darkness. Spotlights cast their beams, summoning us to our feet like cobras rising to their master. We undulated our arms on cue and gyrated in our gold lamé miniskirts. Wearing a counterfeit smile, I drew the pharaoh's headdress back and forth between my elbows in a poor Cleopatra imitation while stagehands lugged in reptile cages. Once the snake master stepped into the spotlight, the dancers rushed out.

Guido waited on the other side of the curtain. I ignored him and dug through the pile of robes for my own. Gone. The other women gathered theirs until the chair remained empty. When I asked Guido what happened to my robe, he just leered.

"Dónde está la bata, Guido?" I asked again.

Guido's swelling smile exposed child-sized teeth. Teeth so stubby they looked ground down, as if he spent his days gnawing on others' peace of mind. Pointing to his crotch, he said, in Spanish, "What you're looking for is right here."

During the rest of the show, Guido cupped his crotch each time he saw me. By the time the finale came around, I seethed from my feathered head to my sequined feet.

"Guido's pestering me," I ranted that night in bed, recounting the robe incident to Stefano as I massaged my feet. Welts from ill-fitting dancing shoes had long since turned to blisters.

"Is messing with me too, Kat'leen. Provoking me. Controlling what I do. Is only talk."

"In America they call it harassment."

"Is not America, Kat'leen. Is their kingdom. Trucks, animals, equipment—Guido's family owns everything. You don't like their rules, you leave, and you are lucky if they don't kick you in the ass on your way out." Stefano turned to me, his face serious. "You should know, is possible the boss hires you because Guido wants you for himself."

"Beata told me. What the hell does that creep do here anyway?"

"The big *testa di cazzo.* Head of dick."

I laughed. "Come on, what's Guido's job?"

"He pretends to help backstage, but only to sniff around the weemuns in leetle costumes. All Guido will ever be is second-in-command since his older brother will always come first."

I lay back down on our bed and watched the elephants sway. "Some of the people here are disgusting if you ask me."

"Most are." Stefano reached his arm around me and pulled me close. "But not Ernesto. He used to perform in a different circus with his own elephant until she gets a tooth infection." Stefano tapped his freshly shaved jaw. "Uses all his money to save her but she still dies. Ernesto loves these elephants, but he grows old before his time," Stefano said through a yawn. "Used to be the first to complain when animals or workers are mistreated. These days, he take his frustration to the bar."

"Why doesn't he just leave?"

"Is not so easy, Kat'leen." Stefano stared at the tent's ceiling, as if he'd find the right words up there. "The circus gives her people *just* enough shelter for them to think is better than the outside world. *Just* enough food to keep the starvation away. *Just* enough money for drink that they forget they are caged like animals."

I ran my fingers over the slick material of our sleeping bag, listened to the nylon swish beneath my nails as I handpicked my next words. "Are you caged?"

Stefano scoffed. "I go when I feel to. Is months I been saving a few *pesetas* each week. Some workers—like my roommate—they come to hide. Maybe they run from police or maybe they run from family. Or maybe they are like Zoltan, running from themselves."

I was running too—but I felt like I was running *toward* something rather than *away from* something. Seeking possibilities, not fighting for survival. Stefano made it sound as if there were nothing here worth finding, as if I were digging for gold in a steel mine.

Tracing the peace sign tattooed on his chest, I asked, "What are you running from?"

"I ran when I was a teenager," he said, "like your *gabbiano*, your Jonathan Seagull. My parents expect me to be different than I want to be. We always fight. I start working at fourteen just to get away. Their house is more like a shelter for me than a home. And then I leave . . ." Stefano's eyes seemed to blur. "Drift around for a while . . ." Then he shot his gaze back to me as if he'd snapped that memory shut. "But I am not running now." Stefano kissed me softly and settled into his pillow. "I been in this circus for one year, and I seen bad things happen, but not bad like I see living on the streets of *Milano*. Caring for these elephants gives me purpose. Makes me feel like I live truer."

Live truer? How could he live truer in a place that cultivated submission? A place where Guido exploited Zoltan. Where the circus exploited everyone. They treated us like property. When I tried to explain that through the example of Helga informing me that I'd ride an elephant in the Christmas shows rather than asking me, Stefano did not share my apprehension.

I don't know what I expected him to do. Had he told me to deal with it myself, I might have felt as though he didn't have my back. Had he offered to confront Guido, I might have told him I could take care of myself. Perhaps I didn't want him to stand in front of me or behind me. Perhaps I wanted him to stand at my side and endorse my do-anything be-anyone American sense of freedom.

But Stefano lay there without opening his eyes. He said, "Is the way they do things in the circus. One day the boss asks you a favor. Next day is your job. Your work gets bigger, but your pay never does. They squeeze you in the circus, Kat'leen, like a lemon in a grinder."

CHAPTER SIX

ELEPHANT RASH AND OTHER RISKS

In the dim backstage light, the circus boss sat at a small table among canvas-cloaked mirrors and drapes bound with ropes. One of the circus goons sat nearby, guarding piles of bills, eyeing each worker suspiciously. He handed over 5,000 *pesetas* when my turn came to receive my wages—just shy of fifty bucks for my first week's work. Grumbling earned me a reminder from the boss that he also provided my room and board.

"Actually, I live in a tent."

The boss looked up from his ledger. He and Guido could have been mistaken for twins if it weren't for the older brother's calculating eyes, for the shrewd set of his jaw that showed through his thinner features. "You going to run off like your friend?" he asked.

"Not yet."

A few days later, Stefano and I moved into an unoccupied step van. Though only a shell with a mattress, its spartan décor came with a preferable level of privacy—unlike the elephant tent, where Ernesto or Zoltan might have walked in at any time during the day. I questioned my intentions as I stacked my clothing beside Stefano's in the cardboard box we would use for a dresser. The circus had begun to feel narrow, static. And I knew better than to count on any lover holding my attention for long.

I hadn't come to Europe looking for men, though I certainly had looked for men in the past. Looked for men, found men, dumped men, been dumped by men. My early experiments had been like three-minute dance-floor interludes—sweat and swirling lights and the thump of a bass guitar that lasted only until the music stopped. Men were fun if you didn't get to know them too well and trouble when you did.

So what if I liked him?

December 16, 1988, Nules, Spain: Is this the place I'm supposed to be—traveling on such a slim line? Moving in space but not in mind?

Beata dropped handfuls of carrots, celery, and onions into the steel sink. "You know how to cook *ragù*?"

I eased away from the old white refrigerator I was leaning against. "I don't even know what *ragù* is."

"I knew the answer." Her thick cutting board clacked against the worn countertop when she set it beside me. "That's why I'm going to teach you. *Ragù* is special, and I cook it only once or twice a year."

Stefano had griped about how this kitchen served garbanzo beans almost every day, as a side dish for lunch and mixed in soup for dinner. He'd eaten little else besides frozen fish, pork chops, iceberg lettuce, beans, and pasta with tomato sauce this past year, and he called the boss's mother, who shopped for the food in her Mercedes and gold and furs, a cheap ass—even more so when it was time to buy food for the animals.

While I chopped vegetables, Beata poured a stream of oil into a heavy pot warming on the stove, filling the kitchen with the fruity scent of ripe olives. She added a chunk of butter and swirled pale yellow and golden green into one color with a wooden spoon. The bubbling oils popped and crackled as Beata added my chopped veggies. She handed me the spoon, transferred a hefty chunk of ground beef into a bowl, and began mashing it with two forks while explaining that doing so kept it tender.

In my opinion, meat was tough no matter what you did to it. Red blobs sizzled when she added them to the pot. I shrank from the odor of warming flesh, but Beata draped her arm across my shoulders and pulled me back. "You see that the red color is going away? It's time for the wine."

White wine turned the mixture into a bubbly mess. I stirred and stirred while she poured a glass of milk and set it next to the pot.

"Milk in tomato sauce?" I asked. "Are you sure?"

"If you don't know how to cook, then you don't know if you're supposed to add milk."

I appreciated Beata's effort to teach me the intricacies of making the perfect meat sauce, but I figured I'd never use the knowledge and would therefore soon forget it. I imagined my mother must have also attempted to teach me a culinary skill or two over the years, back when she'd had the chance, before my father's accident.

Once upon a time, before our family moved to Oregon in

1979, my mother embodied the Southern California version of June Cleaver—blonde, athletic, and educated. She devoted her mornings to earning her second college degree and afternoons to helping with homework, baking bread, or hauling her four children to baton lessons, spelling bees, and football games. Every night, picture perfect tuna casserole, eggs goldenrod, or chicken and dumplings graced our table. Betty Crocker would have been proud.

In those days, all six of us still played together. We flew kites on Glendale's Kite Hill, and we camped in Angeles National Forest, singing songs around the campfire while Mom played her guitar. One photograph in particular comes to mind: two boys in matching red, white, and blue T-shirts that Mom had sewn on her Singer; two girls in yellow sundresses; my mother wearing a matching dress and smiling affectionately at the camera—at my handsome father who held the camera.

Things changed when my father broke his back in 1972. Multiple operations and failing mobility do things to a gallant fireman. He'd saved lives and homes, ducked gunshots while dousing flames during the Watts riots, and roomed for long stretches with his life-risking brotherhood. My father inhaled it all and set his sights on making captain. What a pothole he must have hit negotiating the curve from family provider to disability-collecting house dad, from breadwinner to biscuit maker. And so began his ten-year drift away from us. I remember him alone in the garage, chain-smoking Marlboros and polishing off cases of Budweiser while the gold brick his colleagues had painted for him collected dust on our mantel. Surely those station mates weren't insinuating that my father had cheated his way into early retirement, not when his scars seemed to stretch from his shoulder blades to his waist?

My mother, well on her way to becoming a professional

student, turned her education into a teaching job at a local elementary school. In spite of her efforts to love, comfort, honor, and keep my father, *for better or worse* kept getting worse.

To my young eyes, they lived separate lives. My father joined a barbershop quartet, slicked his hair back, and twirled the tips of his moustache into handlebars. He often spent weekends singing to crowds in California's amusement parks, leaving Mom to care for us kids. Parent-teacher conferences, correcting papers, and compiling report cards consumed Mom's weekday evenings. My father substituted in the kitchen. Pea goozlum, a firehouse mixture of sausage, peas, oil, and onions, was a favorite. Home-from-school lunches were Daddy's specialty—avocado and mayonnaise sandwiches, with more mayo than avocado, and bowlfuls of berry yogurt topped with a happy faces of miniature marshmallows. No matter how much I had loved those lunches, they hadn't encouraged me to follow my mother's domestic footsteps.

Since moving out at seventeen, I'd survived on boxed macaroni and other heat-and-eat meals. Simplicity was key. I may have warmed beans, rolled a burrito, or steamed rice now and then, but what was the point of getting as involved as Beata's *ragù* if it would all be gone in a matter of minutes?

The cook kept a careful eye on the mixture, pouring in the milk after the wine evaporated, then watching the milk bubble away. On cue, I dumped a large can of tomatoes into the pot, covering the other ingredients with mounds of plump redness. Pools of milky meat gurgled into pink mush as each ingredient lost itself in the mix.

"When the tomatoes boil, we'll lower the heat," Beata explained. "Then four or five hours to a wonderful sauce. You'll try some, won't you?"

The sauce smelled good—delicious, even. If only I could

scrape a little off the surface, eat only what I wanted. When I shook my head, Beata flung her hands in the air and sent me away with a bag of old bread for the elephants.

Ten days after Bambi's attack, Stefano finally allowed me within the elephants' reach—as long as I stayed out of Bambi and Kama's range. I touched the others. Sometimes they touched back.

When I offered Mary half of a Frisbee-sized loaf, she plucked it from my hand with a curled trunk and rammed it into her mouth with the tip of her trunk, condensing it into a tennis-ball-sized lump that disappeared down her throat. Then she looked for more, drawing the pink tip of her piglet snout along my limbs, sniffing my arms and my hands. Could she smell the vegetables I'd just finished chopping in the cafeteria? I held my palm near the end of her trunk, playing with the humid breath filtering through my fingers the way I'd played with wind whooshing past car windows as a child. Mary sucked my hand up to her nose with a moist slap. The wall of muscle beat like a heart against my palm.

The elephant tent felt like a hideaway, an incubator that kept my tenuous bond with Stefano warm and protected from outside interference. I enjoyed spending my free time reclining on the straw bales, listening to Stefano sing while his rake rustled across the elephants' wooden decks or his broom swished over their weathered skin. Quiet time passed while he tinkered and I journaled. Sometimes, I just watched the animals sniffing and exploring and scratching their haunches against each other. It touched me the most when the elephants simply shifted their weight and tilted way over to rest against their neighbor. Sixteen thousand pounds in perfect equilibrium, each elephant leaning on the other as if seeking—and finding—sanctuary.

Late that night, as Stefano made the elephant beds, he kept looking up from his work, watching me watch him. "This is supposed to be our first night in our own place," he said, sinking his pitchfork into the dirt and coming to sit beside me, "and you look like you going to miss my elephant tent."

Stefano corralled my shoulders in his arms. His skin on mine sent a jolt through me. I liked Stefano's touch. Liked how comfortable I felt with his closeness. Liked how we'd both left home in a Jonathan Livingston Seagull search for what lay beyond.

This was more than dillydally sex.

"You bring a lot of girls in here so you and your elephants can seduce them?"

Stefano turned me toward him. Hot breath breezed past my neck. "You are here because you are special to me. When I see you that first night, I think, *This is a girl I could fall in love with*. But I tell myself no." He cast his gaze downward and spoke in a hush. "The last person I care for hurt me, and I am not sure I want to know you." Taking his time to work his eyes back up to meet mine, he said, "But all that night I think about you. I do not stop thinking about you since."

As I listened to his stripped-down, bare-metal words, the fluttering in my chest burst into a thumping on my breastbone. Feelings so true and so terrifying whirled through my head. Perched on that high wire of emotional honesty, dizzy and giddy and breathless, I felt on the verge of falling, falling, falling.

"Stop. Stop." Helga yelled at me from the back of the dressing room a few days later. "What are you doing?"

I was topless and held the blue mini skirt at mid-thigh. Couldn't she tell I was getting dressed for the elephant dance?

A flash of pink, my newest costume, landed in my lap. "You're riding the elephant. Tonight."

"But I never— No one—"

"Tonight. Hurry."

As if on cue, someone rapped on the outside of the trailer. The door flew open, and the others rushed down the steps.

"Tonight?"

I sat in my chair, dumbfounded, with the blue skirt still at half-mast and the pink costume covering my breasts. Then an elephant bellowed. I kicked the door shut. Off with the blue. On with the pink. I thrust my feet into shoes and leapt for the door.

I took two steps toward the riderless elephant and froze. I'd grown accustomed to Raya's docility in the tent. Backstage, with the trumpeting horns amplifying the applauding crowd, with her glittering headdress intensifying the wild gleam in her eye, Raya morphed into a Dalí-esque, gravity-defying elephant whose legs stretched toward the sky.

Stefano appeared behind me. "You don't have to do this."

"Help me up."

He shook his head and tugged on the elephant's ear. *"Down, Raya. Down."* Raya bent her front left leg into a step and lowered her chest and head. Stefano held my foot on her knee. *"Up, Raya. Up."* He pushed me against the elephant's flank. My stomach dove as she hoisted her knee and me into the air. "Grab on," Stefano yelled.

I reached my hands over her head and searched frantically, finding nothing but rough skin, prickly hair, and the stiff ridge of one big ear. "To what?"

"The strap around her neck. Anything. Grab on!"

Stefano shoved my bottom up. I latched onto Raya's ear and pulled. The elephant tossed her head in the air. I fully expected to soar over her back and fall face first in the dirt. Instead, I landed in a magnificent belly flop across her haunches. And in the silence that follows a severe blow to the body, I heard the music for the elephant number begin.

"Slide forward." Stefano tugged on my foot. "Get one leg on her other side."

The other elephants marched their experienced riders toward the big top, and Raya followed, unconcerned with the amateur sprawled across her back. I hooked both hands onto the neck strap of her leather headdress, heaved my torso up, and swung my right leg over her back. Pink beads popped off my costume, tumbled down the elephant's sides, and disappeared into the dirt. Scooting toward her neck, my fishnets clung to sandpaper skin. Quill-like hairs shredded my inner thighs as Raya hustled toward her place in line. My body seesawed and my stomach swirled.

Stefano ran alongside. "You sure about this?" he yelled, as if I could stop 8,000 pounds of elephant. My gaze darted from his concerned face to the light blazing through the widening crack in the blue velvet curtains. "Hold on," he called, "as tight you can—"

Spotlights hit my face. Trumpets blared. Children cheered. Popcorn. Dust. Straw. Struggling to keep my legs clamped around Raya as we hurtled into the ring, I screamed, "*But I've never ridden an elephant before!*"

My legs bounced off her neck. My butt bobbed on her withers. Each time one of her front feet nailed the ground, stiff, black neck hairs punctured my thighs. We pounded around the circle twice before screeching to a full stop.

Stefano yelled, "Get ready," and flung his hand up.

A sign? I didn't want to raise my hand, but I did. The elephant lowered her head for momentum and then hurled her front legs in the air until she stood on her back feet. My body catapulted back. My butt saw air. My palm wrenched against the leather strap, yet I held on. Raya landed with a great thud, stabbing her whiskery stubble deeper into my flesh.

As the elephants backed into the rear of the ring, stagehands rolled in great metal stools. Raya hefted the two of us onto one of the stools, and we spun to the left, spun to the right. Off the stool. On the stool. The next time Stefano gave his 'hand in the air' sign, I tightened my grip. Seconds later, Raya kicked her front feet up. She stood vertical. I lay horizontal. We spun and we swung like a mechanical bull ride. Raya danced the two-step and bowed on her knees. I couldn't feel my fingers, I couldn't feel my thighs, and I couldn't wipe the smile off my face.

If I'd had an ounce of sense, I'd have considered how forcefully twenty-four pizza-sized elephant feet pounded the earth. I'd have thought about all the times I'd fallen off a horse, and how if that happened here, I'd be smashed flat. Instead, I beamed like a kid on a carousel as Raya completed her fifteen-minute routine.

With an upward surge of her shoulders, the elephant lifted me high into the air and pivoted until her front feet rested on the closest elephant's haunches. Raya's body lurched when Mary's feet landed just three feet behind me. Above my head, Mary stretched her trunk up and trumpeted into the heights of the big top. Ears ringing, I waved to the gushing crowd as our line of elephants and dancing girls paraded out. My head swirled, my hands ached, and my thighs burned. Where I didn't feel pain, I felt numb. Still, I couldn't stop grinning.

I rode an elephant! A running, dancing, twirling elephant!

Stefano appeared at the elephant's side, instructing me to lie over Raya's head, swing both legs to one side, and slide down her shoulder. I did as he said, but my hands gave out as I hung from Raya's neck strap. Strong arms caught me before I touched ground.

He winced when he saw the hot pink welts covering the insides of my thighs. "Elephant rash," Stefano said. "I never ridden without jeans on."

"I doubt fishnets offer the same protection," I told him, hobbling bow-legged toward the dressing room.

"You have *coglioni*," he called after me.

I turned around. "*Co-lee-oh*-what?"

"*Palle.* Balls," he said, cupping his privates into a tight package. "Is a compliment. Not many weemuns would go in the ring with no practice." Stefano tilted his head back and spoke through his smile, "That's my girl."

His girl.

CHAPTER SEVEN

IN THE LAND OF MATADORS

Nine Days of Hell. That's what Stefano called December 24 to New Year's Day. Three daily shows meant an endless performance from noon to midnight, with one crowd exiting the big top as the next entered. Tensions ran high. Some of the workers believed if the Christmas season went poorly, then a year of bad luck would follow.

A few days before Christmas, we drove into the outskirts of Valencia, our next venue, trading rural orange groves and scrub-covered hills for high-rise apartments and distant church cupolas. Artists spruced costumes, props, and routines for the holiday shows. Workers replaced burnt-out light bulbs, sewed torn curtains, and washed tents. Someone even painted the ticket booth. A single night without hearing big band marches or smelling over-greased popcorn seemed strange.

During one afternoon of preparations in the elephant

tent, Stefano was unusually quiet. Then, out of nowhere, he blurted, "My mother is coming to visit."

I looked up from oiling a red leather strap. Mothers were not a part of my boy-girl equation. Hippie boys did not bring their moms to Grateful Dead shows. In the two weeks since I had joined the circus, Stefano had eased into my life as no man ever had. *But meeting his mother, for Chrissake?* Shouldn't there be a grace period?

"I'm not sure why she comes." Stefano's bobbing Adam's apple seemed to shove his words out one phrase at a time. "I call my grandmother last week. Tell her I meet a girl. Grandma tells the mamma. This morning I call Grandma again. She tells me my mother is coming. Maybe she comes to check up on me." Stefano soaped his brush and focused on scrubbing an elephant headdress. "She arrives Christmas day—but don't worry. She stay only two nights then back to Italy."

I didn't say anything about him acting far more worried than I.

By opening night, the big top sparkled. Colored lights hung from trapeze platforms and iridescent garlands crisscrossed poles. Valencians in holiday finery streamed through pine bough arches to fill every seat. Their fur coats and high heels made the beach towns and agrarian villages we'd passed through seem far away.

Backstage hummed with performers waiting for the opening parade. I took my place next to the juggler and listened to the *thwap thwap thwap* of clubs whacking palms as he warmed up. No one wanted to mess up opening night. Even the clowns seemed on edge.

Finally, the ringmaster donned his red tails. The house lights faded, the crowd applauded, and the velvet drapes whooshed open. Horns blasted and drums boomed as we paraded into the spotlights, waving to the crowd, welcoming them all to Super Circo Magico. When the horns faded, the Tarantella blared from speakers. As everyone else left the ring, the five dancing girls and I hopped on one foot and snapped our fingers in the vigorous dance once believed to cure tarantula bites. *Mamma mia, mamma mia, già la luna è in mezzo al mare* . . . We hopped on the other foot and twirled around in our sexy peasant-girl costumes. *Mamma mia, mamma mia, mamma mia, si salterà* . . . After the Tarantella, I rushed to the dressing room. Off with the flouncy red skirt. On with the skimpy silver bottoms. Off with the red vest and its blue rick-rack trim. On with the metallic bikini top that looked like a medieval WonderBra. I grabbed my silver cape and ran out for the sword-swallower's intro. For me, it was all a countdown to riding Raya.

Thirty minutes later, I stepped onto her raised thigh, and this time Raya swept me onto her back in one swift, liquid movement. My hair bounced behind me as we pounded into the ring. Spotlights! Flashbulbs! Trumpets! And my pelvic bone slamming into Raya's great neck with each plunging step.

Memories of my cowgirl aunt teaching me to ride a horse and instructing me to move *with* the animal flashed through my mind. I couldn't have been more than ten years old. We still lived in California back then, but we were on a summer trip to Oregon. The horse smelled like open fields and warm leather, and I remember feeling as though one of my plastic horse figurines had finally come to life.

Move with the elephant?

The next time the elephant's head went down, I yanked on

the leather strap, forcing my hips forward. It worked. I rolled over her spiked hair instead of it jabbing into my skin.

Move with the elephant!

When Raya raised her front feet, I pulled my chest toward her head. When she stood vertical, I held myself vertical too, with my hand in the air and my eyes open wide. As her body thundered down, I clenched my legs around her neck, using my calves like shock absorbers rather than my butt like a basketball. Raya lurched forward and onto her stool. The trainer twirled his metal rod in the air as the elephants spun circles. First this way, then that way, off the stool, and on the stool—no matter what, my body moved with my elephant.

Children waved, and I waved back as Raya walked on her hind legs out of the ring with her head bouncing in front of me, her lungs ballooning beneath me, and her ears flapping against my legs. Once outside, I leaned forward and ran my hands over the knobby top of her head. She lifted her trunk until its tip floated in front of my face.

"Look at you two." Stefano stared up at us. "Is like you been riding together for years."

At midnight, when I arrived at the elephant tent after the opening show, Stefano suggested we celebrate.

"Because the show went well?"

"Because it didn't go bad," he said as he stashed his tools. "When show goes good, performers get credit. When show goes bad, workers get shit. So far, no shit, so *festa*."

Walking to the bar, I heard small parties in some of the campers. Usually, I couldn't make it from one part of the grounds to another without hearing at least a few arguments, but that night the circus seemed at peace, as if Christmas had come early to our lot in Valencia. I should have known better. Illusion is the circus's greatest feat.

Stefano's gaze swept the barroom and returned to me. He looked down at his glass and then back across the table at me.

"I'm still here," I said, the next time his green eyes met mine.

He slid his vodka away and wound his fingers through my own. "These last few days everything is busy—we are too much apart." Stefano's eyes sought his glass and then shifted back to me. "What I try to say is, has been a long time I don't feel this way about a weemun."

Stefano's simple words filled me with warmth. *I could fall in love with this man.* I tightened my grip on his hands and leaned across the table—

"Por qué, Stefano? Por qué?" Guido's drunken voice boomed from the bar's entrance. "Why do you romance this girl when you know she will be in my bed tonight?"

My lover's face turned to tendons and gristle.

"You hear me?" Guido waddle-walked toward our table. "*My* bed tonight."

Stefano jerked up. His chair crashed to the tile floor. He strode toward Guido, inhaling all the rage and resentment in the room in a whoosh of air that billowed his nostrils and inflated his chest like a fighting cock.

"No—" I reached for him, but Stefano slipped away.

Guido's head wavered. A single punch on the man's smug face would topple him. But if that were to happen, I knew Stefano would be the loser in the long run.

"Can't we just go?"

The room hushed as the battle burned in Stefano's eyes.

"Please, Stefano. For me."

Breath seeped out of Stefano in a slow, angry leak. "Say what you want, Guido," Stefano hissed as we walked out. "Everyone sees she is with me."

Outside, Mediterranean breezes cooled our skin. I hoped the cool air would chill the fire in my lover's eyes. Instead, Stefano darted for a car, roared, and kicked the tire. Primal grunts and snarls sprang from him as he pelted the rubber again and again, rocking the car with his fury.

His frenzy stopped me in my tracks. The boys I had hung out with did beadwork, wove daisy chains, and exhaled life's frustrations in a cloud of pot smoke. It struck me that I barely knew this man.

With a final yelp, Stefano collapsed, shoulders heaving onto the hood of the car. Then he pushed himself up into a straight-arm stance, leaning into the car, wiping his mouth and forehead on his arm as his breathing slowed.

"You just assaulted that tire."

Stefano, his face still flushed, reached for me, but I sprang from his touch. "Is a tire, Kat'leen." His cheeks hopped as if suppressing a laugh.

"But—what if you got that angry with me?"

Stefano's expression morphed from mock to shock as he made sense of my words. "I would never touch you. No matter how mad I am, I would *never* touch you."

This Stefano frightened me. "I can't be with someone who needs to hurt things."

"I didn't *hurt* the tire." He held out his hand. "I want to protect your honor. My honor. I want Guido to answer for his actions. You beg me not to. But my blood is hot. When I feel something, it stay right here." Stefano pounded on his breastbone. "If I don't react, will grow until I explode. So I kick a tire. Now is over. *Finito.* Is this not better than hiding feelings?"

Stefano stared at me without blinking. When I stayed quiet, he slipped his hand under my arm. "Is late. Come back to the circus."

My arms stayed crossed the entire way, my hands tucked from his reach.

In bed, Stefano kissed my shoulder and pulled the covers over us. I still hadn't said a word, choosing to knead my distress instead of letting it go, as he had. Our first disagreement, and I was doing all the disagreeing.

His breath turned to long wisps as I replayed the bar scene. Stefano's touch. His tender revelations. Guido's domineering manner and callous remarks. Just how did I want Stefano to react—sit cross-legged on the floor and meditate? In this land of bullfights and matadors, did I think he could cool his hot blood when it suited me?

My mother once told me a childhood story about how her German aunt had instructed her on the proper way to line-dry laundry. One rule sticks in my mind: Underwear could never—*but never*—be hung anywhere but inside pillowcases. Over the course of her childhood, my mother became skilled at hiding her underwear and her feelings. Learning from her, I used emotional prudence as both weapon and armor. No wonder a roadside display of wounded honor left my brain feeling wrinkled and unable to make sense of what had happened.

Stefano lived by different rules. Undiluted rules. He did not hold back from revealing his anger, his passion, or his vulnerability, and he was always genuine. How could I argue with that?

And yet, I did.

I lay there, torn between feeling so damn certain and so utterly confused.

I wanted to run from him.

I wanted to run to him.

I wanted control of my emotions.

Instead, I was falling uncontrollably in love.

CHAPTER EIGHT

THE GIFT

To begin his morning time-to-wake-Kathleen ritual, Stefano kissed my cheek. His lips meandered across my chin and down my neck. When I stirred, he said, "Wake up. Is Chrees-mus."

I sprang up. "Christmas?"

"Yes. And Beata needs you in the chicken. I mean kitchen."

"This early? What time is it?"

"Time to cook," Stefano said, and he disappeared out the door.

Christmas. I wanted the holiday to be special, as it always had been at home. Even after my siblings and I had gone separate ways in search of our lives, we did everything within our power to reunite at Mom's. Each year, we hung homemade stockings for everyone, enough to turn a window ledge into a rainbow. We doused our coffee with Irish cream and brewed spicy wassail to scent our celebration.

I looked around the step van. Christmas in the circus

would just be another day with my face caked in makeup. Where were the mounds of brightly wrapped goodies waiting under a tree? The drawn out *ohhhs* and *ahhhs* filling the room as my family opened each other's gifts? Three generations of women in the kitchen rolling out pie dough and filling it with scrumptious fruit? No one laughed or hugged, reminisced about past celebrations, or made plans for coming years. And stockings? The only ones around were secondhand fishnets.

Inside the kitchen, I stirred gooey condensed milk into my coffee and held it under my nose. Sweet, strong, hot, and far better smelling than fish at seven a.m. I guzzled the cup and dipped another strip of cod into beaten eggs and breadcrumbs. When I finished breading the fish, I rinsed lettuce until Helga called me for makeup for the morning show.

Returning to the kitchen after the elephant number, I was greeted by the smell of frying fish at the bottom of the steps and a wall of heat at the top.

I caught Beata eyeing my robe. "What?" I looked down at the shabby terry cloth, one of Helga's castoffs. An artist's palette of red, blue, black, and pink makeup stained the top half of the robe, and the lower half looked as if a cat with PMS had used it for a scratching post. "This is what I always wear between shows."

"*Sí, sí.* Put an apron over it."

"With this heat?"

Beata shook her head and passed me her long-handled fork. Firecrackers of oil exploded from the pan. Grease clung to my skin, my costume, my hair. As my heap of crispy fish carcasses grew, so did the kitchen's temperature. Trickling sweat burned my eye. Rubbing it loosened a fake lash, and my knuckle came away smeared with black.

"I need to leave early Beata, look at my makeup."

"No time to fix anything."

I followed her gaze out the door. Stefano approached the kitchen with a well-dressed woman. The ends of her golden scarf frolicked in the breeze. I leapt back from the door. *His mother.*

"Stefano has a surprise for you." Beata hitched my robe closed, tucked under the stained collar, and pushed sweaty curls from my face.

"The eyelash, Beata, the eyelash." She pressed the flopping lash against my lid. "And the liner? How badly did I smear the liner?"

Wiping my eye with terry cloth marred the robe with new streaks of black and beige as Stefano tromped up the steps. I gave him my most sincere *how could you* look and peeked over his shoulder. When Stefano told me of his mother's visit, I'd envisioned a somber woman in a black shawl with a pot of spaghetti in one hand and a wooden spoon in the other. Instead, a fashionably dressed blonde with green eyes as vivacious as Stefano's looked up at me from the bottom step and smiled Stefano's smile.

His mamma took my hands in hers and smooched my cheeks. "Nee-stoo mee-tyoo, Kataleena." She glanced at Stefano who nodded. "Yoo comma loonch weet me?"

"Lunch? I'm so glad you speak English."

"No," Stefano told me. "No English, no Spanish. I teach her the sentence walking over here. The mamma want to greet you in your language. Five minutes she forget everything."

"They're not going to let me go out for lunch," I said. Then, "What's her name? Am I supposed to call her *Mamma*?"

"Angela. And I arrange lunch. That's why you must come working so early this morning. Helga even excuse you from the first finale."

"Vaya, vaya." Beata motioned for us to go. *"Feliz Navidad."*

The three of us headed for the step van so I could change. Navigating her heels through the gravel lot, Angela simultaneously dodged tent stakes, electrical lines, guy wires, and wayward piles of manure. Stefano grumbled at her in Italian. To me, he said, "Who wears Sunday shoes to a circus?"

"Why didn't you remind me of her visit?" I asked, hoping my sweet tone hid my frustration with him from The Mamma. "I look like a tart."

"What is tart? You just look like you work in the circus."

"But she's your *mother*."

"I did not have any gift for you," Stefano murmured. "So I think to surprise you with lunch away from the circus."

Now I felt bad. Days had passed since he'd mentioned her visit, but still, how could I forget? And how could I forget a Christmas gift for Stefano? "Thank you, Stefano, but if you just would have reminded me . . ."

"But then would not be a surprise." Stefano tossed his hands in the air. "Weemuns!"

I caught my floozy reflection in the van's mirror as I climbed in. What could I do? Right after lunch there would be another show. I pulled Levi's over my fishnets, slipped on one of Stefano's T-shirts, and rechecked the mirror. Perfect. A casual floozy.

We ate at a nearby Catalan restaurant. Stefano and his mom ordered *paella,* the house specialty; I settled for a meatless Valencia salad.

Angela looked vibrant and fresh. Perhaps because of the way her gold earrings accentuated the blonde highlights in her hair, or perhaps because of the way she glowed while doting on her son after not seeing him for well over a year. At first, Stefano dutifully answered her questions, turning only occasionally toward me to roll his eyes. But Angela was unrelenting. Stefano's answers grew short. Curt. He fidgeted in his seat and jerked his shoulders, shrugging her off like a too-warm coat.

Angela turned to me and smiled.

"Did you tell her that I don't usually wear makeup?"

Stefano said a few words to Angela, who nodded.

"What about the smell? Did you tell her I was frying fish?"

Angela nodded again. Had Stefano translated correctly? I wanted to speak with her, but what could I say with the few Italian words I'd learned? *Do you agree with your son that I have* belle tete*? You know, he's pretty darn good at* facendo l'amore. *In fact, a* rapida scopata *in the elephant tent would make me feel a lot better right now!* Instead, I mustered a halfhearted smile and turned my attention to the arriving waiter.

The plate of lettuce, tomatoes, asparagus, onions, olives, radishes, and hardboiled eggs he set before me made me crave my family's Christmas dinner. Years of vegetarianism had passed since I'd eaten a slab of the standing rib roast Mom cooked when we could afford it, but eating it wasn't the point. I wanted to smell its hearty aroma while at a table with my family. Then I could be happy with my usual mashed potatoes, stuffed mushrooms, and cheese loaf.

"The mamma says you look sad. I tell her you are missing your family."

I nodded to Angela and reached for Stefano's hand.

Instead of helping Beata between the second and third shows, I slipped away to a nearby bar and called home to tell everyone how much I missed them. Then I spent a week's wages on Moskovskaya vodka for Stefano, chocolates for Angela, and a bottle of Baileys for me. Baileys—traditional, Irish like my family, and guaranteed to warm the bluest mood.

I waited backstage for the opening parade when Stefano came to tell me he'd finagled a box seat for his mother so she could take pictures for his grandmother. Conjuring up an image of Stefano's grandmother straight out of the Godfather movies, I marched into the ring. The woman who raised Stefano would soon be looking at photos of a hussied-up, near-naked dancing girl.

Stefano and his mom met me outside the costume trailer after the show. Hideous makeup stripped from my skin, I could finally meet her face to face.

"Ciao, bella." Angela tugged my cheek. Her hands fluttered like banners on an indecisive wind as her words gushed out. *Foto, balla, costumi, elefanti*. She mimicked me riding Raya. *"Brava, Kataleena, brava."*

"She says she take pictures of you dancing in this costume, you dancing in that costume," Stefano explained. "Her favorite parts are you on the *elefante* and the clown."

The clown appeared next to Stefano smiling broadly. "Could that possibly be me?"

I'd passed the entertainer backstage for weeks, but we'd never met. Stefano had told me of his television stardom in the sixties, and although he and his children currently worked in this circus, he wasn't a relative of the ruling family and didn't act like one. Once introduced, the entertainer crossed the social boundary between artists and workers to invite us to his family's private celebration.

Sparkling glasses of spumante waited when we arrived backstage. I opened the Baileys and offered a round. The way the bottle's base nestled in the crook of my arm comforted me, as if some jolly Irishman had designed it to be carried around and shared. Even after we polished off its contents, I cradled the brown bottle as if it connected me with home. When Stefano draped an arm over my shoulders and held me close, I felt love—whether his or a reflection of my own, I wasn't sure. Perhaps a combination of the two.

Surrounded by love and laughter, the division in my head between strangers and friends, between home and life on the road, blurred. I remembered that family could also be found and forged. By focusing on what I'd missed in Oregon, I had almost missed sharing Christmas with Stefano.

CHAPTER NINE

LOVE IN THE ELEPHANT TENT

On Angela's last morning in town, Stefano and I visited her downtown pension to indulge in a hot bath. Afterwards, sharing a round of coffee in a nearby bar, I felt Angela's gaze hovering on Stefano and me, contentedly studying our interactions. She would tell me one day that her son's eyes smiled when he looked at me.

After Angela got on a train to Barcelona and her flight home, Stefano and I rode a city bus back to the circus. I slid across the plastic bus seat and nudged him. "Did I pass the test?"

He curled his arm around my shoulder. "Mamma says to me, 'Stefano, when you meet this girl is your day fortune.'"

I leaned into his embrace. "And what did you tell her?"

"I do not like to agree with the mamma, so I say, 'Yes, Mamma, but I knowed it first.'" Stefano chuckled. "This way, she is agreeing with me."

Riding past palm trees, flower stalls, and buildings so ornate they seemed to be made of lace, I described my Puzo-influenced image of dowdy Italian mammas and grammas, spaghetti pot and all.

"My mother? Cooking?" He laughed. "She is the only mamma in Italy who doesn't like to cook."

"I thought all Italian women loved cooking."

"My mother is . . . not like other mothers." Stefano paused. "Sure, she cooks for me when I am leetle, but she tells me every time how much she hates it. Makes me feel like I am in her way."

Through the bus windows, Stefano stared at the proud Gothic arches of a nearby edifice and its backdrop of contemporary high rises. He said, "Was my grandmother who raise me, her courtyard I play in after school, her lap I sit on to read books." The arm Stefano laid over my shoulder bounced and bobbed, jostling me as he animated his story. "My mother and I don't talk or play—she just yells to me, tells me what to do, how to act. I don't want to listen. From when I am twelve we are at war. Is still difficult. These few hours are the most time I spend with her since I leave my parents' house."

Though inspired by Hollywood, my vision of The Italian Mamma is not far from her traditional role. She is devoted, adoring, and understanding. Her success is measured not by her education or her profession, but by her family's well-being.

This role gets my vote as probable cause for that peculiar phenomenon in Italy called *mammone*—adult, single men who still live with their mammas. A whopping seventy-five percent of Italian men still clutch their umbilical cords at thirty. Some leave, stretching their mamma-bond as far as they can, reveling in their independence for a month, a season, a year. When they've had their fill of doing their own laundry, mother's caretaking pulls them back to her bosom like a big rubber band. Most eventually leave for good, but only to trade *mamma per moglie*, mother for wife.

When Stefano compared his own childhood against those of his close friends, he felt shortchanged. The stories he told that creased his dimples and crinkled his eyes never included his own parents. By the time we met, they'd been estranged for five years.

His mother may not have been a typical Italian mother, but neither was Stefano a typical Italian son.

Right before the second elephant number, something sent Guido screaming his head off outside the dressing room. I couldn't understand his words, yet they made me cringe. The other riders and I crept out of the costume trailer. No one wanted Guido's attention.

"Andale! Andale!" His hands thrashed in the air. "On those elephants."

The six of us scrambled onto our mounts. Stefano urged the animals into place, but Gooli, the oldest elephant, didn't hustle. Guido stomped toward her, his face blushing from peach to pink to crimson. Ernesto sidled into Guido's path, but Guido knocked him away and ripped the prod from his hand. Gooli bellowed like a thousand psychotic trumpets. She ducked her great head as Guido swung, bellowed again, and trotted toward the other elephants with a frightened rider clinging to her back. One by one we flew into the ring. Away from Guido's enflamed face. Away from his hurled curses. Away from the menace of his prod.

Guido stopped just short of the audience's eyes.

Nausea overwhelmed me as Raya and I twisted and turned through our routine. *He almost attacked Gooli.* My head spun even when Raya stood still. I scanned the back lot as we came out of the ring, looking for Guido. The other riders dismounted and gathered around the trembling woman who'd ridden Gooli. Not one of them glanced at the elephant. I stayed on top of Raya all the way back to the tent, finally sliding down the elephant's side and into Stefano's arms.

"He tried to beat her!" I turned to Gooli and rubbed the soft skin behind her ear. "Is this what goes on around here?"

"Usually is not so bad." Stefano bolted a chain around one front and one back foot of the first elephant and moved down the line. "Except once, with Mary."

"Mary?" My gaze shot to her. "Someone beat Mary?"

"Last spring. Something scares her in the show. Maybe a balloon pop, I don't know. She screams. Runs through the crowd, out of the ring. People get scared. Late that night, when she is chained up, Guido and his friend take a pole and beat her." Stefano's labored breath underscored his words. "Guido was crazy that night."

I squeezed my eyes shut, trying to block images of sweet Mary cowering under Guido's assault. "Couldn't you stop him?"

"When I hear elephant screams, I call Ernesto and hurry to see what is wrong. Guido sees me coming and turns the pole toward me." Stefano spoke fast and angry. "I *want* to hit Guido. I *want* to make him stop. But Ernesto uses his trapeze muscles to hold me back—he won't let go. Says that Guido will first beat me, then beat Mary even harder. Ernesto makes me walk away."

"You walked away?"

Stefano hammered a cigarette out of his pack. "I don't want Mary to get hurt more," he said, bowing his head to his lighter, "so I stop struggling and listen to Ernesto. This is before I understand that Ernesto will drowned himself in a bottle of whiskey before he will fight with the boss's family. If he does, his own family will be living in the street. Ernesto is trapped, and the boss knows. If I had understood, maybe . . ." He pulled hard and deep on his *Ducado* and spewed a cloud of blue smoke. "Maybe I would have hit Guido instead of the truck."

"You hit a truck?"

"I break my hand. Punch so hard a bone comes out the back. First I go to the bar, then I see about medicine." Stefano drew my fingers to the nub of a scar below his knuckle. "After my hand is bandaged I pack my bag." Stefano's hand tensed under mine. "But when I go to Mary I see she is hurting."

"Oh God."

My tears spilled over. Stefano scooped them from my cheeks with curled fingers.

"Is not bruises or cuts," he said. "Elephant skin is thick, does not show the hurt." Stefano's words trickled out, and he sounded far away. Dazed. "Is more how low she hold her head. How Raya and Lola keep touching her with their trunks, gentle around the ears. Like a mamma caresses a baby." Stefano tucked my curls out of the way and traced the shape of my ears with his fingers, over and over, his touch so light, he brought me into his trance. "I cannot leave when she feels pain. Around her, on the ground, I find coins—must have spilled from Guido's pockets. Buying Mary some bread is the only way I can tell her I am sorry I did not protect her."

This tyrannical world, where the powerful amused themselves by tormenting the vulnerable, was despicable—even for a place existing on the fringes. A brisk wind picked up in the evening, cooling the circus and the tensions within. My head stayed hot. That night in bed, each time I closed my eyes

I saw Guido threatening Gooli and beating Mary. The whistling wind morphed into an elephant's scream. I inched closer to Stefano, wedging my face into the warm spot between his shoulder and head.

I wanted to stop Guido or anyone else from hurting these animals again. But this was their world. They created it. They financed it. They owned and controlled everything within its walls, including Stefano. Including me.

When Stefano's lips touched my forehead the next morning, I spoke before opening my eyes.

"Last night. These people. Mary. Gooli." I blurted out my thoughts. "I need to get out of this circus."

Stefano stumbled back from the mattress.

"Come with me," I said.

He looked as if he no longer understood English. "You mean . . . leave the elephants?" He fumbled with his *Ducados*, lit one, and blew the smoke out the door.

"You told me you aren't caged here like the rest of them." I gathered the sheet around my body and stepped closer, gnawing my lip, watching his reaction. "Let's go to Italy, Stefano. We'll visit your grandmother and my friend in Rome. We'll start something different. Something new."

Stefano's thumb flicked the base of his cigarette, sending ash rolling down his shirt. He sucked on the cigarette, then tossed it. Scrunching his arms against his chest, he said, "I want to protect my *elefanti*, Kat'leen. To save them." Then his arms fell to his sides. He said, "The animals will never be free. They will never escape these people. Never escape this life." Stefano pulled another cigarette out of his pack. Then he jammed it back in. His gaze met mine. "But I can."

I threw my arms around him. Stefano pulled me close and whispered, "Today I talk to Ernesto. Tomorrow we escape."

"Escape? What are they going to do, imprison us?"

"No. But they will try to make us stay. Keep our pay. Make trouble. Tell no one."

"Not even Beata?"

"Only Ernesto." Stefano shook his head. "I will miss Ernesto. And my elephants."

"I wish that leaving here didn't mean leaving your elephants, Stefano. Can they do the whole elephant thing without you?"

"For one year, they pile responsibility on me until I become a mountain, but I will not leave a hole when I am gone. Other people will come. Soon this circus forgets I was ever here."

By midnight, twelve hours after the morning show began, my final performance with Super Circo Magico had ended. The lights cascading from the heights of the big top were spent, the vacant seats and velvet drapes lost to darkness. I'd slipped out of my last rhinestone costume, peeled off my last pair of fishnets, and washed away every trace of makeup. Our backpacks waited in the tent, ready for our early morning departure, and Stefano had gone to convince the boss to give us our pay a day early.

Inside the elephant tent, his six girls swayed from side to side. My gaze wandered over them, pondering the subtle differences I hadn't noticed weeks ago. I picked up the bag of old cafeteria bread and started down the line.

"Hey Raya." I ran my hand over the narrow bridge of her trunk and thought about how it looked pinched, as if she'd worn tight fitting spectacles all her life. She leaned in to me as I placed a chunk of bread in her mouth. "Thank you for teaching me how to ride an elephant, Raya. I felt your power. Shared your magnificence." She leaned closer. Warm elephant breath filtered through my clothing to my skin as I said, "I wish this wasn't your life."

Mary. Gentle Mary. Even though she was the youngest elephant here, the soft curves of her head and jowly cheeks gave her a sweet, grandmotherly appearance. "I'd like to take a pole to Guido for what he did to you." She took the bread from my hand and shifted her weight forward until the arch of her trunk rested against my chest. I remembered my first day here, tracing the grooves under her eye with my finger, how she'd lifted my hand back to her face, as if telling me she wanted more. "I'll never forget, Mary. Never." I brushed my fingers across her eye ridge. My throat tightened. Less than two weeks had passed since Stefano gave me permission to approach them when he wasn't present, and my relationship with the elephants had grown exponentially. If saying goodbye generated this much emotion in me, how would Stefano feel after an entire year?

Lola's wide face seemed to give her a perpetual grin. "Take care, happy girl," I said as she scooped her treat from my hand. "And take care of Mary."

The prominent bones above Gooli's eyes arched like the brows of a grande dame. After giving her some bread, I stretched my arm up. Gooli lowered her head, and I ran my palm over her rugged skin. "Watch out for that bastard, old girl."

Tears wet my cheeks by the time I reached Bambi. I stayed a step out of her reach, watching. Bambi watched back. The wide bridge of her nose made her look like a fighter who'd seen too many punches. She curled her trunk up high, pink tongue palpitating in her triangular mouth. "Easy, Bambi." I stepped toward her and set the bread on her tongue. She could have reached me, hurt me if she wanted to, but she didn't.

Kama. The smattering of freckles across her snout made her look like a scheming kid concocting her next hoax. Her alert eyes darted from my face to the bag of bread. Tossing her a portion, I wondered if she'd ever forgive Zoltan.

When Stefano returned, he laced the tent shut and held out a skinny roll of bills he'd pulled from his pocket. "I decide not to ask for yours. If the boss thinks we are escaping, he gives me nothing. We can share . . .

"You're crying."

I glanced at the elephants. "Saying goodbye made me sad."

"You are changing your mind?"

"No. I want to go. I just wish . . . that they could come too." I imagined Stefano and me sneaking a troupe of elephants through the streets of Valencia, tiptoeing to the train station with 50,000 pounds of pachyderm. For the past year, these six elephants had filled his world. How would he adjust to trading them for me? "Are you ready to leave the circus?" I asked.

"You don't see my bag next to yours?"

"Not your belongings, Stefano. You."

He stole a peek at the elephants as he unplugged his portable radio from the tent's power supply and coiled its cord. When Stefano sat beside me on the straw bales, he said, "I don't know how to say goodbye to an elephant."

We reclined onto the straw and held each other. Twelve dark eyes observed us from the other side of the tent. Gooli stretched her trunk toward us until the tip of it bobbed just five feet away. Stefano unbuttoned my shirt, swept his lips down my neck.

"Think they know what we're doing?"

"Elephants know, Kat'leen. Is said they have memories of things they never experience." Stefano pulled my hips against his own. "Is beautiful. Like being one of them. Sharing . . ."

"Yes."

". . . their sensitivity . . ."

"Yes."

". . . power . . ."

"Yes."

I felt their eyes on us, heard them breathe the same oxygen. Rushing air, deep and full, as if all six inhaled in unison. I imagined their breath on my bare skin as air gushed from their lungs. I waited to inhale until they inhaled and then held my breath, waiting, waiting, until they exhaled. My head grew light. Swimming. Swooning. Animal. Straw. Sweat. Stefano. It all merged in my head in earthy bliss.

Soft whispers in the dark. Stefano's voice cracked over his words.

"What I can say?"

Because he spoke English, I presumed he was talking to me. Then I saw his silhouette, naked at the edge of our straw-bale bed, facing his elephants, and I wondered if he spoke to us all.

Shoulders slumped, fingers plucking pieces of straw from the bales, Stefano continued. "I tell her I will follow her if she must go. At first I think I do it for her, but sitting here, I know I do it for me." The straw fell from his hands. "The six of you will always be in my heart. Your sad eyes in my memory."

I awoke a second time to Stefano's hand stroking my cheek. As I dressed, he stepped toward the elephants and stood, arms at his sides, eyes closed, head tilted back. Each elephant stretched her trunk toward him, inhaling his odor. Those who could reach him skimmed their trunks over his body. They touched his hands, his face, his hair. Elephant heads rolled from side to side, and their rumbles vibrated from deep within.

They know.

Stefano shuffled to the far end of the tent. Making his way toward me, he paused to whisper in each elephant's ear. Trunks reached after him, curling around his arm, tugging him back. Stefano kept going, tears slipping down his cheeks and disappearing into his whiskers. When his hand fell from the last elephant, he picked up his bag, lifted the side wall, and ducked under without looking back. I followed him out but held the canvas from falling into place.

Stefano knelt beside me. He said, "Italians say *arrivederci*—until we meet again."

I looked down the line of elephants swaying in the early morning light. "Think we'll ever see them again?"

"Only in here," he said, tapping his chest. "Every creature has his life. For some is possible to change, Kat'leen. For some is not."

Hand in hand, we crept away from the elephant tent and toward our future. A traditional Italian who dove deep and a free-spirited American who kept her emotional toes in shallow water—two expatriates, each searching for something different. We found one another. The surreal atmosphere of the circus had minimized our differences and driven us toward each other. But for two individuals accustomed to plowing through life like glaciers carving solitary paths over rough terrain, creating a life together meant change. Great change.

Falling in love had been the easy part.

I took one last look at the sleeping circus. The mist shrouding the big top made it seem serene, magical. But I knew better. As dawn spread its pink light over Valencia, we slipped away. Stefano's words hovered in my thoughts.

For some is possible to change. For some is not.

CHAPTER TEN

WELCOME TO ITALY

You can tell a lot about a culture from its proverbs. Italians say that while sharing a table with family and friends, one does not grow old. And rather than kill two birds with one stone, Italians feed them with one bean. Creating, sharing, and eating food is tantamount to life and love in Italy. Knowledge, necessity, and anticipation unite, merging past, present, and future to nurture body and soul. The bountiful Italian table urges one to pause long enough to inhale the scents of the season's harvest and feel the heartbeat of the day. To break bread is to forge bonds.

Italian dishes are not complicated affairs piled with ingredients that fight for prominence, but recipes whose few components shine. Each element is sincere, savored for what it brings. However, combining individual ingredients into a delectable dish takes more than a wooden spoon and copper pot, which means the simple act of eating in Italy is not so simple.

Neither is love.

Twenty-six hours after Stefano and I said goodbye to the elephants in Spain, the fog lifted from the rice fields surrounding Milan, and our train slowed under the immense iron and glass tunnel of his hometown's central station. I closed my coat against the winter chill and followed Stefano onto the platform. The mid-morning throng of travelers enveloped us in cigarette smoke and perfume, miniskirts and Armani suits. The humming bustle of the crowd echoed off the ceiling and seemed to push back down, making me feel insignificant and small.

"Hold tight to your bag," Stefano warned. "Things disappear quickly here."

One of my hands grasped my pack's strap, the other Stefano's arm. Above our heads, great black signboards flipped letters and numbers like a Rolodex, listing the ever-changing schedule of trains to every corner of Europe. *Zurigo*, Vienna, Budapest, *Monaco*, *Praga*; just mouthing the names intrigued me enough to check when each train departed. I slipped my hand into Stefano's, reminding myself that I had reached my current destination.

That late December day, as I was poised on the threshold of a new year and a new relationship, Italy unfolded before my eyes. Riding a bus to his old neighborhood, we passed fruit stands with apples and oranges stacked in perfect pyramids, and we passed *salumerie* where rows of dark red salami and marbled pig legs hung like wind chimes. Freshly skinned animals, bared teeth and dark eyes still intact, stared from beds of parsley. A woman strolling down the street in a billowing fur cuddled a coiffed poodle, making me wonder how someone could embrace one small fuzzy animal and wear another. Pouty-faced clerks lounged on sleek furniture in uppity boutiques, and machine-gun-toting guards patrolled in front of marble buildings. Scrolled trims, gargoyles, and wrought iron adorned warm-hued facades, and white statues reached from under blankets of sooty muck and pigeon poop to support elaborate balconies.

I remember noticing how the centuries-old buildings we passed melded into newer ones and wondering if my old, independent life would meld so seamlessly into a new life, a shared life. Stefano yo-yoed up and down in his seat, pointing out old haunts and favorite eateries. As his excitement grew, so did my concern. We hadn't planned beyond traveling to see his grandmother, Maria. In an industrial city such as Milan, how could we hold onto the magic of an elephant tent?

Walking from the bus stop to Maria's apartment, Stefano paused to buy cigarettes—Camels, I noted, rather than the usual black Spanish tobacco—and then steered me along a row of dilapidated apartment buildings that he called *palazzi*, through an archway, past a courtyard statue of Mary in flowing blue robes, and stopped under a first-floor window. Sheer green curtains parted when he called his grandmother's name. Under a halo of soft gray curls, Maria dabbed at tears behind her silver-rimmed glasses.

We looped around to her door and listened to the clankety-clank of her deadbolt. His grandmother wrapped her long arms around Stefano, pack and all. The flurry of our arrival came to a standstill as she pulled him into her chest. The man who always seemed to be on high speed, who hurried to his next task almost before finishing the previous one, stood perfectly still in his grandmother's arms.

"Mio bambino." Maria clutched him close. *"Mio bambino, mio bambino, mio bambino."* When she finally turned to me, Maria stooped to kiss my cheeks and said, "*Benvenuta, Katarina.*"

I have since learned that Maria adores primroses. If I'd only known then how much she loved them or how much I would come to love her, I might have brought her some that day we met, might have thought twice about this traditional Italian grandmother's first impression of a carefree American wanderer. But I strolled into Maria's home empty-handed, past the refrigerator in her foyer and into the main room of her home where I took off my pack, maneuvered around the dining table that took up most of the space, and sat on a small chair at the far end of the room.

The first thing an Italian does for a guest is offer something to drink. It's a gracious custom and generally appreciated. What's not nice is that one cannot refuse the offer without offending the host—as if doing so implies that the offering isn't good enough. I didn't have to worry about that yet as I gladly accepted Maria's offer of coffee as she welcomed me into her home.

The train ride weighed on me. Ragged naps had added up to nothing, and I needed a shower, but I'd already seen the bathroom: unless his grandmother kept the shower or tub in the entryway with her refrigerator, there simply wasn't one here. I settled for splashing cool water on my face and retreated to Maria's bedroom, the only other room in the house. I fell asleep under a cross-stitched bust of Mary and a wooden crucifix, listening to the muffled words of Stefano and his grandmother in the other room.

I had barely closed my eyes when Stefano kissed my forehead. "I thought you'd want to help cook," he said. "I tell the *nonna* you want to learn all about Italian food."

After three weeks in the circus kitchen, eating dry beans and raw vegetables sounded more appealing than ever cooking again. I pulled a pillow over my head. "Who's even hungry?"

"Is almost lunchtime, Kat'leen. Everybody is hungry."

Everybody meant Stefano's mother, father, uncle, aunt, and cousin, who would all converge upon Maria's apartment in one hour. Where eight of us would fit, I could not imagine.

I peeked out from under the pillow. "Did you tell her I don't cook?"

Stefano nodded. "She didn't believe me."

Inside the kitchen, steam from a boiling pot moistened the air, and sizzling onions and oil filled the tiny space with their fragrance. Maria presented me with a bowl of floating brown things that smelled like my brother's socks. *Funghi Porcini*, as in fungus. I was supposed to squeeze them as I fished them out so their juice stayed in the bowl. The point of wringing fungus until dark liquid oozed out baffled me.

"*Nonna* says not to strangle the mushrooms," Stefano called from the TV chair. "Next, rinse them under water until no more grit comes off."

Maria motioned for me to watch as she added handfuls of white rice to the oil and onion mixture.

"Always Arborio rice for risotto," Stefano said, translating her words. "Two handfuls for each person, plus a few extra because Stefano eats a lot."

Maria flipped the mixture around with her wooden spatula for a few minutes, ladled in steaming liquid, and motioned for me to add more. Bits of flesh floated in the broth. She passed me the wooden spatula. My turn. Maria shook her head as

I stirred and wrapped my hand in hers. I hesitated, but the warm, motherly pressure of her hand on mine melted my resistance. She guided the spatula in slow swirling motions as if frosting a cake. "*Bene*, *bene*," she said, when I finally got the hang of it.

She poured the mushroom liquid over the rice as the last bit of broth was absorbed. Her gnarled fingers flew as she minced and added mushrooms. Maria bobbed between the stove and the counter top, breading chicken breasts and frying them in oil and sage. Between dipping and frying, she set the table. Stefano paused watching TV only to unwrap bundles of cheese and cured meats to sample the contents.

He waved off my suggestion that he help. "Would upset the grandma. She like to cook and clean and prepare for the family."

"Accepts, maybe. But *likes*?"

"All Italian weemuns do—except my mother."

Testing a kernel of rice, Maria shook her head and motioned for me to add more broth. My wrist was tired, but when I switched stirring hands, Maria clucked her tongue. Switching back, I longed to be somewhere else. I'd never felt at home in a kitchen if not baking. *Shortening, sugar, eggs, vanilla, flour, soda, salt,* I would have told Maria if I spoke Italian. *I've known the recipe for chocolate chip cookies since I turned four. Shortening, sugar, eggs, vanilla*—

The next time Maria tasted the rice, she added grated Parmesan and a pat of butter, declaring it *finito* as The Family began squeezing through her narrow doorway.

Angela entered first and reached for her son. Then she turned her smiles and golden highlights toward me. "*Benvenuta*," she said, offering me two kisses in proper Italian fashion. As we parted from our embrace, Angela entwined her arm in mine, holding me close as if I might try to slip away.

Voices and outstretched hands filled the room. With Angela at my side, I planted *due baci* on the cheeks of Stefano's aunt, uncle, and cousin, managing to bump each nose in the process. Months would pass before I concluded that most Italians do not actually kiss each other's cheeks—they kiss *at* each other's cheeks. But nobody tells you that, leaving the uninitiated to smooch countless numbers of perfumed cheeks, sculpted beards, and grizzled jowls.

Stefano's father, Angelo, entered last. I remember how formidable he looked—cropped hair, square jaw, wide shoulders—every sharp angle conveyed sturdiness and durability. Strength, like I saw in Stefano. Strength that one man cultivated chasing a little white soccer ball, the other man from turning his back on everything it symbolized.

Father and son stood eye to eye, neither more than a few inches taller than my own five-foot-five, and greeted each other with quick kisses and pats on shoulders. As they parted, Angela seemed to propel me toward her husband. "*Piacere*," he said. It's a pleasure. He smiled and reached for me, and all the hard angles turned soft.

Everyone talked simultaneously as Stefano's father poured bubbly red wine into stubby glasses. Hands moved faster and voices grew louder—and they all seemed directed at Stefano.

"Why are they mad?" I whispered.

"Who is mad?" he said. "We are just talking."

I caught words such as *Americana* and *elefanti*, but the one word Stefano kept saying was Angelo. I'd never heard a child call his parent by name. My own father was never anything besides Dad or Daddy to me, titles of deference and of tenderness. Even during my late teens, when I often felt like ex-family of his ex-wife, I still called him Daddy.

Angelo fired question after question. Stefano's movements became jerky, his voice shrill. In Angelo's banking world, two plus two could only equal four. Apparently, Stefano's answers did not add up. I didn't have to understand their language to recognize the distance between them.

Food would ease Stefano's anxiety, and I welcomed its arrival, but when Angela handed me a ceramic bowl mounded with risotto, I passed it on.

"*Mangia, Kataleena, mangia*," Angela said, directing the bowl back to me.

I didn't know what to do. Shuffling food around my dish wouldn't fool anyone, and no canine vacuum hovered underfoot to help with the dirty deed.

"Help, Stefano. Remind her that I don't eat meat," I said, and slid the dish away.

Everyone hushed. The swish of the bowl across the tablecloth sounded like the great north wind as Angela pushed the rice back toward me.

"She says there's no meat in it."

"Yes there is. From the broth. I added it myself." I pushed the bowl away.

More silence, then everyone spoke at once. Maria handed a plate of fried chicken breasts to Angela who set it in front of me. I shook my head.

"Grandma says is *pollo*. Chicken. Not meat."

"If it eats and breathes and poops, it's meat." My face felt hot. "Doesn't *carne* mean meat?" I looked at Angela and said, "*Grazie. No carne.*"

Stefano's mother went to the refrigerator and came back

dangling a salami by its string. I shook my head again. Angela looked stumped—certainly she meant only to satisfy me. Perhaps if I'd spoken Italian then, I would have explained my reasons for not eating meat. Or perhaps I was too young, too immature, and felt as offended at her insistence that I consume flesh as she may have felt at my refusal to eat it. Yet even with my current understanding of the importance of food to Italians, pleasing her would not take precedence over my convictions, though I would feel the weight of being caught between those convictions and her eagerness to please.

I pointed to the plate of cheese and the mound of rolls at the center of the table. "I'm fine with those, *bene, bene*. And *vino.*" I raised my short, sturdy glass of wine. "*Vino.*"

"*Salute,*" someone said, and the toast echoed around the table. Soon, the clatter of forks and table banter took over, and everyone forgot my refusal to eat their meat. At least I thought they had.

Hours later, lunch over and the dishes washed, Maria packed a bag and went to stay with Angela and Angelo, leaving us her apartment. Stefano did not blunt his disappointment as he cranked Maria's deadbolt into place.

"You should have eaten the rice, Kat'leen."

"You know I don't eat meat. Why didn't you help me?"

"Everyone expected you to eat. *Nonna* cooked special for us."

"*We* cooked," I corrected, following him back into the living room.

"*Tre giorni sotto la neve*," Stefano said, dropping into a chair. "Three days under the snow!"

I planted my palms on the table and leaned toward him. "What the hell is that supposed to mean?"

"Is what my grandparents learned during the war. Hiding

from the shelling in the countryside with two babies. Was not enough food, so they eat anything. Everything. Pears, mostly, and the occasional cat."

"What?"

"My *nonno* told me once—to make cat meat tender, you leave it three days under the snow."

"Cats?"

"To survive, Kat'leen. You think they want to eat cats? Was war. People do what is needed. Fifty years pass—Grandma still doesn't understand when people refuse food."

I slipped into the chair beside him. "Listen, Stefano, I'm sorry about your family's wartime hardships, but I won't eat meat because of them."

"Is customary in Italy that when someone offers you something, you accept." Stefano's voice turned harsh. "You need to understand that Italians don't just eat, we eat well." He stood tall and threw his arms out as if to collect the entire kitchen and living area in an embrace. "Food is to be celebrated."

I flung my back against my chair so hard, it rocked onto its rear legs. "Food is nutrition. It makes no difference whether it's cut and stirred and babied for hours before you eat it. In fact, our bodies do best with less-prepared, plain and simple food." I stared at his unsympathetic face. "And what the hell is your problem anyway?"

"You are the different one," he said, moving away. "This is the way *we* do things in Italy."

For the last month, *we* had been Stefano and me. But at that moment, his *we* became him and the rest of Italy. I didn't understand how traversing borders changed alliances or why *different* didn't attract him anymore.

"When did different become bad?"

Stefano raised his arms and opened his mouth, but no

words came out. The lines of his face shifted from firm to flexible. "I am with you because you are different. Because I look at you and I see life's *possibilità*." He leaned against the wall and dug his knuckles into his eyes. "People here get caught up in the way things are supposed to be—the jobs, the clothes. Angelo asks me over and over what I am doing with my life. Around him and my mother, I start thinking like Italians—putting everything into *compartimenti*. I leave Italy because I want to let all of that go.

"I'm sorry, Kat'leen." Stefano reached for my hands and pulled me toward the bedroom. He tugged at my shirt, kissed my neck, and said, "What you think about making love in a real bed?"

"Your grandmother's?"

The bed creaked beneath us.

"*Nonna* would be happy if she knows."

The warmth from his lips quashed my concerns. "Just don't go and tell her."

"Is Italy, Kat'leen. I don't *need* to tell her."

Half an hour later, our heads lumped together on Maria's pillow, Stefano said, "Your hair smells like food."

I snuggled closer. "Did your gramma say anything about my cooking?"

"Mmm," Stefano mumbled into the pillow, "no . . ."

"She must have said something."

He opened one eye. "Is not important."

"Tell me."

"Maybe she say a leetle something about not understanding how you get this far in life without learning to cook.

And maybe she say I shouldn't worry because everything comes in time."

"In time for what? I don't cook, Stefano. I have no desire to *learn* to cook."

"How you going to eat for the rest of your life?"

"I've made it to twenty-three, haven't I? And as you can see," I flung the covers off my curves and lifted myself to my knees, "I'm showing no signs of malnutrition."

Stefano pulled me back down, muffling any further elucidation with a wet, lippy kiss.

That evening, his parents' table overflowed with salad, sautéed greens, artichokes, broccoli, half a dozen cheeses, and a large basket of fruit.

After thanking Angela, I asked Stefano, "Didn't you tell me she doesn't cook?"

"There is putting food on the table and there is cooking." He stabbed a pink slice of prosciutto with his fork and curled it around his tongue. "*Nonna* probably help."

I didn't understand many words spoken during the meal, but I understood the rhythm—Stefano's father or mother would ask him a question and then one parent would interrupt Stefano's reply and the other parent would interrupt the first interruption. All three voices grew louder and louder as each tried to speak over the others. Whatever everyone said must have been either often repeated or unimportant, because only his grandmother and I listened.

Stefano had told me about growing up in this apartment as an only child, how he'd never hosted a sleepover or a birthday party and how playtime with friends occurred either at a friend's house or outdoors. According to Stefano, Angela had tried to keep her son's life as neat and tidy as her home. Stefano shared her enthusiasm for order, so he found other ways to rebel—such as the time he'd lobbed raw eggs from their kitchen balcony onto every fur-wearing woman who passed below until someone called the *polizia. Tremendo*—tremendous in the overwhelming sense—is how Angela explained her son's youth to me. Even toddler-sized doses of his vitality would have been a challenge for a young mother. I can imagine Stefano daring Angela to control him, provoking her to try harder, and keep trying harder, as their tug-of-war matured.

One reason Stefano loved working with the elephants is that not many people came around. He needed his space—and in this small house, he hadn't had any of his own. The room we ate in that night had doubled as his bedroom. This was common for European families, but I had American expectations of space. Growing up in a family of six, I understood sharing a bedroom with a sister. I hadn't experienced sharing it with the dining room table.

Stefano seemed defensive that first night in Italy, just as he'd been at lunch. After weeks of watching him play den mother to six elephants—cooing in their ears, scratching their chins, attending their every need—his discomfort in his childhood home put me on edge. The anxiety in his voice made me wish I spoke enough Italian to back him up.

As the meal wound down, Stefano bid me to follow him down the hallway, through Angela's eight-by-six-foot kitchen and onto a standing-room-only balcony that overlooked the neighborhood park. And there I saw it. A circus. Its blue-and-white-striped big top looked as small as a patio umbrella from our sixth-story view. I gazed over the queue stretching out from the tent's entrance, over the dozen trucks and trailers spread around the park, past the solitary woman warming up a horse, to the small animal tent beyond her. I could almost see Kama's freckles, feel Mary's skin.

"I wonder if they have elephants," Stefano whispered from behind the warm glow of his cigarette.

We skirted the toy-sized circus while walking back to his grandmother's apartment, smelling its peaty smells, scanning the darkened grounds for familiar signs. Stefano pulled himself away. "Come on," he said. "Beyond this park is the *naviglio*."

I rolled the word nah-*veel*-yoh around in my mouth while Stefano explained how, starting in the fourteenth century, horses walking beside Milan's canals pulled long boats filled with marble to build the Duomo, the city's grand cathedral. Even Leonardo da Vinci had left his mark on the canals, designing a system of locks intended to make them navigable from Milan to Lake Como, some forty miles away.

"Were still used when my mamma was a child," he told me. "People even used to fish in them. Now is a place where people dump trash. Sometimes there are animals floating. I see a dead man once. These days, I think you going to died if you just touch the water."

At the *naviglio*, we strolled out over an arching marble bridge that blushed in the moonlight. I couldn't see the blackened depths of the canal, but I heard the water whispering its way out of the city.

Stefano leaned over the guardrail. "Growing up, I always want to escape the city. Was my dream to be a *guardia del parco*—the guy in the green suit that lives with Yogi and Boo Boo and watches deers eating in the meadows." Scoffing as if the likelihood of living in the middle of nature were as unattainable as living on the moon, Stefano said, "As a kid, I can never leave, but the water could. So I stand here and watch it go."

Listening to how Stefano had found solace watching contaminated water flow away from his city aroused the same protective instincts I'd felt in his parents' apartment. I wanted to take him to a mountaintop surrounded by a sea of hundred-foot Douglas fir trees. *One day, I'll show him the herd of wild elk that grazes in the foothills around my Oregon home. I'll take him—*

I cringed. I'd been thinking about the future. Not tomorrow, not next week, not next month. The Future.

For years, I'd been running my own catch-and-release program with men. Stefano was different. I admired his passion for his elephants and thrived on his passion for me. More than that, he made me feel like I mattered. I felt connected to him, and I wanted to share with him and soothe him. The emotions he roused disarmed me. I felt lightheaded and grounded and—

I slipped my hand into his, touched his callused palm with my fingers. My voice hesitated in my throat, tripped over my tongue, and tumbled out of my lips. "I'm falling in love with you."

He gripped my hand. A tear on his lash reflected the light of a distant streetlamp. I brushed it away with my lips, tasted his salt in my mouth.

"Is many times I think of telling you the same words." His breath quickened. He stared into the shadowy water, raking his fingers through his hair, turning his curls to frizz. "That girl I loved played games with me. Hurt me. Left my heart feeling dead." Stefano looked up, his hair framing his face like a halo. "I want to love you," he said, "but I don't know if I can ever love again."

CHAPTER ELEVEN

WEALTH TO TRASH COLLECTORS AND GYPSIES

December 31, 1988, Milan, Italy: Revealing feelings from so deep inside, coming face to face with what is happening between us. As a relationship grows, does the fear ever lessen?

Italians believe New Year's Day is a chance for *rinnovo*, renewal. To assure the new calendar brings all they desire, many Italians throw out their undesirables. Literally. At the stroke of midnight, passersby beware. Streets normally packed with cars empty quickly. Families fling open apartment windows, and silverware flies through the air. Glasses explode on sidewalks. Pots and pans bounce off forgotten cars. Furniture splinters on streets. Women toss entire sets of dishes, pausing between stacks of bowls and plates to raise a glass of bubbly to the ruin below. Men enlist friends to force washing machines over balconies. They cheer the crashes reverberating off nearby buildings and trust that the new year will replace all that is lost.

Stefano said that New Year's morning brings wealth to trash collectors and gypsies; I hoped it would bring something valuable to me.

Before meeting Stefano, my only direction was *anywhere but here.* But he made me want to linger—right up until the moment on the *naviglio* bridge when he admitted that he didn't know if he could return my feelings. The love that had opened my heart the night before now made me shrink back in on myself. Love made me worry that I had something to lose. What does an emotionally prudent young woman do when the man she wants has made her feel as if she were a million miles away from him?

She runs.

On New Year's Day, I left to meet my friend Helene in Rome. Perhaps if I let go of Stefano, then he could let go of his past. For all he knew, it had taken me only four weeks to say, "I love you."

I knew it had taken twenty-three years.

When we said goodbye in the train station, I searched his eyes, looking for some clue that Stefano could love again, could love me. I wanted him to ask me to stay. Instead, he kissed me and said, "Go, Kat'leen. I just hope you come back."

Hours later, I could still feel the weight of his rejection, the pressure of his lips on mine.

Romans ran out of space long ago. As rulers and religions changed, they crushed old structures into the ground to make way for new. Most of ancient Rome sits far below her modern streets. In the walls bordering the buried remains, one can see strata of soil and ruins, of time and history. Though each level locks the past further away from the present, the top layers still cling to what lies below.

My train rolled into town as the sun began to set, past remnants of city walls and crumbling aqueducts. Buildings scrunched against buildings as far as I could see, and throngs of antennas sprouted from every rooftop, making the whole city look as if it needed a shave. They say you can't see Rome in a day, but I did my best to see it in three: Helene and I wandered the halls of the Vatican Museum, gazed at the ceiling of the Sistine Chapel, and pressed our bare feet into the cool marble floor of Saint Peter's Basilica. We ran our fingers over the Pantheon's ancient brick walls, marveled over the Colosseum's magnificence, and stood over scattered segments of the Forum's once great columns.

Everyone and everything in Rome made me think of Stefano—from the thickly accented flirts who prowled the city's sights to the intense stares and muscular arms of her statues. I wanted to be with him, but I needed to give him a chance to figure out if he wanted to be with me. On my third afternoon in Rome, while watching sunlight reflect off the Fontana di Trevi and dance across the stone sculptures, I told Helene that I could wait no longer. I sought the nearest payphone and dialed his grandmother's number.

"Kat'leen." Stefano's voice crackled. "When you are coming back?"

"Now. I'll pack my things and catch the first train."

"It make me happy you are coming so soon."

Happy . . . because he missed me or because he loved me? When I looked in his eyes, I would know. "I'll call along the way with my arrival time. See you soon."

"Yes. Soon." He paused then said, "Kat'leen—me I love you."

Descending the rocky hills of the Northern Apennines onto the frosty Padana Plains, I fidgeted in my train seat. I pulled my pack over a shoulder and maneuvered through the travelers, weaving from car to car, bumping, banging, smiling my way to the head of the train. The locomotive rumbled to a stop. Stefano stood at the front of the platform, his eyes flickering from face to face until he found mine.

The train door whooshed open. I rushed into the cold Milan air, into Stefano's warm arms. He picked me up, pack and all, and whispered the words that conquer the most sovereign of hearts.

"I love you."

Years of wandering had led me to this moment in time—this kiss, this embrace, this man.

Stefano wiped away my tears and said, "Why you cry?"

CHAPTER TWELVE

PRETTY GIRLS ARE ALWAYS BALLERINE

Venezia is a town where *palazzi* actually look like palaces, where marble seems to float on water. In winter, the evening mist that envelops the city's ornate monuments makes Venice seem as fragile as the blown-glass artistry that fills its galleries. Stefano took me there on a honeymoon of sorts soon after I returned from Rome. Wandering over bridges and down narrow streets, my hand laced with his, we avoided the main thoroughfares and intentionally lost ourselves in the quiet spaces Stefano called *angolini.* Even waking to the early morning calls and pungent odors of fish vendors on the Cannaregio Canal, their crates of silvery catch sparkling in the sunlight, charmed me.

For four days, we wallowed in each other and shared the perfection of new love. I remember one lovemaking moment in particular when Stefano looked so peaceful and our unity felt so complete that the sense of fulfillment left me breathless.

I wanted to stay in that moment forever, but forever is short-lived when you're twenty-three.

There in Venice, in a hotel room with pink walls, a gilded mirror, and a lopsided chandelier, Stefano stared out the window overlooking the canal and asked, "Where we go from here?"

"We're seagulls," I told him. "We should float free with the wind."

Stefano harrumphed and flicked his shoulders. "Sometimes the wind takes a *gabbiano* places he doesn't want to go." He turned from the window and leaned against the wall, watching me sort through a handful of postcards. "When I leave my parents' home," he said, "I find myself in bad company. Was too much time on my hands and I get into trouble." Stefano scrunched the bridge of his nose between his thumb and forefinger as he spoke. "The elephants in Spain helped me as much as I help them, Kat'leen. They keeped my attention. Give me a roof and food—"

"You want to go back to the circus?" I did not, and even if I had wanted to return, it would not have been so soon. All the new sights and experiences had made the few weeks since leaving Spain pass far too quickly. "I thought we left Spain to start something new."

"The circus is not perfect, Kat'leen, but I'm not ready to go back to a normal job. Circus is the only work I think I can keep—the only work where we can be all day together." Stefano climbed onto the bed and reached for the chandelier, tugging on it here and there, as he had already a few times, trying to make it hang straight. "Maybe we get a job with Moira Orfei—one of the most famous circuses in Italy."

"Moira Orfei? I saw that name on posters everywhere in Rome. It said '*regina degli elefanti*.'"

"Moira is called Queen of the Elephants."

"But does she treat them well? What if—"

"Moira will be different than Guido and his family. I promise."

She supposedly had gypsy blood, Stefano told me, and had maneuvered her way onto the silver screen and beyond, eventually becoming one of the most famous personalities in Italy. Between excursions to Rome and Venice, my travel savings had dwindled, and I would soon need to start earning a living. If I had to work for someone, a gypsy elephant queen seemed better than most.

Stefano released the chandelier. "Maybe one year of working with the elephants is not enough experience for Moira's circus. Maybe I'll have to tell them I work in the Spanish circus for *two* years."

"The second they see you with the elephants they'll give you a job. But what about me?"

Smiling down at me, he said, "Pretty girls are always *ballerine*."

"More bikinis and blue eye shadow?" I tossed the postcards aside. "I have only nine months left until my plane ticket expires. That's the last way I intend to spend them."

Stefano knelt beside me on the bed. "Circus weemuns either cook, clean, dance, or perform. You don't perform. You don't want to dance. Is clear what you think about cooking. Is no free ride in the circus for anyone, so what you will do? Clean?"

"Women are good for more than cooking and cleaning and shaking booty, you know." I moved over to the window and stared down at the quiet, still water of the canal. "I know," I said, turning to him. "I'll work with the animals."

Stefano's hands flew up. "They don't let girls work with animals—too dangerous."

After four weeks in the Spanish circus, I understood the danger. Handlers risked being stomped, kicked, bashed, and smashed. Clawed, bitten, spit on, and shit on. Still, it beat my other options. "If Moira's the Queen of the Elephants, then she works with the animals."

"Performing."

"Hell." I flopped onto the bed and collapsed into his lap. "Why do I need to work? I still have a little money left. Won't they let me just be your girlfriend until I find a job I like?"

"Kat'leen, I tell you you'll have four choices and what you pick? First the fifth, then the sixth. Always different you are, *Americana*."

"And we concluded back in Milan that different wasn't a problem, remember?"

He tipped his head down and kissed my forehead. "Not a problem."

For Stefano, joining the circus was an escape from his old life and the Old World, but that didn't make it the New World, either. Catapulting myself into their backwards culture did not strike me as a good way to move our relationship forward. Although I understood that compromises could save a relationship, I did not yet comprehend how finding that shared existence can also save one's spirit. When I finally agreed to join another circus, my reasons were much more self-centered.

"'All day together,' you say?"

Stefano nodded. "I promise."

We hitchhiked south two days later. By that night, Giuseppe Nones, Circo Moira Orfei's award-winning animal trainer, was gripping Stefano's outstretched hand and flashing a grin as brilliant as the rhinestone lapels of his baby blue tuxedo. From nearby rows of eight-by-eight-foot cubicles, twelve tigers riveted their eyes on the trainer.

We made our way around one of the largest big tops in Europe, past yellow and blue trucks, yellow and blue trailers, yellow and blue living quarters, and into the elephant tent. I lifted my chin and inhaled as Giuseppe pushed aside the flaps covering the door. Squeals, rumbles, and flapping ears greeted the trainer. Pointing to each elephant in turn, Giuseppe said, "Whiskey, Babati, Bimba, Katia, Banana, Shiva, Jenny."

"Their beds," Stefano whispered to me, "look how thick."

Two workers fluffed piles of straw between the elephants; a third distributed flakes of green hay. Three caretakers for only one more elephant than the Spanish circus. If Circo Magico was a Motel 6 for elephants, Moira Orfei equaled the Hilton.

"*Ciao,* Banana," Giuseppe cooed as he approached an elephant with skin as flawless as gray velvet. Banana reached for the animal trainer, curling her trunk loosely around his arm and then draping it over his shoulder. Giuseppe introduced us to the crew captain, Hassan, who made Banana's bed. From what I gathered, the three men discussed elephant food, elephant feet, and Stefano's experience. One of the trainer's hands bounced in the air, accentuating his words. The other scratched behind Banana's ear and on top of her head, patting, rubbing, fingering her skin. His caresses seemed spontaneous, natural to him and to the animal.

Stefano soon stroked the elephant's jowl, moving with her as she swayed in the same side-to-side dance as the elephants in Spain. And as in Spain, their wooden decks creaked and groaned under their weight. One difference struck me: The chains binding their ankles were not bolted to stakes driven into the ground, but anchored to hefty eyebolts welded to the metal frames of the very decks they stood upon.

These elephants held themselves captive with their own weight.

Their own physical weight. To me, it seemed even more degrading than the chain-to-stake system used in Spain. Of course 8,000 pounds of force could break these chains to bits . . . if only they believed in their own strength.

The next time Giuseppe shook Stefano's hand, I knew he had a job. When he glanced my way, I hid my apprehension. *Is this how I want to spend the rest of my European adventure? Any of it?*

"I start in the morning," Stefano told me.

"Just like you wanted."

"And you don't have to work yet," Stefano said, "just like you wanted. Giuseppe says watch out for Moira—if you get in her eye, she make you dance. Tomorrow he finds us our own room. I tell him is okay we sleep in here for now, but he insist I ask you."

How could Giuseppe know that I'd feel more at home in an elephant tent than the metal sleeper boxes where most workers lived? There weren't a whole lot of Italian words I could say knowing it was the right place and time. This one I knew.

"*Perfetto.*"

CHAPTER THIRTEEN

LIONS AND TIGERS AND BEARS — AND SHARKS?

The first time I saw him, the gangly redhead took my breath away. Our curious eyes met, and he leaned ever so slightly in my direction. He stepped toward me, his muscular body flowing, his gold-flecked hair twinkling in the morning sun. We each inched closer until his dark eyes stared down at me. Whiskers protruded from his chin at every angle, and his upper lip drooped over his lower as if he'd been given an unmatched pair. He moved them as though he had something to say but mumbled it away instead, perhaps knowing I couldn't understand his language.

"You like zee giraffe?" a hulk of a man said as he approached, his stout chest wobbling like a giant penguin. He spoke in gruff English, jabbing the stubbed remains of an index finger toward the animal as it skittered to the far side of its pen.

The strip of coarse mane shooting down the giraffe's neck twitched as he observed us from afar. I looked into his gaze, and I knew I could get lost in those large brown eyes. "I've never seen such a beautiful animal."

The man scrutinized the giraffe, then shrugged. "If you say, but Baros is too stupid to do anything more than run around zee ring. I am Erich, from Germany. I care for zee tigers." His hand swallowed mine when he shook it.

I eyed the splattered blood on his shirt. "I'm Kathleen. My boyfriend got a job—"

"I know. I know. Italian, vorking vith zee elephants. You are American, but you don't vant to vork."

"I'll work," I said, crossing my arms over my chest, "soon as I figure out what I want to do."

He pointed his stump at me. "You stay away from Moira, or she figures it out for you." Erich waved off my thanks with a jab of fleshy arm and said, "You vant beautiful animals, you come see my tigers." Sunlight reflected off his balding head as he lumbered away.

The giraffe clip-clopped closer. I noticed how icy rivers of white hair flowed between the umber islands of his coat. When I reached for the fuzzy knobs on his head, his long ears flickered and his bony legs looked poised for flight. I lowered my hand and backed away.

Animal cages surrounded me. To the left of the backstage entrance, two railroad cars of tiger cages hugged the big top; to the right stood a pen made from four-inch-thick steel poles. Opposite backstage, spread between the tigers and the hefty cage, a crescent of yellow and blue pens completed the circus zoo.

The giraffe, Baros, watched me wander past the enclosures of his truck-mates—a bubble-eyed ostrich, a fluffy emu, and a raggedy North American buffalo that snorted and pawed at the dirt as I passed. I soaked up the giraffe's attention while perusing the truck housing a fuzzy llama, two ragamuffin camels, five antsy zebras, and five doe-eyed African antelopes. When I stopped to study a mural of a voluptuous woman surrounded by razor-toothed sharks, the giraffe peeked over the semi. Under his watch, I circled around until I came to a large truck connected to the enclosure made from four-inch-thick poles. Something big lived here.

The gate into the pen was wide open. Curiosity overruled common sense, so I ambled in, sidestepped an impressive mound of dung, and contemplated the gashes that left swaths of bare metal on the truck's walls. Right then, a tall blue-eyed, blond man ran out from the back of the tent. Hooves thundered behind him. I'd come looking for a massive beast to match the massive poles, yet the last thing I expected to see was a rhinoceros charging toward me. The blond shrieked and waved me away. I slipped between the bars and out of the enclosure just in time. A heavy chain clanked against the gate as the man secured it. The rhino snorted and spun inside his cage. Another man holding a whip raised his chin as if to take on airs and proceeded to scold me.

"Nino asks why you are in his rhinoceros cage," the blond man translated.

"I was just leaving," I said and headed for the elephant tent. The last thing Moira needed to hear was that I had nothing better to do than get in the way.

"Stefano?"

He appeared from between two elephants, scrub brush in one hand, a pail in the other.

"You have to come see—they have a giraffe, an emu, an ostrich, even sharks!"

"Sharks?" He lit a cigarette and stepped toward me.

"Either that or some half-woman-half-shark. Plus there's a buffalo and a rhino. Zebras and—hell, I wouldn't be surprised if they had a caterpillar on a mushroom."

"A what?"

"Come on." I pulled him toward the door. "They won't shoo me away if you're there too."

"Kat'leen." Stefano set his jaw in an unfamiliar way that made me feel like I was bothering him. He said, "I'm cleaning elephants."

"Right. Well . . . later, then." I looked away, then turned back to see the stern look still there. Straightening my back, I said, "Maybe I'll explore outside the circus."

"Giuseppe says we'll stay here at least two more weeks—plenty of time to look around." Stefano's expression softened as he set his pail down and stepped closer. "He finds a habitation—a lodging—for us, but it needs scrubbing." Stefano stamped out his half-smoked cigarette. "I find you a bucket and a brush."

"A scrub brush?"

I did not intend to come off as a spoiled American, but *scrubbing* and *lodging* were not words I used in the same sentence. I hadn't had my own apartment for over two years. Between moving out of my VW bus and living in an elephant tent in Spain, I'd flopped on couches, sneaked into squats, and slept in fields. My sleeping bag was my abode. Scrubbing? No. I was more likely to kick beer bottles and cigarette butts out of the way and then snuggle in for the night. I wouldn't have called those places clean, but I did call them home for a night or two.

On top of that, "habitation" sounded like a hamster cage to me—and that was just what our new home looked like. The end cubicle matched the tiny workers' bunks in Spain, except this one came with an outdoor carpet of empty vodka bottles strewn between our neighbors' steps and ours. A whiff of cigarettes and old sweat met me at the threshold. Considering the places I'd crashed on my journey south from Amsterdam, I shouldn't have been so dismayed, but something told me we'd be bedding down here a lot longer than a few nights. Propping open the window opposite the door and lugging out the soiled mattresses helped. I scrubbed the ceiling, walls, and floor with cold water and grew thankful that the room measured barely fifty square feet.

I met Stefano in the cafeteria at noon. The squat cook eyed me while Stefano explained that I didn't eat meat. She said she would do what she could to provide for me, and on that day offered spaghetti with tomato or spaghetti with butter and Parmesan cheese, accompanied by a single-portion box of wine. I glanced around—all the workers had little, employer-provided boxes of wine. *Food plus wine? Not bad*, I thought, unaware that my menu wouldn't change for months.

In Circo Moira Orfei, one crewmember was obligated to guard the elephants day and night. We would relieve the worker who'd been the *guardiano* while we ate, Stefano told me on our way back to the elephants, and then he and I would have the tent to ourselves while the others took their after-lunch break elsewhere.

Sitting behind me, straddling the same straw bale, Stefano draped his arms around my waist and spoke softly next to my ear. "Banana—third from the last—is the mean one. Giuseppe says stay away—she beats all the workers except the crew captain, Hassan. She try already to slam me this morning with her trunk. I raise the shovel in my hand to block her. She must think I'm about to hit her because next thing I know, she grabs my shovel with her trunk and is swinging at me. If Hassan wasn't watching . . ." Stefano's laugh conveyed more relief than humor. "And Shiva, the leetle one to the right, is dangerous too, but not bad like Banana." Stefano's hand wandered along my thigh. "Jenny, the big one on the end, is nice to people but hates Banana. Today she stretches over, pulls on her chains, and swings at Banana with her trunk. Poor Shiva in the middle gets hit instead." Stefano kissed my neck. His hand slid under my shirt to rest against my ribs.

"Tell me about the others."

"Whiskey, the first one, is the oldest. She seem calm, easy to work with. Then comes Babati; she is the hungry one. Keeps looping her trunk on my arm when I walk by, then pushing me toward the food. Is funny the way she does it—soft and strong all at once."

Someone behind us interrupted, saying, "You again."

I turned to see the English-speaking blond man from the rhinoceros pen standing in the door, looking surprised at the sight of Stefano and me entwined on the straw bale. "Don't tell me I'm not supposed to be in here, either."

"I could care less where you are," he said with a German accent, "but Nino is Moira's son. He'll break your balls no matter where you are or what you're doing."

Stefano stood up. "What happened?"

"I may have been a little too curious this morning," I explained.

Stefano grunted and stuck out his hand. "I am Stefano."

"Dieter. I run the horse tent and everything else Nino needs a hand with. Time to unload a delivery of hay. Let's go."

Stefano pecked my cheek and left.

"Hay," I told Hassan in Italian when the other workers

returned before Stefano did. I didn't know how to say that Dieter had called him away or that I'd guarded the elephants in the meantime. "*Fieno*," I repeated and returned to our future room to scrub the walls again.

Returning to the tent a few hours later, I found Stefano between two elephants with a sandpaper-wrapped block of wood in his hand. White dust cloaked his hair, skin, and clothing. Trickling sweat mixed with the powder, forming a paste that settled in his jaw stubble.

"That elephant dander all over you?"

Stefano wiped at the grime, baring a few pink stripes on one cheek. "We are cleaning the *elefanti*."

"Again?"

"First we clean their beds. Then we scrub them with soap and water. Now that they are dry, we sand their skin to an even shade."

"With sandpaper."

Stefano nodded and returned to the animal's hindquarters. "Is like the rubbing stone my *nonna* use on her feets. Hassan says we do this every day there is a show."

I ran my fingers back and forth along the ridges of the elephant's trunk. "What's her name?"

"Katia."

"Sure you're not hurting her?"

"After one and a half elephants, is hurting me, not them."

I followed him around the rear of the animal. "Giuseppe and his wife came by the room. She speaks English—said she couldn't see how a couple could fit on one bunk, so she told Giuseppe to have someone build us a bigger bed."

"Is good, no?"

It wasn't good; it was great. I just didn't expect anyone to care so much. Nor did I think to question why they might.

Sanding elephants to the perfect hue kept Stefano occupied right up to the four p.m. show. I sat out of the way on a pile of straw bales. Listening to workers' banter, I realized how much Italian I'd already learned—at least in certain fields. Conversing about day-to-day life, I would be lost. Discuss elephant menus or manure, and I could follow right along, if not join in. As the days passed, more and more words clicked for me. The trick was correlating Italian words to their English counterparts. *Acqua* sounded like aquatic and meant water. *Cavallo* sounded like cavalry and meant horse. *Spettacolo*, spectacle or show. *Indovinare*, to divine or guess. *Stelle*, stars. *Tenda*, tent. Picking apart the words helped me to understand. To make myself understood, however, I learned that adding a vowel to the end of the English word usually communicated what I intended. Elephant—*elefante*, tiger—*tigre*, animals—*animali*, machine—*macchina*. The technique wasn't failsafe, of course. Once, when asked about vegetarianism and my penchant for salads, I explained that I preferred to eat my food more natural—without preservatives, "pree-ser-vah-tee-vee." Dropped jaws and howls of laughter stopped me mid-explanation, and Stefano promptly informed me that I'd just said I preferred my food without condoms.

Fumbled meanings were only one hurdle to learning Italian. Even when armed with the accurate word, correct pronunciation and proper lilt were a completely different sport. The only reason for consonants in the Italian language is to trampoline vowels into the air, and I learned to speak as if orthodontic rubber bands kept my jaws bouncing. *Ciao, bella. Mamma mia. Amore mio.* But I was just as likely to wish someone *Buon Anno*, Happy New Year, as I was to wish them *Buon Ano*, Happy Asshole.

Regardless of the tribulations of learning a new language,

I soon graduated from waving my hands around a pertinent word or two to forming sentences—which presented a new problem. Word order was hell. Italians say *I you love* instead of *I love you* and *elephant gray* instead of *gray elephant.* My attempts to form sentences came out disjointed and garbled, as if whirled in a blender. After each effort, I had to ask the person I spoke with if he or she understood. At least saying *te capi*—the Milanese version of "do you understand," pronounced "take a pee"—left me grinning every time.

But on that first day in the circus, forming proper Italian sentences had little importance, as I had no one to talk with.

When Stefano finally paused for dinner before the eight p.m. show, I asked, "You always going to be this *occupato*?"

Stefano wolfed down his pasta. "How could I know, Kat'leen? Is only the first day."

I pushed the noodles and tomato sauce around in my bowl. "How late do you have to work?"

Stefano's pork chop disappeared in two bites, and he set his sights on my dinner. "You done with that?"

I pushed my pasta toward him. "Will you answer my question?"

"Not if I don't know the answer."

Under the big top, inside the *pista*—the performance ring—a cherry-lipped contortionist wrapped her body around itself like a finial on a wrought-iron fence, five pairs of zebras and African antelope do-si-doed in an exotic square dance, and the ostrich hauled a leprechaun around the ring. Inside the elephant tent, I waited for my lover to finish his day so we could finally make good on the pledge he'd made in Venice to be 'all day together.' But Stefano had also promised the elephants that he'd improve their lives. Promised the circus that he'd work for their paycheck. Promised himself that he'd earn Giuseppe's respect. I was blind to all but one of his promises.

When I brought his after-dinner coffee from a nearby bar, Stefano told me to stand aside and watch as he poured one packet of sugar into his coffee and stuck the second into the breast pocket of his work shirt. He stirred the sugar and espresso into a syrupy solution, gulped it down, and stepped toward Shiva, the littlest of Moira's elephants. Shiva stretched her trunk toward his mouth, paused inches from Stefano's lips, and then wriggled the tip of her trunk into his pocket to pull out the sugar packet and pop it in her mouth, paper and all.

"You see?" Stefano looked proud. "When she smell coffee in my mouth she knows there is a sugar in my pocket." Bobbing her head up and down as if asking for more, Shiva frisked his pocket again. "I think she is my favorite," Stefano said, laughing as the elephant patted him down. "Is all day I am working to teach her that." I must have looked jealous, because he immediately added, "In between all of the work, of course."

It was long past midnight before he laced the elephant tent shut, turned out the lights, and slumped onto the straw bales.

"At last," I whispered, snuggling into his arms to watch the elephants. I could have easily mistaken these vague figures swaying in the dark for the elephants in Spain. Recalling the romantic nights we'd spent in their company, I said, "Close that door and the whole circus disappears, don't you think? . . . Stefano?"

I listened to his sleeping breath and let the rhythmic creaking of elephants swaying on wooden planks croon me to sleep.

CHAPTER FOURTEEN

MOVING IN

Circo Moira Orfei was an encampment with nearly 300 people filling its ranks. The set-up, complete with telephones, cisterns, and refrigerator trucks, a schoolhouse, a box office, and a laundry truck, easily covered an entire city block. In addition to a 3,000-seat big top and huge tents housing elephants and horses, another *tendone* accommodated two tire specialists, three welders, and six mechanics. Most of the electricity to power everything inside and outside of the show came from tapping into city lines. Multiple generators backed up the local supply, the largest a rumbling beast that produced 700 kilowatts an hour. The circus consumed almost 4,000 gallons of diesel during a typical winter week *when still.* Moira's circus was an island on wheels, an all-inclusive gated community—just not one where I belonged.

Stefano assured me that I could be in the tent with him whenever I wanted, as in Spain, but the two elephant tents had different vibes. There, I'd been Stefano's lover, his confidante; I felt involved. Here, I was a spectator—or worse, an intruder. It didn't help that three men had already propositioned Stefano in three days—a manager's stout-bodied domestic help; the old ticket-man with the barest fringe of hair circling his pate; and the stylish set designer who'd offered Stefano some clothes if he could watch while Stefano tried them on. Their advances unsettled me. Not because I doubted Stefano's sexuality, but because I shared their need. The circus was a fishbowl where people begged attention in extreme and bizarre ways—both from the public and from each other. Three hundred souls packed so close you couldn't get naked without the whole place knowing, yet everybody was left wanting.

The first time I ventured beyond the circus fence, I stayed away one hour, the second, four hours. By my third excursion, Rome won, and the teeming city filled my empty days. I lingered among the flower vendors in Campo de' Fiori, writing letters from a sidewalk café while opera cascaded like geraniums over a balcony and into the square. I lay in the sun on the slopes of Circus Maximus, writing in my journal while watching elderly women cut dandelion greens with stubby knives and deposit them in their black aprons.

February 5, 1989, Rome, Italy: Roma, Roma, bella Roma! Six-week anniversary with Stefano. Six weeks! Love is grand, but I have so much to learn about being in a relationship—when to give, when not to take . . .

In Rome's museums, plazas, and ruins, I found the Italy of dreams and postcards, a stolen vacation. Eating breakfast and dinner in the circus and sleeping in the elephant tent, I could have survived for days on a couple of dollars' worth of cappuccinos and public transportation. Instead, I wandered crowded markets buying odd bits of clothing—a secondhand, black wool vest that might have belonged to a diplomat and some gauzy Indian scarves for our room. Rome enchanted me, but each time I returned to the big top, to the yellow and blue city within a city, I felt alone.

The monotony of the elephant tent eased when we moved into our room. A week's worth of scrubbings had conquered the odors. With the upper bunk removed and the lower bunk widened from two feet to three and a half, topped with a new mattress, and clothed in crisp red sheets, our *abitazione* looked . . . inhabitable. I drummed my fingers on the rickety stand by the door and made a mental list—replace the scrap of wool draped over the window with my new scarves, find a privacy screen for the door and a washbasin for the stand . . . My eyes paused where Stefano had already written his name on the wall. I dug my journal out of my pack, found his seagull drawings, and taped them above his name. *Home.* Before putting my journal away, I jotted down how comforted I felt to have a place of our own.

I transferred the clothes from my pack to the plastic fruit crates we'd use as shelves and recalled how hitchhiking south from Amsterdam through Belgium, France, and Spain, my pack had always felt like an entire dresser strapped to my back. Its contents barely filled two crates. Stefano's clothes didn't even fill one, as most of them were crammed into a laundry bag. In Spain, Stefano had done his own washing in a bucket. I appreciated that he never asked me to do the job, but regretted that his clothes never came clean.

Grabbing the bulging sack and his last clean pair of jeans, I headed for the tent. "Change your clothes," I called to Stefano as I marched in. "It's time to do the wash. How do you say 'Laundromat'?"

Cantaloupe-sized balls of elephant dung rocked the wheelbarrow as he heaved them in. "What is, Kat'leen?"

"Coin-operated machines to wash and dry clothes."

"I never seen a machine that dries clothes, and *lavatrice* are only in people's houses."

Since ancient Romans used aqueducts thousands of years ago, it seemed preposterous that modern Romans didn't have Laundromats in 1989. But as hard as I tried, I couldn't recall seeing one during my jaunts around Rome.

Katia inspected my laundry sack as I eased between her and Bimba. "Hey girl." I rubbed her trunk and pulled the sack from her reach. "So how do less-fortunate Italians wash their clothes?" I asked Stefano.

"How you think?"

"I'm not giving up so easily. Drop your pants."

On my way off the lot, I passed by our room to pick up the Italian travel guide I'd found in Rome. Farther down the row of rooms, Neil Diamond blared from Dieter's cubicle. Long ropes of plastic garland hung in the open doorway, keeping out flies and prying eyes. When I knocked on the exterior wall, Dieter peeked through the tendrils.

"Got any Grateful Dead in there?" I asked.

"Who?" Dieter's smile exposed teeth so tangled, they looked more confused than his eyes. "I've got everything Neil Diamond's ever done."

"Thanks anyway." I eyed the neatly made bed, his stacks of books, and folded clothing. "You ever seen a Laundromat in Italy?"

"Haven't looked. Erich lets me use his machine." Dieter motioned to the railcar's tongue. "It's under that tarp."

"Lucky you. So where do I find a Laundromat?"

Dieter shook his head. "Doubt you will."

I opened the back cover of my guide and held it out. "You mind writing down coin-operated washing machine and dryer in Italian for me?"

Dieter scribbled a few words. "Waste of time," he said and turned back into his room.

Stefano and Dieter would learn what a woman with information at her fingertips could accomplish. I stopped outside the circus fence to search the travel guide's index. Under L, I found Lake Garda, Last Supper, Leonardo da Vinci, and Lesbian Travelers. Under W, I found Water, Wine, and Willy Wonka. Under C, I found Climate, Coagulated Blood, and Coffee. I flipped to the front of the book. Under Essentials, I found Clothing, Packing, and eventually Washing. *Washing!* Reading further, I found the suggestion to use my hotel sink.

Every block surrounding the circus seemed to have a dry cleaner, and every clerk shook her head as she read my note. Each time, I held out Dieter's note more tentatively than the last. Half a mile away from the circus, a young woman working alone in a dry cleaner took pity on me.

"I have traveled to America," she told me in perfect English as she studied me with vibrant green eyes. "I know the drying machine you're looking for. You won't find one here, but I do have the machine to wash clothes. Let's load your things."

"Tell me," she said after learning what brought a foreigner so far from the touristy center of Rome. "What are you circus people like?"

"I'm not one of them. My boyfriend . . . It's temporary."

"I saw Moira whip a man in a movie once—and now she whips elephants in the most famous circus in all of Italy." Steam clouded her face as she pressed an industrial iron into a pair of slacks. "How is she in person? As beautiful as she looks when I see her with the Pope or Prince Rainier on TV?"

I explained that I hadn't seen Moira, much less spoken with her, and told the young woman about giraffes and riding elephants instead. Forty-five minutes later, my wash finished, I thanked her and loaded the wet laundry into my sack.

"Come back to visit," she said. "Wash your clothes whenever you need to. And try to talk to Moira."

The Queen of the Elephants presented only her splendorous side to the public, and displaying laundry meant a stiff fine against paychecks. Empty equipment haulers were strung wall to wall with clothesline, their doors latched shut to hide the drying laundry. It seemed silly to me. Ropes studded with colorful plastic clothespins laced half of Italy's apartment buildings together. Across the land, neighbors' sheets tickled one another and socks played footsie in plain sight. In the circus, we had to tuck ours away, as if to hide our humanity and prove that we lived to work rather than worked to live.

Inside one of the haulers, I draped a pair of jeans over the line and ran my palms over the cool, wet denim to smooth the wrinkles. I was having more physical contact with Stefano's pants than I'd had with him lately. Good thing he considered working with the elephants a labor of love, because not much energy remained for other labors of love. I half expected Boredom to creep up behind me, tap its know-it-all finger on my shoulder, and urge me back toward the open road. But I didn't want more independence; I wanted more Stefano.

This time, running away was not going to get me what I wanted.

"I came to see your tigers."

Erich looked up from the long-handled shovel he was squirting with a hose. He said nothing. Beyond him, golden eyes tracked his movements. A pacing tiger rubbed against the bars of his cage, his tail hovering behind him like a cobra, his barbed tongue glistening as it slid between white fangs. *Pddth-ddth-ddth-ddth. Pddth-ddth-ddth-ddth.*

"What kind is he?"

"Zimbali is Bengal, but there are Sumatran and Siberian as vell." Erich leaned the dripping shovel against the end of the trailer.

"What do they eat?" I asked.

"Lucky you, I'm feeding them late today. Come vith me."

I followed him beyond the zoo to a small blue tent tucked between two trucks. When Erich propped open the tent, the bouquet of raw, tepid flesh oozed out with a cloud of flies. He donned a plastic apron, hefted a slab of fresh meat onto a stout chopping block, and hacked at the seeping carcass with his cleaver. He held a bloodied chunk up for me to see. After finding me loitering around the animals almost every morning since we'd arrived a week ago, did Erich want to know if I'd cringe when exposed to the down and dirty of caring for them?

"Thanks," I said, "but I'm vegetarian."

The German hewed through meat and bone, splattering blood on himself and the walls of the tent.

"That how you lost your fingers?"

Erich paused his whacking. "No. Bitten off."

"Musta hurt."

"Not as much as this."

With a blood-crusted hand, he lifted his T-shirt to bare a mishmash of suture lines and scar tissue. His torso looked like a puzzle.

"Jesus." The bravado I'd mustered vanished. "A tiger did that?"

"Polar bear." He let his shirt fall back into place.

"There are polar bears here?"

"No. Vorking in America. Vun swipe crushes my shoulder, leaves my arm dangling. Mostly metal now." His blue wheelbarrow rocked as Erich tossed in goose-sized hunks of meat. "Vun second. My attention goes away from her for vun second and look vat she does."

He stretched what remained of his arm, as if reassuring himself it was still there, and then maneuvered the wheelbarrow out of the tent and back to the tigers.

"Is how things happen in zee circus."

Erich lifted a small hatch at the front of an empty cage on one end, pushed a chunk of meat onto the floor, and slid open a divider between the first and second cage. The tiger pounced on the meat and circled the cage before settling in a back corner. Erich shut the divider, lobbed the next piece of meat in the newly emptied second cage, and slid open the divider between the second and third cages to let in the waiting tiger. The cat inhaled deeply and lay down, steadying the fresh meat in her claws as she slurped it clean of blood.

Glancing my way, Erich said, "Be careful here."

CHAPTER FIFTEEN

SOUNDS OF THE WILD KINGDOM

"Moira knows you're here." Stefano tossed what remained of his cigarette as he climbed the steps to our room.

My grip on the toothbrush I offered him went limp. *"Minchia."*

Technically, the word means penis in Sicilian, but it expressed "wow," or, in this case, "oh no." Ten days in Moira's circus and I'd already learned to cuss in Italian, German, Polish, and Arabic. With the few choice verses I'd imported from Spain and my American repertoire, I could offend almost anyone, intentionally or not. The problem was that parroting words trumped grasping their meaning. When the Arabs said *zeppe*, I thought zippy, as in happy or energetic. They meant penis, and they considered the fact that it sounded similar to Giuseppe's nickname, Beppe, one hell of a bonus. At the slightest provocation, the Poles would cry *kurwa jebana*, and I thought curve, as if they'd hit an unsuspected curve in the road, which is one hell of a difference from what it really means: a whore, doing what whores do.

During our early days together, Stefano had to adjust to my penchant for latching onto words whether or not I felt their emotional weight. Words such as *scurnacchiat'*. To this day, I love the way it rolls off my tongue—*skuurrr-na-kyat*. Unfortunately, it is Neapolitan for *cornuto*, or horned, and not to be confused with the English horny. Considering that Italians "grow horns" when their spouses sleep around, it is safe to say that being *cornuto* is bad for Italians and definitely *not* a wise response when a burly Neapolitan customs agent asks if you've learned any words in his dialect! One day, Stefano would label me his *scaricatrice di porto*, his dockworker, but on the night he informed me that Moira had learned of my presence, he just chuckled and reached for his toothbrush.

"Nice," he said, noticing the scarves I'd hung over the window and the candles flickering on the stand beside the door. "Moira stops Giuseppe twice today, asks why you haven't been to see her yet," he mumbled through toothpaste.

I sank to the bed. "Did she say anything about me dancing?"

"I don't think she has a chance."

Stefano rinsed his mouth, spat out the door, and sat on the edge of the bed to slip off his clothes. Although the circus provided a shower room for workers, Stefano rarely spent half an hour in line at the end of a long day, choosing a sponge bath instead. Dunking a washcloth in the bucket of water I'd warmed with the homemade heating element we'd brought from Spain, he worked his way from his face on down, over the peace sign tattooed over his heart—because that is where peace comes from, he'd once said—and the tummy that had noticeably grown since our arrival in Italy.

"Feels good," he said, finally easing his feet into the bucket.

"Don't worry about Moira. Giuseppe tells her he needs you to feed some animals."

"Which animals?" I sat upright. "What am I supposed to feed them?"

"So many questions, Kat'leen." Stefano dried his feet and pulled the covers over both of us. "For the exotic troupe. The regular workers don't do it right. Giuseppe says he needs someone who cares."

I sat up again. "How does he know I care?"

"I tell him you do." Stefano pulled me back down and wrapped his leg over mine. "So does Erich the tiger man. I think everybody in the circus knows."

"Everybody? Who's everybody?"

"Shhh." Stefano stifled my questions with a sloppy kiss.

"Shhh," I whispered back. From next door, Izaak and Borys's drunken conversation sounded so clear, it seemed as if they sat on the creaking bed with us. "They'll hear."

"If they heard that, then they definitely going to hear this." Stefano smooched my neck. "And this." Another kiss on my shoulder.

Passion. Heat. *Amore.* I forgot about who could or couldn't hear us.

Many of the exotic animals ate their share of hay during the day, but the antelope, giraffe, llama, buffalo, ostrich, emu, and camels required additional meals at eight a.m. and four p.m. It was my new job to make them.

ANTELOPE: 1 scoop oat bran, 5 carrots, 5 apples.

GIRAFFE: 2 scoops oat bran, 5 carrots, 1 scoop wheat bread, 2 heads lettuce. Moisten.

LLAMA: ½ scoop oat bran, 3 carrots, 3 apples. Moisten.

BUFFALO: 1 scoop oat bran, 5 carrots, 5 apples, 1 scoop white bread chunks.

OSTRICH: 1 scoop oat bran, 5 carrots, 5 apples, 1 head lettuce. Cut small. Moisten.

EMU: ½ scoop oat bran, 3 carrots, 3 apples, ½ head lettuce. Cut very small. Moisten.

CAMELS: 1½ scoops oat bran, 5 carrots, 5 apples, 1 scoop white bread.

I looked over the list of detailed recipes and sighed. I'd wanted to work with the animals, but this seemed a hell of a lot like cooking.

All animal eyes focused on me as I plopped down on an overturned tub between the crates of fruit and bread. I tossed two heads of lettuce on the chopping block and unsheathed the paring knife Giuseppe had given me. Mina, the poofy brown and white llama named after a soulful Italian singer, curled her lip and pelted me with sour mash every time I moved. I flicked the chunks off my shirt and dragged my ingredients closer to Baros, the giraffe.

When traveling, the giraffe hauler was a standard-height truck. Baros had to sit down to fit. As soon as the circus parked, workers used a pneumatic lift to raise the outer shell of the giraffe's custom digs, doubling its height to twelve feet and allowing the animal to stand inside. Baros poked his head out from his tower of a truck. I pushed my fingers through his chain link fence and waved a dark green leaf. He took a few tentative steps down his ramp and inhaled. A few more steps and warm breath wafted over my skin. The giraffe twirled the tip of his tongue around the leaf and succeeded in ripping some off before lurching away. Baros studied me from behind lashes that would shame Max Factor. Unfolding my fingers, I revealed another strip of Romaine. Baros came closer and lowered his checkered cheeks. When I didn't push the lettuce through the fence, he finessed his tongue through a link and licked my hand like a lollipop as he tried unsuccessfully to take the leaf. Finally, he lifted his head over the fence. Baros extended his tongue farther and farther, wriggling it between my fingers, prying the treat from my grip. Gazing at my distorted reflection in his obsidian eyes, I realized there were far worse things to do in the circus than make animal food.

In addition to the room and board I already received, Walter, Moira's husband, deemed an hour and a half of preparing the exotic troupe's morning and afternoon food worth 10,000 lire a day—a whopping seven bucks. Stefano made only four times that much plus room and board for working up to sixteen hours a day. The circus kept ten percent of our paychecks—a retainer, they called it, a *cauzione*. The word sounded like caution to me, as if intended to give the worker caution before fleeing. It was a leash that Moira held snugly in her hand.

"Did you know the giraffe's tongue is so gray it looks purple?" I giggled and leaned across the cafeteria table during lunch, eager to share my experience with Stefano. His face reflected my glow. I lingered in the moment of mutual happiness before saying, "I never imagined making friends with a gir—"

Izaak called my name from the other end of the lunch truck. When we looked up, he rattled in broken Italian and laughed. A few others laughed too.

"What?" I asked, chuckling along. "Someone dancing on TV last night?"

Stefano shook his head. "Don't listen to him."

"*Ti-vu ballando,*" Izaak said again, standing up to rut his hips back and forth. That time, the whole cafeteria laughed. Brows arching over intense blue eyes, Izaak asked, "*Capito*?"

I did understand. When Stefano and I made love the previous night, not only were Izaak and Borys along for the ride, but also the other two workers in the center room, Dieter in the fourth room, and Erich on the far end. I struggled for some spirited comment to toss back at Izaak, but his jab had hit me where I hurt. It exposed my greatest need and my greatest fear. Left me feeling empty and alone. Stripped me naked in front of forty men.

I would never have Stefano to myself.

Izaak's *shreek shreek shreek* simulation of our creaking bed chased me down the cafeteria steps.

"I hate it here," I told Stefano when he caught up. "We almost never make love, and when we do, we can't even keep it to ourselves."

"Shhh." He closed his hands around mine and pulled my fingers to his lips. In the midst of this slow-motion kiss, Stefano stole backwards down a narrow corridor between vehicles. When we arrived at the hay truck, he swung open its back door and pulled me into two feet of gloom between a wall of hay and the metal door he shut behind us.

"I don't like this."

"You will." Stefano hoisted himself up and disappeared between the stack of bales and the roof of the truck.

Ten feet away, in the halo of a flashlight, he motioned for me to follow. I wormed through the crawl space, ignoring the hay scratching my arms and snagging my hair. Three bale-lengths in, the hay opened up into a cave just large enough to allow us to lie down. Hazy sunlight from a pair of air vents showed Stefano's sleeping bag piled in a corner.

I smiled. "You did this?"

"Loading the truck this morning." Stefano helped me out of the crawl space, and his kiss chipped away the humiliation I'd felt minutes earlier. "Now you like?"

I did like. No, *I loved.*

The heady aroma of hay engulfed us for the next half hour and most of our after-lunch rendezvous over the following week. No matter how many bales workers hauled into the animal tents during the coming days, Stefano kept our hay cave partitioned off. Elephants, bosses, and coworkers claimed most hours of Stefano's days, but those thirty minutes belonged to us. Though we both reveled in our restored intimacy, my days revolved around those lunch-hour trysts and the hope that we just might find a way to carve room into this life for us.

"We leave Rome in two days," Stefano said one day as he reached over and plucked a pale green blade of hay from my curls. "This truck is going to be loaded with gear tomorrow."

I stopped buttoning my shirt. "But it'll empty out again, won't it?"

He shook his head. "Hassan says is used for hay only when we stay in long towns."

For the sake of privacy, our future lovemaking would be shared with seven elephants and limited to his turn as guardian every fourth day.

CHAPTER SIXTEEN

RASTA

During our first cafeteria meal in the new *piazza*, Stefano scrutinized the tomato-drenched noodles I slid from one side of my dish to the other. "I know," he said, "cooking. That's what Italian weemuns do when they are bored. We could buy a leetle burner. Set it up on our steps."

Splendid. I want a lover, he offers a propane camping stove. "I don't want a hobby, Stefano. I want you."

His hands flew up, then crossed over his chest. "Just trying to help."

"If you want to help, then touch me. Hold me. *Be with me*." I eased my hand into his. "Find the time to take a walk or something. *Anything*."

"Is my turn at *guardiano*."

"Then I'll come to the tent."

"A load of hay is coming."

"Of course, work."

"Is the nature of the circus, Kat'leen."

Funny how only the most unnatural entity around could keep to its nature. The rest of us, man and beast, were bound to follow its course by need, desire, or chains.

Though Stefano dedicated his day to his job, I counted on him dedicating his night as guardian to us. But moments into our midnight tryst, I pulled away from a fizzling kiss to discover Stefano sleeping with his arms stuck in the air as if I were still in them. His workload gave him every right to be exhausted. At the time, however, I knew only of my need to be reassured and his inability to do so. I crept back to our room and curled into one corner of a bed built for two.

Longing for that childhood sense of security my father's love once provided, I reminisced about how he used to put me to bed with great fanfare. How he used to flap the sheets and blankets so their breeze tickled my cheeks before he tucked me in snugly enough to keep out any threats to his baby girl's dreams.

Sometimes, I wonder if I loved my father more than I loved my mother when I was young. It's not that he loved me more than she did; he just showed it differently. My father, the great creator of pet names that oozed affection, doled out tender monikers such as Weeblit, Wicktil, Leekus, and Roonis to his children—and every stuffed animal, baby doll, and gerbil we toted home. I remember the countless times Daddy cuddled me on his beer-belly lap to keep me company or quiet tears.

My mother showed her love in other ways—such as homemade cookies and Singer-stitched dresses. She turned whole grain from her parents' ranch into beautiful bread; stretched a small budget to feed, clothe, and entertain four children; and she hid the painful distance between her and my father. Efficiency pulled her face as taut as the strings on her

Martin guitar. Affection, the type that fills a child with giggly warmth, remained trapped beneath my mother's struggle to make the best out of what life dealt her. She is, of course, the parent who stayed the course.

At twenty-three, I still sought my father's showy brand of attention. In the currency of young love, Stefano's kisses were more precious than his enduring integrity, and I calculated the depth of his emotion by the quantity of his affections rather than the quality of his actions.

Early the next morning, Stefano peeked in the door. I lifted my head and unwrapped my arms from his pillow.

"Sorry I felled to sleep," he whispered. He pulled a ball of wiggling white fuzz out of the pocket of his work coveralls: a scrawny puppy. I reached for it, felt its heartbeat in my hands, kissed the velvety black smudge on its forehead. Laughter bubbled out of me while he licked my face with puppy abandon and bathed me in warm puppy breath.

Stefano looked as radiant as a new father. "The mamma was so skinny her bones stick out. No way she has enough milk to grow two babies." Stefano reached his arms around both the puppy and me and said, "We're going to save him."

Only three weeks old, his eyes still cloudy, the English setter mix needed constant supervision. When not eating, the *cagnolino* slept in my arms, lounged across my neck, or snuggled inside my shirt, consuming my spare hours as quickly as his meals. Giuseppe lent us a baby bottle used to feed rejected tiger cubs, and I forayed into town to buy a small propane burner. Stefano's eyes brightened the moment he saw it.

"The puppy needs his milk warmed," I told him.

"Of course. Is only for warming milk. You think of a name yet?"

"All afternoon I've been listening to Bob Marley sing about joy coming from within. This puppy makes me feel warm inside."

"You want to call him Bob?"

"I was thinking Rasta."

"For Rastafarian?"

"It's better than Bob, isn't it?"

Our stint in the following *piazza*, Caserta, lasted only three days. It took over 200 men five hours to set the circus up, and with an evening show that first day, two shows on the second day, and two more on the third day followed by a three-hour takedown, life outside the big top soon mimicked the fast-paced show within.

While Stefano worked, I hauled Rasta around the zoo, introducing him to the animals. The giraffe licked him; the llama sniffed once and then spit on both of us. In front of the tigers, Rasta burrowed into the crook of my arm and whimpered while Erich explained the intricacy of shepherding twelve tense tigers the entire length of their conjoined cages, through the tiger tunnel, and into the *pista*. The puppy curled in my lap while I prepared the exotic food in the mornings and afternoons, and during the hours in between, we roamed fields surrounding the circus and made forays into town to replenish his supply of milk and other necessities.

"Soap," I said the word louder this time, but the shopkeeper just stared. "Soapa?"

She pulled a can of minestrone off a shelf and handed it to me. *"Zuppa?"*

"Not soup." I shelved the can.

I'd finally conceded to hand wash the beyond-dirty clothing heaped in a corner of our room, but I lacked the cleanser to do so. Setting Rasta down, I studied plastic bottles and cardboard packages. All dish soap—which I supposed would do. "Soap," I tried one last time, pretending to squirt something on my shirt and scrub it.

The shopkeeper's eyes lit. *"Sapone?"* She snatched a box from another shelf. *"Sa-po-ne."*

Eying the stack of folded clothes pictured on the container, I said, "Yeah, *sapone*," and thought it wasn't a far stretch from *soap*. I added a few bottles of Peroni beer and grabbed a blue tub from a stack in the corner. In the meantime, Rasta piddled on the floor.

The woman lifted a roll of paper towels out from under her counter. *"Scottex."*

"*Scottex*," I repeated, cleaning the mess and adding two rolls to my pile.

On the way back to the circus, I stopped in a dairy for Rasta's milk. The cheese display caught my attention. I'd eaten nothing but pasta with tomato or pasta with butter for weeks, so I added a block of fontina and a ball of fresh mozzarella to my order and thought, *Making sandwiches isn't really cooking, is it?*

Minutes later in a bakery, I stared at my newly purchased loaf of bread and wondered where to carry it. I'd left my knapsack at the circus and would never make it all the way back carrying the *cagnolino* in one arm and everything else in the other. Rasta rolled more than he walked, leaving me one choice: nestle the puppy down the front of my T-shirt and into my bra. The shocked baker laughed.

Before leaving town, two apples, four blood oranges, and a salami for Stefano overloaded my bags. I ignored the locals' stares as I toted my purchases down the streets of Caserta in my paisley skirt and silver bangles, with my corkscrew curls bouncing around my face and the head of a white puppy peeking out of my V-neck. Stefano had warned me that most foreigners never make it to Italy's lower regions, and the farther south we traveled, the more of an oddity I'd be. I don't think he realized how odd.

Stefano froze in the doorway of our room.

"It's only fruit and sandwiches."

"But is food. *You are making food.*"

"Don't get any ideas. I spent two days' wages on one meal. We can't afford to cook for ourselves, even if I wanted to."

Stefano slipped his knife out of his pocket and opened it more slowly, more ceremoniously, than usual. He sliced the tip off the salami and peeled its skin in small, careful strips, as if peeling overripe fruit. He may have managed to control his hands, but he did a poor job of restraining the lilt in his voice when he said, "You saying you want to?"

"No."

It wasn't *no* with anger or malice or to withhold something from him; it was *no* to save something for me. On one hand, Stefano loved that I was different; on the other, he wanted me to slip into the Italian-woman mold, cooking and cleaning for her man. The old have your cake and eat it too — or, as Italians say: your barrel full and your wife drunk. I said *no* to preserve my identity and my independence.

On our final day in Caserta, Stefano's crew simultaneously prepared for the show and dismantled the tent. Giuseppe conferred with Stefano before leaving him in charge while the trainer and Hassan led the elephants to the ring. Stefano rose to the occasion. He kept Izaak and Borys on the ball—even made them refold a section of tent that didn't look just right. When the animals returned after their performance, Hassan and Borys fed and watered the beasts while Stefano and Izaak grunted and strained to heave unwieldy bundles of perfectly folded tent onto the steel-framed elephant decks. I watched my lover pause more than once to dig his thumb into his lower back and knead the spot where Bambi had walloped him in Spain.

He asked me later if I'd seen when Giuseppe had put him in charge. I nodded and told him that I'd also seen how he and the animal trainer had started to seem more like friends than employer and employee.

Though many Italian artists worked for the circus, few were laborers. Most of Stefano's countrymen thought the job too menial, the hours too long, the work too dirty. But having a *paesano* in the tent clearly pleased Giuseppe, just as receiving Giuseppe's trust pleased Stefano.

Just as nurturing Rasta pleased me.

Stefano's not-so-sly attempt at diverting my attention from him was a huge success. The dog brought joy into my days and gave me something besides Stefano to care for. Maybe Rasta would never provide the secure fatherly companionship my dad once had or the constant romantic companionship I desired with Stefano, but he did a helluva job of making me feel needed. Even more, he unfurled a motherly instinct in me that I hadn't known I possessed.

The day he brought Rasta home, Stefano had said that we were going to save him. Little did we know that, one day, the puppy might save us.

CHAPTER SEVENTEEN

ANIMAL RIGHTS AND WRONGS

The circus could easily fill a few acres, but not every town had that much space to offer. When logistics separated elements of the circus, the elephants were the first to relocate. They were the most intelligent circus animal and didn't panic easily, as if understanding what the circus demanded from them lessened their fear. Moira's elephants may not have scaled Alps and stormed Roman territories as Hannibal's elephants had, but the chains that bound them still seemed insufficient. I often wondered why none of them ever threw a four-ton tantrum and broke free. Perhaps they had long ago, before their confinement had become routine.

The whirl of Giuseppe's metal whistle punctuated the grumble of semis arriving in Catanzaro Lido, and the sprinkling of parked vehicles became an intricate web around a 250-foot-diameter clearing the big top would soon fill. To this day, it riles me to hear anyone correlate a disorganized mess with the finely tuned instrument that is a circus. Every facet of its existence—man, woman, animal, vehicle, tent, performing act, hosting town, and attending public, magnified by the incredible potential for the unknown—is figured into every equation, every day. Like a perfectly designed Rube Goldberg machine, should one aspect end up an inch or an instant off its mark, if men such as Giuseppe and Walter were not constantly harnessing its explosive and implosive energy with painstaking precision, this whirling twirling machine could stop cold, potentially leaving hundreds of people without work and thousands of attendees in harm's way.

When the forty-foot elephant truck Stefano and I rode on was summoned to the front of the positioning line, Giuseppe waved his sinewy arms in exaggerated directions through dust-filled air, instructing the driver to park a third of a mile down the road, next to a gravel decline that led to the beach. Drivers had already parked the railcars that held our room and the elephant tent along the shore. Beyond the railcars, the turquoise Ionian Sea sparkled in the mid-morning sun. The Greek Isles were some 300 miles out to sea from the arch of Italy's boot, yet this rocky stretch of beach looked like paradise to me.

With Rasta in my arms, I sprinted across smooth stones to the sea and flicked off my moccasins. Cool, clear water lapped against my knees as I waded in, and the hem of my skirt floated on the surface. Stefano watched from the trucks.

I waved him over, yelled, "Jump in." But he shook his head and swung open the rear doors of an elephant truck.

After dipping our squirming puppy in the water and bringing him back to shore, I looked up again to see Stefano at the back of the second elephant hauler staring toward the main *piazza*. He looked down at me and then back at the *piazza*.

Choose me.

Giuseppe's whistle called like a far-off bird.

Choose me.

I lingered another moment before wading back into the water.

His footsteps pounded across the beach. Barely pausing to shed shoes, socks, and jeans, Stefano dove into the cool water. Laughing, splashing, frolicking, we slipped under the surface. The circus disappeared. Bubbles gurgled between us as we sank to the pebble bottom. I wrapped my legs around him, and we drifted from shore, holding our breath and our embrace for as long as we could before shooting up for air, still in each other's arms. The moment my ears broke from the water, I heard the chugging forklift and Rasta yapping from shore. Izaak and Borys were perched on the back of the tractor; Giuseppe piloted it over the beach.

I clung to Stefano as if I could stop him, but he slipped from my arms.

"You drive a forklift?" Giuseppe yelled over the engine.

Stefano pulled jeans over dripping underwear. "No."

"Then you'll learn." Giuseppe showed him how to maneuver the gearshift and operate the lift. "Keep control of your load, Stefano," he warned as he left, "always keep control of your load."

"Where's Hassan?" I asked, stepping up onto the tractor.

"Izaak says two trucks are broken down. Maybe he's on one." Stefano shrugged as I stepped back down. "Maybe."

He coaxed the battered yellow forklift into gear and began unloading the tent with all its poles and coils of rope from the trailer. After a long walk down the beach, Rasta and I returned to find the tent complete and the crew cleaning all the elephants except Banana. Dinnertime came and went; Hassan never arrived.

Whistling some classical tune as he often did, Giuseppe showed up early to make sure Banana didn't strike Stefano as he tidied her hide and fastened her headdress. The animal trainer sounded pleased, and he spoke to Stefano in the same reassuring voice he used with his animals. When he said the words *grande responsabilità*, Stefano lifted his chin and straightened his back. He stood as proud as a flagpole.

"Everyone believes Hassan has escaped," Stefano told me as he unchained Banana.

"I hate that everyone says *escaped* when someone leaves."

"I told you before, you don't just leave the circus. They pressure you to stay—then steal your deposit or keep your papers if pressure doesn't work." He looked up from the elephant's leg irons. "When is time to go, we go, no matter what. But I want to talk about staying." Holding his gaze on me, he said, "Giuseppe asks if I will take Hassan's job."

The tent closed in on me so fast I fought to breathe. "Crew captain?"

"Giuseppe values my work." Stefano's eyes widened when he said, "He values me, Kat'leen. *Me*."

"What will that mean?" I squeaked more than spoke. "Even more time for the elephants?"

"It means my opinion will matter," he said slowly, as if savoring his words. "*I* will matter."

When Stefano and Giuseppe returned after the performance, seven sets of elephant eyes followed Stefano as he divvied up bales of hay for their dinner. Whom else would the animal trainer choose to take over Hassan's position? Stefano attacked his work and didn't stop until he finished. And he understood elephants, recognized who wanted what and when. He knew the order of their bowel movements so well, he often parked his wheelbarrow under the rump of the next one to go. He'd inserted the full length of his arm up rectums to retrieve swallowed bailing twine, and an elephant had once splattered him so forcefully with diarrhea, it stenciled his silhouette in green on the tent's back wall. Still, he didn't shy away from giving them the care they deserved. He fed and bathed them, commanded and consoled them. In turn, the elephants treated Stefano like one of their own, elephant aunts adopting a wayward child, often greeting him with rumbles that vibrated like tribal drums in our bones and called to the marrow of our beings.

Late that night, I sat on the edge of our mattress as Stefano settled under the bedcovers. Little over a year ago, he'd happened upon a circus in Spain and developed a symbiotic relationship with elephants, turning them into his family, their tent into his home—at least until I came along. Three months had passed, and I was still dangling, unsure of where I belonged, or if I even wanted to. In one afternoon, Stefano's sense of place had surged. He was the one person here I had any connection to, but the centrifugal force behind his promotion made me worry that the coattails I held onto would slip from my grasp.

"You really want this, don't you?"

Stefano's eyes flew open. His breath rushed out of him in a resounding *Yes.* He inhaled slowly, as if composing himself, and then, with a hand splayed over his heart, said, "Working with elephants is something I feel inside of me."

"Can we have a trial period? See if it works for us?"

"If I say yes, is a commitment."

"How long of a commitment?"

"Is late, Kat'leen, I don't know." His chest swelled with a yawn, and he dropped his head back into the pillow. "Six months. We save our money for six months, then travel like you want."

Six months—twice as long as Stefano and I had been together—seemed eternal. At the same time, I knew the seven months remaining on my plane ticket would flee in an instant. I grabbed my journal and slipped out to sit on the bottom step and watch the moonlit waves roll in.

Ten feet behind me, Stefano purred. Even in his sleep he emanated stability—the kind of stability that comes from having strong convictions, from believing in what you do down to your soul. Stefano's spirit was as tangible as the earth, his sincerity as solid as the rocks beneath my feet, his pull on me as strong as the moon's pull on the tides.

February 23, 1989, Catanzaro Lido, Italy: It's we now, not I. Ours, not my.

"Giuseppe needs to know if I'll take the job."

I looked away from Stefano and toward the animal trainer who stood in the doorway of the tent. Giuseppe seemed to study my uncertainty.

"You told him I don't want to stay, didn't you?"

Stefano shook his head. "Giuseppe sees that nothing here holds your interest."

"Nothing but you." I took a deep breath and said, "Tell him yes."

Stefano stopped straightening Banana's headdress. He eased his gaze toward me as if a quick movement would scare my acceptance away. His mouth twitched.

"Tell him yes."

A handshake and the job was his.

Giuseppe lifted a red thigh-length over-shirt from his arm and handed it to Stefano. It wasn't a fancy "show" shirt—more like a lab coat. Something Stefano could put over a white T-shirt and black jeans and look presentable enough for the audience. "Brush off your jeans," Giuseppe said. "Stay in the back of the ring. Learn the elephants' routine."

Stefano's already-broad shoulders spread even wider as he slipped on the shirt.

Watching him lead elephants trunk to tail, trunk to tail, up the incline and along the road toward the big top, I had a vision: no matter how tightly I held onto Stefano, he would still hold onto the circus, and she would drag us along until he let go of her, or I let go of him.

With the new job came the offer of a new place to live. Two rooms took up the front half of the trailer that hauled the elephant tent; Hassan had lived in one. Giuseppe's housekeeper lived in the other room, and it wasn't difficult to figure out that rooming next to one man offered more privacy than rooming next to six.

Instead of one-fifth of a railroad car, the room filled an abundant one-quarter—eight more square feet of living space—plus it had a shower *and* warm water. I spent one afternoon cleaning. The next morning, I replaced the single bunk with our big bed, hung a new curtain on our en suite shower, draped my scarves over the window, and taped Stefano's seagull drawings to the wall. Splinters jutting from the leaning-tower-of-cabinets enclosing Hassan's mini refrigerator convinced me to leave our plastic clothing crates on the floor.

Six months. To make life tolerable, I needed something to do beyond making the exotic troupe's food and toting a puppy around—and it certainly wouldn't hurt to earn a bigger paycheck. I still didn't want to dance, and Giuseppe kept Moira from insisting that I do, but he cautioned me not to push it by hanging around the front lot.

Circus folk find many ways to round out their incomes. Officially, Walter increased his take by charging curious patrons to view dozens of zoo animals in unnatural habitats and watch a long Slavic woman swim with a couple of even longer sharks during intermission. Giuseppe and his wife ran the concession bar—his bonus for keeping company with tigers, elephants, and the rest of Moira's menagerie of biting, kicking, stomping beasts. And any woman who participated in the show could usher guests for tips.

Unofficially, just about anything goes, and just about everything went. In the nooks and crannies its spotlights do not illuminate, the circus holds many secrets. Stefano ran what he called the Manure Mafia—bartering the elephants' "gifts" for local farmers' wares, from unlabeled wine to uprooted tobacco plants. Thievery was not as prevalent in Circo Moira Orfei as it had been in Spain, but bicycles, mopeds, and car batteries were easy prey, and a few workers here certainly helped themselves to whatever necessities the immediate neighborhood had to offer. And in deep dark corners during deep dark hours, Third-World workers sold their bodies for cold hard cash.

Pippo, the photographer, operated somewhere between official and unofficial. He flung baby animals into children's arms, snapped a shot, and then coaxed their parents out of seven bucks for a claim ticket at a local photo shop. The circus sanctioned Pippo's profession as long as he kept its destruction discreet. In the back of his cargo van, puma, lynx, and tiger cubs mewed for their mothers' milk. Sweet-faced chimps hunched farther and farther forward as they outgrew their cages. The stench of tight quarters and soiled bedding permeated the air. Sickness often turned the cubs' blue eyes crusty and colorful coats mangy. Then they disappeared. Some animals survived the torment of ping-ponging in and out of children's arms and living in squalor without catching some disease. Still, their teeth would eventually grow too long or their tempers too short, and they too would disappear. Pippo always imported fresh-faced babies to take their places, keeping his income rolling in and the circus's weighty percentage on track.

Perhaps that's why Walter and Giuseppe averted their eyes. Later that year, after the death of a cub, Stefano threatened to call the Italian version of the Animal Protection Agency, only to have Giuseppe implore him to reconsider. The Agency had told Circo Moira Orfei repeatedly that if all circuses cared for animals as well as the Nones brothers did, there would be little need to regulate their actions. Still, Giuseppe thought it bad business to ask the inspectors to come calling. Defying him would have cost Stefano his job. Though frustrated and angered, Stefano kept his mouth shut. And Pippo continued his daily exchange of blood for gold.

But I didn't know any of that the day in Catanzaro Lido when I found the photographer at the back of his van feeding his animals. I heard the mews and smelled the dirty bedding and asked if he needed an assistant. Pippo scoffed and sent me away, but I moved closer. Peeking around one door, I followed a diapered chimp's black finger as it stretched through the bars of his steel prison to poke at the silver lock that kept him captive.

"Ohhh," I sighed and stepped closer.

The chimp's dark eyes begged for attention.

Pippo ordered me away.

"But you look as if you could use some help," I countered.

"*Via*," Pippo ordered again, slamming the van doors shut and using his squat, square body to steer me away.

I should have done something. I should have pushed past Pippo and freed his entire menagerie. Or called the protection agency myself. But I didn't. Not on that day and not on any of the days I spent in the circus.

Over the years, I have tried to make sense of my involvement in a world where such behavior was accepted. At the time, I believed that befriending a giraffe and making his food improved his life. Although that is true, it is also true that I willingly lived in the company of exploited animals. I took pleasure in their presence, even when I knew it was given against their will. My intentions seemed respectable at the time. Today, they seem naïve. Clueless. I cannot claim to have shared Stefano's hopeful—and hopeless—responsibility to these beings. Today, I ask myself how my curiosity differed from circus-goers whose money provided wages and food and fuel.

It didn't.

Whether through patronage, ignorance, or silence, we all enabled this prison-on-wheels to continue rolling on.

Pippo would eventually fall out of Walter's favor and lose the photo business to one of Walter's brothers, but not before the man who helped put the sleaze in circus created a dot-to-dot of animal graves across the Italian countryside.

After dismissing the possibility of a job with Pippo, I walked back to the beach and tucked myself in our new room. The more I thought about the diapered chimp, the more suffocating my own room felt. I propped open the window, swung the door open wide, and let the sea breeze bathe our miniature home. I needed air. And space. I crammed our clothing crates into a corner, kicked moccasins and flip-flops under the bed, cleaned toothbrushes and Stefano's razor off the counter. When there was nothing left to put away, I sat on our front steps and let the sunshine warm my skin. I listened to the waves tumble against rocks and willed them to wash the futile plight of Pippo's animals from my mind.

An entire day had passed since we'd moved into our new room, and I still hadn't seen our new neighbor. One hundred fifty feet and an elephant tent separated us from our old neighbors. I liked the seclusion. Farther down the beach, a fisherman pulled his blue dinghy ashore. Seagulls swirling above him announced his arrival, and dark-haired women in housecoats materialized out of nowhere to cluster around his boat and scoop the day's catch from its depths.

"I need a bag. I need a bag." Stefano bounded up the steps and rummaged through our room. "Where you hide the plastic bags?"

He leapt past me and tore down the beach, returning ten minutes later with a dripping sack. "Time to celebrate. New job, new room, everything." He showed me a collection of finger-sized silver fish wriggling among squid tentacles and black-eyed shrimp. "*Frutti di mare.* Fruits of the sea."

I wrinkled my nose. "But they're alive."

"Fresh from the *Ionio* this minute. If you ever going to eat fishes again in your life, these should be the ones. We need lemons, oil, and flour. If you could walk to town for some things, tonight I cook for you."

Stefano arranged the propane burner on our front steps and tossed some seafood in flour he'd seasoned with salt—as his grandmother used to do summers on the seaside, he explained. I hoisted my Levi's up from my hips and sat down. Rasta watched from our doorway, wondering, perhaps, why we were using his stove for something besides warming milk.

After Stefano dropped the first batch into the bubbling oil, he passed me the bag of flour and then added a second handful of seafood to the bag. It landed with a thump against my palms. I considered the limp weight in my hands, juxtaposing these creatures' lifelessness against the fact that just that afternoon they were swimming free in the Ionian Sea. I wanted to feel bad. I wanted to feel certain of my vegetarian convictions. But I was hungry. So very hungry.

"What do you think, Rasta? Should I eat the meat?" The puppy hopped into my lap and licked my chin, surely telling me that if I didn't want the seafood, then he'd be happy to help.

In a country famous for its food, I'd been losing weight without even trying. I watched the seafood turn golden as Stefano moved it around in the pan, thought about the fisherman nourishing himself, his family, his community. I smelled the fresh-cut lemon, the hot fried batter. I closed my eyes. Breathed in again. And then I shook the shit out of that plastic bag.

Stefano speared the first batch of golden brown loops and crescents from the hot oil with the tip of his Opinel knife, dribbled fragrant lemon juice, sprinkled salt, and offered a ring of squid to me. Salt and citrus exploded on my tongue. I bit into the warm meat, cutting through the robust tissue, exercising my long-neglected incisors, devouring Stefano's offering in one ravenous, carnal moment. I felt its essence, its vitality, its stamina. I was sinking my teeth into life itself.

Swallowing with carnivorous zeal filled me with a deep satisfaction, as if this bounty could satiate the hunger within me.

Stefano studied my face, waiting.

"It's chewy."

"Food is supposed to be chewy. You like or not?"

I swigged pinot grigio straight from the bottle. "I think I do," I told him, hesitant to admit how easily the flesh went down as I peeled the pink shell from a shrimp. "Definitely do."

Stefano watched me scrape out the shrimp's black vein with my thumbnail before I ate it. "Why you are always picking stuffs apart?"

"Because it's poo."

Stefano pointed to the head I'd set aside. "What about that?"

"You want me to eat its head? That's worse than poo."

"Not eat, suck on. Is where all the flavor lives." He slurped on my discarded shrimp head. "Try one—it tastes like the sea. *It tastes like Italy*."

"I'm not going straight from three years of vegetarianism to sucking brains."

"Then eat the leetle fishes."

"But they're *whole*."

"Mmm." He popped a few into his mouth, then held one out to me by its tail.

"No poop, no brains, no guts."

"At least you try the squids and shrimps." He lifted his plastic cup of wine in a toast. "*Cin cin* to eating meat."

"*Cin cin* to your new job," I added.

First our cups met, then our lips.

"My new job." Stefano shook his head. "Giuseppe knows me six weeks and he trusts me with his elephants. I can't remember my *parents* ever putting me in charge of anything."

Stefano's eyes changed. His irises looked backlit, as if a flash came from within him. I wondered if the fire in his eyes spoke of pain or pride. Or was it purpose?

Be careful here, Erich had insisted.

CHAPTER EIGHTEEN

HOW DIFFERENT COULD IT BE FROM RIDING A HORSE?

"Giuseppe wants to know if you are afraid of the ostrich."

I looked from Stefano to the animal trainer as the three of us strolled the perimeter of the elephant tent in the *piazza* following Catanzaro Lido. "What kind of afraid?"

Stefano hesitated before saying, "You remember the exotic number from that time you see the show? Moira's son stands in the middle of the ring and—"

"Zebras and antelope together, and later the giraffe runs through . . . I remember."

"You are watching when the ostrich comes out?"

"Yeah." I didn't get Stefano's gist. "He runs around the *pista* with a kid on his back."

"Not a kid, Kat'leen. Hassan." Stefano pursed his lips. "Giuseppe asks if you will try riding the ostrich."

My imagination soared to a land where rhinestone cowboys rode hulking birds with flamboyant plumage. I could almost hear my decorative spurs dragging in the dust. An incredulous chuckle gave way to sheer joy. "Hell yes."

When Stefano came to call me for a trial run, he found me donning Levi's and muttering *shit shit shit* over and over.

"You don't have to do this, Kat'leen."

"I want to," I said, belting my loose jeans with a scarf. "I'm just preparing myself to deal with whatever might happen in there."

"By saying *sheeet*?"

I looked up from lacing my moccasins. "It's something I learned from my mom."

Despite being a well-heeled churchgoer, my mother had taught me my favorite stream of curses from the front seat of her two-door turquoise Corvair—one of a long line of rattletrap cars my father hauled home. I remember Dad herding his four children into the car so Mom could drive us to our various lessons or Sunday services. His handlebar mustache twitched and wiggled under fleshy cheeks as he ridiculed us for squabbling over the front seat since its unlucky occupant would likely die first in an accident. But we didn't listen. We didn't ponder the scar on his cheek from a car crash some years earlier, and we didn't heed his warnings. We cared only for the thrill of the road rushing at us in blurs of gray and black, for the honor of sticking our tongues out at siblings crammed into the back seat.

Victory wasn't always sweet. The problem wasn't the cracked upholstery leaking bits of itchy yellow foam that clung to bare legs. It wasn't the lap belt our safety-minded father insisted on cinching down until we couldn't breathe.

The volatile variable was whether the car would start. No one wanted to sit next to Mom when it didn't. I can still hear the whine of the starter bouncing off the garage door, radiating down the street, disturbing Southern California suburbia as it struggled to turn over the engine. How I'd cringed against the passenger door as my mother cursed in time with the cranking engine. *Shit-shit-shit-shit-shit-shit-shit!* Both terrifying and hilarious, she rattled like the lid of a boiling pot. *Shit-shit-shit-shit-shit-shit-shit* to the sound of the recalcitrant starter.

Mom could have saved for a decent used car with the portion of her teaching salary my father let her spend. Instead, she bought a membership to AAA and used her allowance on baton lessons, football uniforms, and summer vacations. I lived for those summer vacations. By the time I'd lost my baby teeth, embers from my father's firefighting accident had singed my parents' alliance, so my mother hauled her children around solo in a weary four-wheel-drive International, another of her uncommon, outdated heaps. Roaming the western states, Mom made us kids pee in coffee cans for fear that stopping the truck meant losing half a day to get it going again. She bargained with the free-swinging shift stick that had long since lost its collar, Pierre the poodle slept on our laps, and Misty the malamute hurled lemon-yogurt barf on every curvy highway. While her kids learned to ride mules down the Grand Canyon and fish the wild lakes of Idaho, pan fry trout in cornmeal and bake sourdough biscuits over a campfire, Mom learned how to bind broken fuel pumps with yarn and bandage leaking radiators with duct tape. We heard *shit-shit-shit-shit-shit-shit-shit* in the generous shade of a Giant Sequoia. *Shit-shit-shit-shit-shit-shit-shit* in the broiling heat of Zion National Park.

It's not the hours spent stuck on the side of the road

that I remember from those trips. I remember Mom playing guitar and teaching us songs around campfires, the expanse of America's national parks, and the freedom of the open road. In light of my mother's shabby cars and her frustration when they broke, *shit-shit-shit-shit-shit-shit-shit* could have been a motto of defeat. Instead, it was a cry of determination. My mother's first step toward triumph on a bad car day. And on that morning in Crotone, Italy, it was my way of steeling myself for the forthcoming challenge.

Backstage, Dieter waited.

"Why the blue tarp?" I asked, looking over the closet-sized, chain-link ostrich cage.

"New people upset him," Dieter said. "It's better he doesn't see the commotion."

"Like putting a dishtowel over a parakeet."

"Yes. The ostrich tends to be nervous."

"Nervous?" I plunged my hands deeper into my jeans' pockets.

"You sure you want to do this, Kat'leen?" Stefano's whispered concern reverberated through me.

"It's okay, Stefano. I can do it."

"I know you can. But I be right here watching in case you can't."

I nudged him toward the ring. "If strangers upset him, then you could make it worse." As I kissed Stefano's cheek, it occurred to me that the ostrich probably had no idea that I mixed his meals every day, making me a stranger as well.

Stefano squeezed my hand and headed for the bleachers with Giuseppe to watch the practice session.

"This is how it works," Dieter told me. "Caesar, the ostrich, is shut inside that pen before the exotic performance begins. The zebra and antelope are in the ring with Nino first. You're next. When you hear the exotic music begin, you must be here, in costume, ready to go. Understand?"

"So far."

"Good. Nino's waiting, so let's get going." Dieter pointed at a red plastic chair. "You'll need that."

"Yippee-kai-yay," I said, grabbing the chair and wishing I had a cowboy hat.

"As I open one side of the cage," Dieter explained, "another worker and I will pin the ostrich against the other side of the cage. You be ready with the chair. Put it between me and the other worker and use it to climb on top of him. Your knees go down. Your feet hook over his butt. Don't let your legs hang. When you're ready to ride, say *go*. I'll swing open the front of the cage and you're off."

"How am I supposed to hold on?"

"He's wearing a saddle."

"Perfect," I said, imagining a western saddle lashed onto the bird. "Will he go after me with his beak?" I thought the rattling I heard was the ostrich scraping his mouth back and forth across the links.

"Only if you're in front of him. Look here." Dieter pointed through the bottom of the cage. I bent down in time to see the ostrich shoot one foot forward and rake the cage with T-Rex claws. "He can raise those prongs as high as your face and slice you open. If he tries anything, protect yourself with the chair. Understand?"

I wasn't sure I did understand about the slice 'em and dice 'em feet. The noises inside the cage surpassed nervous. Recalling the neck-to-waist, stuffing-spewing slashes I'd seen on the jackets of the exotic-troupe workers, I fingered gashes in the chair's back that I'd previously disregarded. My stomach turned squirrelly. This schizophrenic eight-foot pterodactyl threatened my rhinestoned, fairy tale image.

"What happens after I get on?"

"We herd him into the show. You hold on. He runs around the ring." Dieter slipped on a pair of leather gloves. "Remember: when I open the cage, it's time to move. Ready?"

I clenched the chair as Dieter opened the cage. Caesar's back shimmied in front of my face. The other worker pushed his chest against the tail end of the bird. Dieter pressed against the front. I shoved the chair between them and stepped up.

"Where's the saddle?"

Dieter's biceps bulged as he struggled to keep the bird still. *"Under the feathers!"*

Plowing my fingers through silky black plumage, I found nothing under the fluff but a stiff leather band. The quaking mass of man and bird wobbled my chair. *"This is a handle, dammit, not a saddle— "*

"You ready?"

I lifted my leg over the ostrich and sank through his feathers to his writhing body. I felt as if I were trying to grip my thighs around a mound of Jell-O. Somehow, I yelled "Go."

The one time I'd seen Hassan ride the ostrich, it seemed as if the bird had run straight forward, as a human would. But when Dieter swung the front of the cage open, Caesar lurched to the right. I slipped backwards and dangerously to one side until his foot pounded against the ground and jolted me in the opposite direction. The ostrich zigzagged toward the ring in a spastic duck waddle, with his head tick-tocking like a metronome and me sliding on slick feathers.

Forget the horse. I'm riding a 300-pound chicken!

Caesar careened into the ring. I barely caught Stefano's worried blur of a face as the bird wound around the *pista* and out through the exit curtain. That's when the question I forgot to ask struck me. *How do I get off?*

"Push." Dieter ran beside me as we streaked through backstage. "Slide off his back."

The ostrich sped out of the big top, into the zoo, and toward his open pen. I let go of the handle and pushed. An instant later, I was flat on my back in the center of the zoo, staring at the big blue sky.

Dieter's face above mine. "You okay?"

Stefano on his knees at my side. "Kat'leen!"

My heart thudded and my hands trembled. I monkey-hooted more than giggled, but I was definitely laughing. Relief eased into Stefano's eyes.

"Can I do that again?"

"Tonight," Dieter said, offering me a hand up. "In the show. You can wear either a sequined girly suit or Hassan's leprechaun outfit."

Stefano recommended Hassan's costume. Having left my flashy bikini days far away in Spain, I was quick to agree.

"Get it from the costume trailer. Eight o'clock, backstage. Don't be late."

Stefano and I headed for a bar right outside the circus grounds to celebrate. I wanted to call my mom right away, but it was still the middle of the night for her, so I settled for yelling, *Shit-shit-shit-shit-shit-shit-shit Mom!* as I lifted my bottle of Ceres beer to meet Stefano's. *I'm in Crotone, Italy, and I just became the new ostrich jockey!*

At eight p.m. sharp, I presented myself backstage in shiny green pants, a long-tailed coat, and a matching top hat. The Polish woman in the costume trailer had insisted on at least minimal makeup and painted my lashes with mascara, drew two bright pink circles on my cheeks, and smothered my mouth with lipstick. Staring into the backstage mirror, I looked at my laughable face as I straightened my gold bow tie. At least here they called it funny. In Spain, they'd made me up worse and called it pretty.

I peeped through a hole under the orchestra. When I'd snuck into the show in Rome, the contortionist had performed first. Tonight, zebras and antelope opened, prancing in time to the big bass drum.

Dieter appeared beside me. "You're almost on, and this time there will be a real audience watching. No time for questions. We open the cage. You get on. You ride into the ring. Got it?"

When Dieter opened the cage, I practically leapt on top of that ostrich. The cage swung open, the velvet curtain parted, and Caesar and I hurtled into the ring.

"*Yee-haw!*"

The fifteen seconds it took us to cruise around the *pista* seemed to pass in slow motion. Applause from thousands of hands undulated over us as Caesar's body swung to and fro under my own. Nino stood center ring. In his eyes, I thought I saw apprehension, as if he didn't expect me to make it around the ring without falling off.

High on adrenaline, I soared through backstage. Planting both hands at the base of Caesar's neck, I heaved myself backwards and slammed into the ground squarely on my butt. The llama galloped past inches from my head on her way into the ring.

"Hey—the llama almost nailed the leprechaun! Good

thing the rhino wasn't coming." Dieter offered a hand up. "Try not pushing so hard. When your feet started to slide off, your shoulders were already too far back. Watch out!" Dieter shoved me out of the way. "Giraffe coming in." I leaned against the back wall of the tent and brushed off my costume while the giraffe loped past. "At least *you* made it around the ring," Dieter said. "That's what counts."

I started to ask him why he sounded surprised, but the giraffe ducked out through the exit curtain and Dieter took off to escort Baros to his pen.

Walking through the circus grounds felt different after performing in the show, as if I might be a part of it all. Thing was, I didn't know whether I liked that feeling. Six-month commitment or not, I considered this situation short-term.

Back in our room, stripping away black and pink makeup, I considered getting Stefano's evening coffee from the circus bar instead of an outside bar as I usually did. It seemed absurd to keep out of Moira's sight after blazing through the big top on the back of an ostrich. Shouldn't a leprechaun be able to waltz through the gangway, that corridor of hustle and bustle that separates the ticket booth from the big top, with her head held high?

At the front of the big top, a wide red carpet stretched all the way from the tent's draped doorway to the turnstile. Moira's seventy-foot trailer lined one side of the carpet, the office, the concession stand, and the toilet truck lined the other. I strolled up the metal walkway to the concession platform, ignoring the group of showgirls on the far end eyeing me from under their big hair.

Giuseppe's wife minded the bar. "So you didn't fall off," she said.

"I don't get why everybody seems to think I should have." I grabbed one sugar packet for Stefano and one for Shiva. "Coffee, please."

"I thought someone would have told you," she said over the humming espresso machine. "The contortionist tried to ride the ostrich in Catanzaro Lido, the day after Hassan escaped. She fell off before reaching the ring. Landed on her elbows, injured both arms pretty badly. Hasn't performed since."

Apparently, hiding from Moira had its consequences. I grabbed the coffee and took off for the tent.

"Stefano? Where are you?" He stepped from between two of the elephants. "I just found out that the last person who tried to ride the ostrich practically broke both her arms!"

"Giuseppe and I discuss it this morning." He poured one sugar into his coffee and pocketed Shiva's. "Hassan rides this ostrich for years, no problem. Nino's wife rides in practice, no problem. But when she rides the ostrich in the show, she has . . . how you say . . . shiny things on her legs."

"Pantyhose?"

"Yes, yes, some of those." He chuckled as Shiva patted him down, looking for her sugar. "Too slippery on the feathers, so she slides off. Giuseppe thinks is more costume problem than animal problem—and I agree. I would have told you if you pick the other costume."

I heard Giuseppe's signature whistle outside the tent. He strolled in, tuxedo jacket slung over his shoulder, white towel draped around his neck. "Tell Giuseppe someone should have told me about the risk."

Stefano spoke with the animal trainer and then translated: "He says look around you. Each time you come into this tent there is risk. Every day you walk through the grounds, you are at risk." Speaking for himself, Stefano added, "We all are, Kat'leen. Giuseppe with his tigers. Flyers on the trapeze. Workers scaling the big top. Everybody." Giuseppe added a few words. "He says you been in the circus long enough to know this."

Giuseppe cocked his ear, listened to the trumpets calling from the big top, and signaled to Stefano.

"Don't forget, was you that insisted on riding the ostrich." Stefano bent down to remove an elephant's leg chains. "We have a saying in Italy," he said as he marched the elephants out of the tent. "You wanted the bicycle, now pedal it."

CHAPTER NINETEEN

BUILDING BLOCKS

Screeching metal invaded my dream and dragged me toward the new day. The room rocked, swinging the shower curtain out from its stall and toppling our stack of clothing crates onto the floor. The puppy burrowed further under the sheets. Over the din of the reassembling circus, I heard, *Sorrrrry*. The seventeen Rs made Stefano's apology sound especially heartfelt.

"Your daddy needs practice unloading with that forklift," I told Rasta as I slid out of bed and kicked clothing aside until my feet reached cool linoleum. I pulled a shirt and Levi's from the heap of clothes, heated milk for Rasta's puppy chow, and headed out into the unfolding circus.

Beyond the rising animal tents, the giraffe's Creamsicle head stretched up from the back of his truck. I waved to him and picked up my pace with Rasta bounding behind me in his wiggly puppy-dog way. In the area surrounding this new *piazza*, mountainous terraces overlooked strips of white beaches and turquoise shallows that quickly turned to sapphire depths. The early March sun promised to warm the day, and I contemplated finding my way to the Tyrrhenian Sea after I finished making the animal food.

Baros curved his neck down, searching for a handout as I approached. Though finding nothing, he stayed, flexing his lips while I scratched his bulbous chin and let his prickly whiskers tickle my palm. I was well on my way to becoming the giraffe's first, and only, friend. He would soon let me walk into his cage when he was sitting down—his most vulnerable state. Not long after that, he'd allow me to brush his haunches. Within days, I would work my way up the giraffe's neck, currying his hide and massaging his neck with stiff bristles until he rested his jaw on my shoulder and draped his chin over my back. I would brush Baros's cheeks with a tender touch and rub the hard-to-reach furrows between his knobs and ears until dirt caked my fingertips. When word of our friendship reached Walter's ears, he made grooming the giraffe my job.

But on that March day, I still worked toward earning Baros's trust. He stretched his purple tongue and curled it around my fingers in his search for a treat, and I laughed. That morning, it felt good to be in the circus.

I divvied up apples, carrots, and bread and sank my fingers into the tubs of oat bran to blend the water. The warm smell of wet oats reminded me of the cost-effective version of hot cereal my mother used to serve us kids. Ralston, she'd called it, a grainy brown and white mash made by Purina. Mom couldn't bamboozle us though—what kid would willingly eat cereal manufactured by a dog food company? But food is food. With nothing else on the table, we were able to wash some down with our glasses of powdered milk. The rest we squirreled into the trash, the dog's mouth, or "hid" on the ceiling.

I can still picture the brown and white splatters my brothers spoon-flicked up there. As soon as I was old enough to say no to Ralston, I did, and have never eaten hot cereal again.

Burrowing the last bits of dry flakes out of the corners of the ostrich's tub, I glanced across the zoo at Caesar. To no one's surprise, I'd stuck with the number. I loved everything about riding that bird—the anticipation as I lowered myself onto his back, the blast of adrenaline as the cage door flew open, the swish of heavy velvet curtains parting, and our thrilling run through the ring. Most of all, I loved that it was different.

It was also different to find myself playing Suzy Homemaker later that morning, back in our room, refolding and reorganizing our mess of clothes. Regrettably, Suzy Homemaker was not the right kind of different.

Stacking our clothing-packed crates back on the floor annoyed me. With a mere sixty-four square feet to live in, every inch counted, and the lack of floor space made our sleeper feel claustrophobic. Crates on the floor annoyed Stefano too, but only because they made the room disorderly.

When I saw Giuseppe heading for the elephant tent, I hurried over. "Stefano, will you ask Giuseppe if I can rip out the old cabinets in our room and build new ones?"

Stefano shook his head.

"We need that space. Ask him."

Stefano turned his pained expression toward his boss to translate, and he came back with, "Giuseppe says the wood smiths are not available to build us new cabinets."

"Who asked the wood shop to do it? Lend me a measuring tape and a hand saw, and I'll build them myself."

Stefano repeated Giuseppe's response in English. "He doesn't want you to injure yourself. Have you ever used a saw before?"

"So riding a crazed ostrich is fine, but he's concerned I might nick myself cutting a piece of wood? *And you're agreeing with him?*"

The two of them conferred. After Stefano told Giuseppe he thought I could manage, the animal trainer said he'd arrange for the wood shop to give me their scraps and loan me a few tools.

"I hope it doesn't turn out any worse than it already is," Giuseppe commented as he walked away.

Stefano nodded in agreement. Apparently, the only things women made around here were dinner, the bed, and love.

For the rest of our stay in Paola, I sweated and sawed and sanded until my hands turned pink and my corner of the circus smelled like a lumberyard. Passersby looked sideways at the scattered wood and sawdust. I didn't care. From Broadway singers to concert violinists, photographers to wood carvers, creativity—whether professional or practical—coursed through my bloodline. My mother's parents built two of their homes and the furniture to fill them. During my father's down-and-out youth, if he and his brothers didn't imagine it and manufacture it or find it and fix it, they couldn't have it. I remember gazing up at Dad's drawings of hilltop mansions until I had a crick in my neck. And to the awe of her young children, Mom brought handmade wooden stepladders and cottage-shaped ceramic planters home from evening classes at the community college. From the first time Play-Doh oozed between my fingers, my parents encouraged me to create with my hands. More than creativity, they instilled self-sufficiency.

Unfortunately, my only hands-on building experience was when I bought my first van. My parents weren't eager for their child to travel America in a twenty-year-old, air-cooled metal tube guaranteed to overheat every summer day, but they accepted my decision, just as they had accepted my decision to join a circus when I called each of them with the news. My mother and I sewed the Volkswagen's window curtains and bed cushions at her house; my father taught me to adjust the carburetor, correct the timing, and set the valves at his. Dad also saw to it that I toured in style. Together, we fitted the inside of my bus with a bed, custom-made chests, and a retractable desk where I made the beadwork to support my travels. During the few days my father taught me the proper way to measure wood, cut with a circular saw, and sink a sixteen-penny nail, I felt like daddy's little girl once more. Years later, building the cabinets for our circus room, I tried to recall all he'd taught me.

I hadn't realized how much I missed the creative process until this project came along. The growing stack of cabinet pieces rekindled my interest in making watercolor greeting cards and intricate beaded jewelry. But my watercolors and my beads were 6,000 miles away in Oregon, boxed up in a corner of Mom's converted motel along with the books, clothes, and music that didn't make the cut from Volkswagen van to backpack. Stefano overplayed the two tapes I'd brought with me until I could barely stand hearing them. *He'd love more Clapton tapes—and I could introduce him to the Dead. As long as Mom was shipping some beads . . .* I chopped off the thought. In 25 weeks, I'd be moving back into my backpack.

For two nights, Stefano avoided staring at the bare corner of our room. On the third, he asked how the construction progressed. Scraping a smudge of pine sap off my forearm, I assured him he was right to tell Giuseppe I could do it—he'd see for himself in the next town.

Early on our first morning in Cosenza, I fastened three waist-high uprights to the wall between the door and bed, one next to the bed, one mid-way, and one beside the door. The bedside half would hold shoes and Stefano's work wear; the other would enclose the mini-refrigerator that Hassan had left behind. Half of the long piece of plywood I screwed on top of the uprights would be our countertop; the rest would support a short storage area, complete with sliding doors, for any foodstuff that might accidentally find its way into our room. I screwed our clothing crates to the wall above the cabinet and called it done. Though neither square nor symmetrical, a functional wall unit emerged from the mishmash of plywood, pine, and plastic crates.

When I invited Giuseppe and Stefano to come see, Stefano ran his hand along the countertop and opened one of the sliding doors. "Look what I found," he said, pointing to the lonely bag of leftover flour from our fish fry. Wood swished against wood as he used the hole I'd carved in the sliding door to open and shut it a few times. I liked the proud way Stefano nudged Giuseppe and motioned toward the cabinet with his chin.

"We need bungee cords to stretch across the crates so our clothes won't fall out when we travel," I said. "The bottom of the door needs to be waxed so it will slide easier, and that finger-hole would be round if I'd had a real drill, but I could try sanding it some more."

Stefano shook his head. "Is beautiful."

Giuseppe studied how I'd screwed five thin pieces of wood together to fashion channels for the sliding doors and then gave the cabinet a shake.

"He says is good and solid," Stefano translated.

When Giuseppe spoke again, Stefano nodded but didn't translate.

"What?" I asked, as the animal trainer strolled away.

"He admires your determination. He also said is looking like you plan to stay awhile."

If one of them had asked me right then why I'd spent a week building a cabinet I'd use for fewer than six months, I may have said I was only making do. Ask me today, and I'll tell you how the ostrich number changed my relationship with the circus, how that promise of daily adventure was the first of many strings binding me to Circo Moira Orfei. Strings that would eventually become a formidable rope.

CHAPTER TWENTY

BIG TOP BLUES

"Americana." Walter's voice boomed across the zoo.

I looked up from making the animals' breakfast to see Moira's husband striding toward me. He spoke so fast, I understood only *Moira, struzzo,* and *problemi.*

Problems? Wasn't I feeding the ostrich correctly? What could it have to do with Moira? The bird, who was scratching dirt and studying it with bulging eyes, looked fine to me. I shrugged at Walter. *"Struzzo tutto bene."* Ostrich all good.

Telling me to stay put, the circus boss marched off.

I leaned back against the giraffe's pen and lifted my face toward the mid-March sun. As spring announced its intentions with blooming flowers and budding grapevines, I worked on my own fresh start, on making peace with the circus.

A leaf straight into Baros's waiting mouth, a handful of leaves for the tubs. A leaf into . . .

Walter returned with Giuseppe and Stefano. I stuck my

knife into an apple and stood. Walter crouched, took a few strained steps across the dirt, and acted short of breath.

Stefano translated, "He says you're too heavy to ride Caesar. Is hurting the bird."

"Too heavy?" I yanked at the loose waistband of my jeans. "I've lost at least five pounds since we got here. Tell him I'll exercise. Lose more."

"Moira told him you've lost weight. You still weigh more than Hassan did. You can't ride the ostrich."

I glanced at the bird. He clearly wasn't all that big under his fluff of feathers. Immersed in my own gratification, I'd never noticed the poor animal struggling to cart my 145 pounds around the ring.

Giuseppe laid his hand on my shoulder and said, "*Tutto* okay."

Everything was not okay. I should have known I would never find happiness here.

"What am I supposed to do for five more months, Stefano? Be the head vegetable-cutter?"

"She wants you to dance."

"What?" I jabbed my fingers through the links of Baros's pen and rattled his cage. Stefano watched my tantrum steely eyed, but I persisted. "What if I say no?"

Walter said, "You dance or you leave."

Later that morning, the costume crew fitted me with a sequined royal blue bikini for the opening and closing parades. Moira's grand entrance required a fringed silver number with a matching wig that made me look like a disco queen discard. Besides dancing, I would also usher spectators to their seats. The Polish seamstresses issued me a gold-sequined jacket, a black beret, new fishnet stockings—for which I owed Moira two days' wages—and a list of supplies to purchase: black pumps, black knee-length skirt, black long-sleeved blouse for winter, short-sleeved white blouse for summer, oodles of makeup.

After lunch, I bound my sleep-flattened curls into a fuzzy ponytail and presented myself for practice wearing Levi's and one of Stefano's button-down work shirts. The empty big top felt cavernous and cold. Six dancing girls wearing makeup on their faces, rhinestone combs in their coiffed hair, and form-fitting outfits that left little to the imagination scrutinized me from their gaggle in the box seats. Their slow-motion appraisals made it perfectly clear that I didn't meet their fashion standards. Hanging around the back lot of a circus, I didn't fret over clothing. I'd never dressed fashionably in my life—unless I counted wearing an old Mexican blanket as a cape at Grateful Dead concerts.

Bernardo, the gay ringmaster who resembled Pee-wee Herman with a brush-over, pranced into the tent with his blouse floating around his thin frame. He scanned the dancing girls, who stared back at him without moving from their seats. Bernardo's head listed to one side, making him seem bored with their inaction. "Up, girls, up," he said. *Clap! Clap! Clap!* "Moira's coming!" Sleeves billowing and fists jiggling, he urged us out of our seats.

The Queen of the Elephants swept in.

Dusty white stilettos. Shapely calves. Playfully swirling hem. Legs women half her age might envy. But things went south the farther north I looked, and I struggled to wrap my brain around what I saw: pink, post-menopausal baby doll dress, complete with lace neckline to frame her round sixty-year-old face. Three red cut-glass marbles bobbing from each ear. Lashes thick and bristly enough to sweep a floor. Pearly white lids, flashier than the egg-sized jewels on her fingers. Arching brows penciled well above nature's intentions. Black beehive, more like a helmet than a wig.

And this was just her daytime getup.

Moira stopped. Her gaze prowled over me. She pointed a hot pink talon at me and said, "You."

My head jerked back. I met the gypsy elephant queen's eyes and offered a feeble smile.

In a flutter of pink fingernails and lacy sleeves, she rapid-fired commands in Italian and steered me into the *pista*. Bernardo clapped the beat and mimicked the trumpets on Moira's cue. I watched the other dancing girls, each perched on a chrome elephant pedestal, bounce their hips and swing their arms. Moira didn't want me to watch; she wanted me to dance. Maintaining her torrent of instructions, voice jabbing me like one of her long pointy nails, she focused on my arms—pulling them here, pushing them there—and bounced her own hips until her baby doll shimmied around her thick body.

I focused on Moira's face. Behind the sludge of mascara, her eyes shone. Her crimson Rocky Horror lips curled at the corners when she spoke, as if she had a secret and she wasn't sharing. For one instant, I saw through her scaffolding of rouge and foundation. Moira was beautiful. Stunning. Then her eyes caught mine. Her face contorted with frustration at my inability to grasp her instructions, and the beauty I'd glimpsed withered beneath her scowl.

I climbed on top of my pedestal and mangled my way through the two-minute number. Then Moira sent us to practice our entrance from backstage. When I ran up the ramp into the *pista*, she screeched, "Do not run like a man. Swing your hips like a woman." Glares followed me as I retraced my steps and started over. Again Moira flung her hands in the air and ordered me back to the starting line. "*Il culo*," she yelled, slapping her own bottom. "I want to see it move!"

The third time, head bobbing, arms flopping, ass swinging like a pendulum, I flounced into the ring like a dancing spaghetti. Moira allowed me to proceed. She soon announced that in two days, we would travel hundreds of kilometers up the eastern side of Italy, almost to Venice. I had until then to collect my supplies and be ready to perform.

Moira Orfei was a woman who broke boundaries. She was both the Queen of the Elephants and the Queen of the Circus, the boss of her own show and a woman who'd utilized her physical beauty and brawny personality to trailblaze her way into Italian hearts and modern Italian history. Yet for me to occupy one small corner of her world, I was doomed to the traditional role of parading in teensy costumes before gawking men. I figured I might as well be humping a pole in a strip joint.

"*Ciao.*"

The giraffe skittered to the far side of his enclosure. I stopped chopping carrots and followed a pair of powerful legs up to the familiar face of a dancing girl. A shock of bleached-blonde bangs accentuated her dark hair and brilliant chestnut eyes. Perfect body, princess nose, generous lips, and flawless teeth—she looked as if she'd strutted off the cover of *Glamour*.

The teenager flipped her brown locks over her shoulder and held out her hand. "Giada," she said, then, "Speak little English." She knelt beside Rasta, who napped at my feet. "Dog?"

"Dog," I confirmed. "Rasta."

At the sound of his name, the puppy sprang up and

covered Giada's hands with kisses. We both laughed. The giraffe strolled over, and I handed a lettuce frond to Giada, who giggled when he plucked it from her fingers.

"*Gonna, trucco, camicette*—" Listing the ushering supplies, she asked, "You like I help shopping?"

Giada found the skirt, shoes, and blouses I needed in one shop and then brought me to a makeup store where boxed perfumes lined the walls and a rainbow of eye shadows glittered under glass. She chose the perfect hue of foundation for my skin, positioned me in front of the *profumeria* mirror, and spread the creamy liquid across my cheeks. Then she insisted on dusting me with powder so the spotlights wouldn't make my face too shiny.

When I told Giada that she seemed like she'd been doing this forever, she compared three blush samples against my skin, settled on one, and said, "Circus is what I know."

Giada's entire family lived in this circus, even her grandparents. Her grandfather had trained her father and uncle's acrobatic duo until her father's accident, at which point Giada's brother stepped in to keep the family working. Her sister, the contortionist and one-time ostrich rider who had since healed from her injuries, had married Moira's son, Nino. Giada trained with hula hoops, but she didn't perform yet.

When I asked if she'd start performing soon, Giada shook her head and said, "I hope not. Once I start, is no stopping until I am too old or too hurt."

The following day, the circus left the turquoise waters of the Tyrrhenian Sea and traded southern Italian warmth for a crisp northern spring. I dutifully arrived at the big top that first night in Rovigo only to have the other ushers scold me for not wearing enough makeup. Compared to me, they looked like raccoons. I took my place in the row of gold-sequined girls at the big top's entrance. Giada explained how one usher greeted each group that entered. Then, as she passed the tickets to another usher who would lead them to their seats, the greeter would inform the patrons that, if they'd like, they could give their usher a tip.

"I'm supposed to *ask for a tip*?"

"Not for you," Giada clarified, "for girl who takes to seats."

Circus patrons paid a premium for their tickets, only to be hit up for Pippo's pictures, snacks, trinkets, programs, and the intermission shark show. Figuring Italians handled gratuities differently, I swallowed my pride and stumbled through learning the greeting. Over the next thirty minutes, I shrugged off indecipherable questions and concentrated on not tripping over bleachers in my new heels. Once the line thinned, Bernardo called the dancers to dress, while a few performers that didn't have to dance remained to seat stragglers. The wad of 1,000 and 5,000 lire notes stuffed in my pocket would surely help me overcome the embarrassment of requesting tips.

Exchanging blazer and blouse for the blue-sequined push-up bra in the crowded dressing room, I did a double take at my bulging bosoms and was surprised that I didn't mind showcasing them as much as I had in Spain. It had taken until my early twenties, but I was discovering that ample breasts could be a pleasure. And they were still a pleasure in my thirties. It wasn't until my forties that things changed, and I started wondering how many more years I'd have to lug the damn things around.

Backstage was thick with performers—trapeze artists, gymnasts, dancing girls, and one old clown who practically begged you to laugh. Light years ahead of the performers in Spain, Moira's men looked as slick as the gel that pasted their hair in place. And Moira, dressed in enough rhinestones to shame Liberace, patrolled from an elephant's stool. Her Tammy Faye Bakker makeup concealed rather than complemented her aging beauty. At the far end, Caesar clawed at his cage; the chair I'd used to climb onto him had vanished.

The ringmaster launched the horns with a flick of his hand.

Moira screeched, "Arms higher—point your toes—fingers up—*smile*," and ordered the curtains drawn.

Through the parting velvet. Into the swarm of color and noise. I was once again a dancing girl.

Stefano made it to bed before me for the first time. "How did it go?" he asked.

"I stood on a chrome elephant stool and shook my booty for a few thousand people with a silver pompom strapped to my head. How do you think it went?"

"So bad?"

I jammed a toothbrush into my mouth instead of answering. Cook, clean, dance, perform; these were the "weemuns jobs." I'd yearned to break that circus standard and felt that I had with the ostrich number. Though some called that fifteen-second whirl through the ring performing, I called it adventure. But Walter had taken it away, and I didn't have much faith in Giuseppe's promise to make *tutto okay*.

Stefano lifted the covers and welcomed me into bed. "You heard Borys is in the hospital?"

I sucked in my breath. "One of the elephants?"

"Fiat. He was behind the tent fixing the fence along the street. Car speeds around the corner, smashes into him."

"Oh Christ." I imagined Izaak's roommate as I usually saw him—watery blue eyes, skin pallid as an overcast sky, vodka-cluttered mind unable to hold his wiry frame straight up and down as he worked. "Is he going to be okay?"

"Is returning to Poland after the hospital."

"Was he drunk?"

As if searching for a way to soften what we both knew, Stefano paused before saying, "In three months I never seen him sober."

Even with their constant cycle of plummeting into bottles of vodka at night and crawling back out the next morning, the muscle and bone of circus grunts took Moira from packed trucks to packed houses over 300 nights a year. Without them, the circus would have had difficulty keeping the wheels rolling. Contracts bound fifty-some Poles to their jobs, contracts that verged on indentured servitude. It was all about survival—if they survived here, their families survived back home. Three-quarters of their meager earnings went directly to Poland to divvy between family and government, barely leaving the workers enough for daily doses of vodka and cigarettes.

On binge days, everything changed. At least once a month, Izaak, Borys, and their compatriots pooled funds to pull an all-nighter. They'd start drinking in the early afternoon and continue pounding drinks till morning light, drowning their nostalgia in grain alcohol, gulping spirits from tall glasses as if it were nectar, and latching onto each other's shoulders, crooning for home.

I remember the time Izaak lost his mind and almost his life. Stefano was on guard that night and had already laced the tent shut when Izaak lurched in.

Circus elephants detest drunks. Keepers under the influence are prone to forgetting elephant etiquette, and many animals have seen the wrong end of a shovel when "caretakers" over-imbibe. Whether alerted by alcohol on the breath, swagger in the step, or a gleam in the eye, Moira's elephants knew to be wary.

Stefano yelled *stop* when Izaak beelined for Banana. The man was long past listening. Banana flipped her head up, cocked her trunk, and lashed out. Wham! The Pole flew twelve feet. Stefano rushed to hold him down.

Strong with spirits, Izaak heaved Stefano away, insisting, "Banana loves me!"

Slam! Smack! Bam! Four times the man flew. He bled from forehead, nose, and mouth, dragged one foot, and clutched his arms to his chest. Stefano tried to hold Izaak back, but he refused to stay down. With all the elephants on their feet, whacking their trunks against their wooden decks, vibrating the tent's walls with war cries, Stefano realized that if he didn't stop Izaak, the elephant would end up hurt, or the man would end up dead.

Stefano sandwiched himself between idiot and elephant and hoped she wouldn't attack from behind. Banana never swung at Stefano. He believes Banana began to trust and respect him that night, making Stefano one of the few who could work within striking range without risking his life.

The following morning, Izaak didn't remember a thing. Stefano and I weren't surprised. We'd seen open-handed thunderclaps across Izaak's and Borys's faces fail to wake them the morning after one of their pining-for-Poland binges.

At least Borys would be going home.

I didn't appreciate it then but, sordid or not, the circus was still an adventure for me. Even if I felt like a ballerina in a snow globe, I chose whether to dance or walk away. The money I made ushering for an hour averaged more than what Stefano earned for an entire day's work—and probably twice what the Poles made. Add the seven dollars I earned for making the exotic animal food, and I fared damn well considering how much free time I had.

Looking back, having whined about the dancing makes me feel like Cinderella complaining that her glass slippers were too tight.

CHAPTER TWENTY-ONE

HOW DIFFERENT COULD IT BE FROM RIDING AN OSTRICH?

Mephisto, the muscular black stallion, pounded past me. He flicked his raven head and yanked against his reins, sending his wavy tresses into disarray. I inhaled the scent of sweat and leather and thought of Oregon. But this was Udine, and the snowcapped mountains I saw in the distance were not the Cascades, but the Dolomites.

Stefano worked more than ever. When Borys first left, the remaining crew had to cover his duties. Since then, Giuseppe depended on Stefano to teach Borys's Moroccan replacement the ropes and make sure the elephants didn't trounce him.

After two weeks of dancing, I didn't enjoy it any more than the first night. From the time I applied my makeup an hour before the four p.m. show until the last finale at midnight, performances leashed me to the circus grounds. A dash to the closest coffee bar or market might fit in somewhere, but it meant traipsing around in call-girl makeup, so I usually chose not to.

Loitering around the zoo watching Dieter and Lara, Moira's daughter, warm the horses for the equestrian number helped pass time between dances. At first, I'd observed from afar, but each day I moved closer.

That day in Udine, leaning against the zebras' pen and watching the two stallions circle the zoo, I thought how petite Lara's white horse seemed next to the black Friesian that Nino would ride. Lara noticed me. She called something to Dieter, who then trotted over to ask if I had riding experience. I nodded, more interested in his mount's fiery eyes.

"How much?" Dieter wanted to know.

"Enough to ride an elephant *and* an ostrich."

"Come to the zoo after tomorrow afternoon's opening parade. Lara wants to see you ride her horse."

I hooked my hand under the saddle where there should have been a horn, swung myself onto the white stallion, and urged him into a gallop. Zebra and antelope lifted their heads as we zoomed toward the rhinoceros pen. The wind cooled my face, the stallion's mane whipped my hand, and his feet drummed beneath me. Sitting in the saddle felt like home.

It hadn't always been that way. The only horses I'd grown up with were the dime-eating, spring-powered jobbies you find in front of supermarkets. Then, soon after I turned thirteen, my father decided our family would leave California for the Great Northwest, precisely as his own father had done thirty years earlier—except that my grandfather went without his wife and seven boys.

By 1979, Mom had spent years of saving and months of spending to redecorate our suburban Los Angeles house, as if beautifying her home would return the luster to her marriage. The extravagance of picking out new carpet is still fresh in my mind: I see my mother and her four children kneeling on the living room floor, clustered around sample boards, poking and petting cubes of color with names such as Summer Day and Bed of Roses. At the time, my brothers shared a bedroom, so my sister and I each had our own. I picked Midnight Blue, an endless color, as infinite as the oceans, as eternal as the heavens. I barely had a chance to enjoy that deep blue dream before my father sold our house. A few days before my mother's teaching year ended, we loaded up a yellow Ryder truck and headed north to Oregon. Mom packed up Great Aunt Maude's china and said goodbye to the fruit trees and landscaped yard of the home she'd poured so much into in hopes of saving the marriage that had drained so much out of her.

My father had purchased the motel property on a solo trip, and when the rest of the family saw our new home, it was a shock. Two of its four front doors had holes kicked through them. Smashed flies polka-dotted the drywall inside. On Mom's orders, no one was allowed to sleep inside before the place was scrubbed and sanitized from floor to ceiling. Outside, brambles and poison oak strangled massive Douglas fir stumps. And the delaminating plywood walls of a barn blew in the breeze, revealing a collection of desiccated deer legs strung up from its rafters.

We were definitely not in Kansas anymore.

For my sister, who was starting her senior year of high school, leaving Los Angeles was traumatic. But for me, cashing in my savings bonds to buy a chestnut Arabian/Quarter Horse with a flowing black mane and full-length tail that streamed behind him when he ran made Oregon heaven for me. Pretty Boy Ben was his name, and he left his cattle-cutting days behind to become a fine trail horse and a faithful friend.

Galloping through the circus on Lara's stallion, I laughed. Any decent cow-poking, trail-riding horse would have been ashamed of Moira's gussied-up, rhinestone steeds.

"Warm him up," Dieter yelled as we rounded the bend. "Don't tire him out."

A tug on the red leather reins slowed the stallion. Lara nodded her approval and Dieter announced, "Warming her horse just became your job."

In the middle of our seven-day run, Stefano's mother came to Udine. Angela and Stefano had shared a handful of truncated phone conversations in the four months since we'd joined the Italian circus, and during one of their recent talks, Stefano brought up his inability to renew his passport. In Italy, the city of one's residence, their *comune,* controls passport status. Due to Stefano's plethora of unpaid motorcycle violations, his documents were revoked—at least until his father offered to have a soccer buddy who worked for the city of Milan smooth things out.

En route to Udine's passport office, I felt like a ball bouncing between Angela and Stefano. I'd long since accepted that I lived in a country where no one pronounced my name correctly, but Stefano insisted that his mother try. *Is not Kataleena, Mamma,* he would correct each time his mother called my name. *Is Kat'leen.* Then Angela would loop her arm around mine, call me *Katreen*, and speak to me in simple, sweet sentences, as if being gracious with me would ease her

Stefano hanging out in the elephant tent with two of his "girlfriends." Summer 1988.

Stefano and me in Sagunto, Spain, soon after we met. December 1988.

On a jaunt with Paco to some nearby ruins in Sagunto, Spain. December 1988.

Deepening my friendship with Baros as we share a quiet moment in the giraffe pen. Italy, 1989.

Baros landing a kiss on my cheek in Potenza, Italy, soon after I joined Circo Moira Orfei. March 1989.

Giuseppe attempting to keep Rasta on Katia's back in Castelfranco Veneto, Italy. Summer 1990. (LIZ CHALCROFT)

Trying to keep up while riding Raya in Valencia, Spain, during Stefano's mother's visit. December 1988.

(ANGELA FONTANA)

Breakfast time in the elephant tent. From right: Jenny, Shiva, Banana, Bimba, Katia (hidden), Babati, Whiskey. Italy, 1989.

Stefano cuddling a day-old tiger cub in Trento, Italy. Spring 1989.

Getting ready to approach Billy Bob, a nine-foot shark. Fall 1989.

Gliding through the salt-water tank with Billy Bob. Italy, 1990.

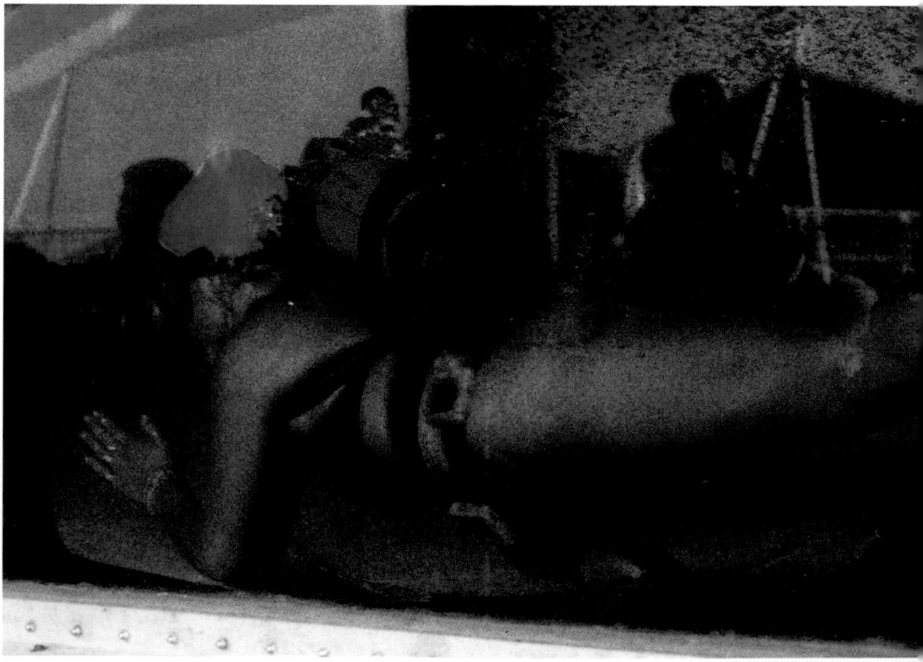

Showtime in Circo Moira Orfei! Stefano, Babati, and Giuseppe ready to head into the big top. Italy, 1989.

Stefano encouraging Shiva, his favorite elephant, to smile for the camera. Italy, 1989.

(l) Finally, some time off in Greece! June 1990. (r) Stefano and me at our wedding, with Rasta nearby. Devil's Elbow Beach in Florence, Oregon. July 22, 1991. (MAUREEN HEYLER)

Stefano and me at home in Oregon, January 2015.

interactions with her son. Before long, Angela would say something that ruffled Stefano, and he would latch his arm over my shoulder, disengaging me from his mother's embrace.

Maneuvering through governmental red tape contributed to the stress. Once fines and fees were paid, statements signed, and pictures snapped, things relaxed. His mother offered us pizza for lunch, which Stefano gobbled in his attempt to return by two p.m., as he'd promised Giuseppe.

"That went well," I said after Angela left to catch her train. When Stefano agreed, I explained that I'd been kidding. "Your mother sounded as if she wanted to bend you over her knee and spank you more than once."

"I'm sure she did. My mother always used her hands on me."

"For no reason?"

Stefano's lips curled in on themselves, making him look a tad guilty. "I did stuffs. Firecrackers in churches, flatten the tires of teachers, eggs on fur coats . . . but I had my reasons too."

"So you really do think today went well."

"You forget that before Christmas in Spain, I don't see her in more than one year." Stefano took my hand, hurrying me back to the circus. "Compare to old times, this day goes good."

Despite his conflicts with Angela, the day had gone well, especially since Stefano would soon receive his passport. That he'd even accepted his father's help reassured me of Stefano's intention to leave the circus at his commitment's end. Until then, I had my new job of warming Lara's stallion to quicken the tick of the clock. Overall, I left Udine more content than when I'd come.

As the days and towns passed, I eased into my role of dancing girl, even if getting along with all the dancers wasn't easy. The troupe varied from six to eight or more girls, depending on how many approvable bodies Moira could glean from her selection of young women. Those either related to Moira or born into the circus wore their pedigrees like crowns. Their sense of importance baffled me. Why carry on as if the circus was their world, yet never make much out of it? Perla—blonde, slender, young, pretty—surely she could have had a performing career. She'd tried once, before my arrival. Moira's son had set his wandering eyes on her and promised her the spotlight. In a rare moment of confidence, Perla told me about the long, hard hours she'd trained at Nino's side to become a *trapezista*. Her eyes grew wide as she relayed the bruises and blisters, the aches and pains. Right before her debut, Nino snipped her from the team—blaming his jealous wife. To my knowledge, Perla never again tried to become a real performer.

Even with her purebred circus blood, Giada was different. The world outside of Moira's blue fence fascinated her, and she wanted to explore all of it. Before summer, she would add four new holes to her ears, for a total of six, and point out that she still had six more to go before catching up with me. I remember how Moira's niece cautioned Giada that piercings could puncture nerves and shrivel ears—she'd seen it on TV. That crap didn't faze Giada. She wanted to take life by the horns and the hoops. At that point in our lives, Giada may have been carrying on more like me than I was. She was curious, adamant about what she wanted, and willing to gamble to get it. She was fearless about falling down and eager to dust herself off after a fall. Giada refused to fit into anyone's mold. Years later, I would read about her being the "premier hula hoop artist in the world," her "dominatrix black-leather outfit," and performances that seemed "more like a rock video than a circus number" as she traveled the world—first as a solo act with her husband, and later performing a different number with Cirque du Soleil. The circus may be her life, but Giada struck the deal on her own terms. And she's doing it with her hair dyed jet black, a bountiful collection of tattoos, and a hell of a lot more than six earrings in each ear.

Although I would always be an outsider to some, over time I made friends with a couple of other dancers. Lisetta, a straightforward Romanian girl, taught me to camouflage rips in my fishnets by weaving miniature macramé with fine thread so I wouldn't constantly have to buy new tights. Her parents were workers, which made it unlikely that she'd ever become an actual performer and probably contributed to her down-to-earth attitude. And Trina, who had black hair to her waist and emerald eyes that glistened when she spoke of the family she'd left in Yugoslavia. She lived with a portly accountant twice her weight and twice her age. Trina had a habit of twisting her hands when she spoke, curling them up, over, and around each other as if trying to find someplace for her fingers to hide. I never learned how she came to join the circus, but she never stopped plotting her escape.

Giada, Lisetta, and I often met in Trina's camper for coffee, where we painted our toenails and traded makeup tips. Inside the big top, we clowned around while showing spectators to seats and told goofy jokes backstage. The night torrential rains flooded the show tent, we spent more time laughing than dancing. Drops smashed against the trucks and trailers and bounced back off, surrounding the circus in a halo of rain. Water gushed through the *piazza*. It sloshed against caravan wheels and seeped under tents. The whole place turned into a mucky, manurey mess. We held onto each other for support on the slick pathways into the big top. And while the local fire department pumped the lake out of the center ring, we waited backstage dabbing mud splatters off each other's fishnets. The *pista* was no place for sequined stilettos. That night, we performed in G-strings and galoshes and turned Moira's choreographed cha-chas into bungled burlesque.

Regardless of my camaraderie with a few of the girls, I wanted to two-step off the chorus line the first chance I had. One night, leading his elephants into the ring, Stefano waved to get my attention and yelled that Giuseppe wanted to speak to me during intermission. Anticipation tingled my toes. Though too pessimistic to hope Walter would allow me back on the ostrich, I still ached for something equally exciting. Waiting in the elephant tent, I couldn't come up with a single realistic idea. The animals finally strode through the door, each hightailing it to her deck and turning a quick 180 as if part of the performance.

"Giuseppe asks if you enjoy riding the horse," Stefano said as he chained Banana and removed her headdress.

I nodded. "But not as much as the ostrich."

"He sees how much the giraffe likes you, says you've gained his *confidenza*."

"*Tutte e due*," I said to Giuseppe. The affection and trust were mutual.

"What do you think about riding Baros?"

My gaze shot from Stefano to the trainer and back. "People ride giraffes?"

"Not that Giuseppe knows. Is a new number for the trip to Japan next year."

"*Japan?* We're going to Japan? Is Moira famous there too? How would we get there?"

"Ship," Giuseppe said. "We'd load the equipment, animals,

and everyone necessary to care for them, and set out across the seas."

"All these animals on a ship? Whoa. How long would that take?"

"So many questions." Giuseppe shook his head, told me to concentrate on the giraffe, and left to dress for the tiger show.

"Dieter will be the one to break Baros," Stefano explained. "If he succeeds, you ride him in the show." He brushed his finger against my cheek. "Is dangerous, Kat'leen. You would be three meters in the air." Stefano flipped his thumb, index, and middle finger in the air. "Three."

My father would have told me either to *exercise caution* or to *remain calm, cool, and collected at all times*. Believing that his knowledge would come back to us when we needed it the most, my father had repeatedly offered these and other bits of wisdom to his children. And that day in the elephant tent, I did hear Daddy's deep, resonating voice and his thought-provoking pauses between each word, yet I carried on as if a sirocco had blown common sense from my mind.

"But it's riding a giraffe!" I said as much to my father as to Stefano.

Stefano reached for my arm. "We need to talk about this—just not now. Giuseppe says I have to help get the tigers into the ring—like is not already enough work I do in here."

In preparation for intermission, Stefano stacked food buckets, straightened tools, and ordered Izaak to cordon off a small viewing area inside the door. For twenty minutes in the middle of the show, the elephants and any personnel in the tent were on display for audience members willing to pay extra to see the circus's back lot. Stefano didn't like outsiders in the tent, especially zoo-goers who were too busy scorning tent aromas or worker appearances to comprehend the elephants' magnificence.

Once Stefano put everything in order, I followed him to the tiger tunnel. As the second half of the show commenced, a handful of ultra-trusted performers and workers persuaded twelve tigers through the tunnel that led to the brightly lit cage constructed center-ring during intermission. While the tigers performed, the men stayed nearby, ready to whisk the tigers back to their cages in case of an attack or fights in the ring. Stuck in the shadows between the end of the grandstand and the beginning of backstage, at least the tunnel offered some privacy.

"I don't like the idea of someone breaking in the giraffe," I told him while he waited for the tigers. "But maybe Baros will take to it."

"Baros isn't an ostrich. What if you fall off?" Stefano reached for his lower back as he said, "You want your body broken like mine?"

"Have you seen him flow through the ring? It's almost in slow motion." From the dim area surrounding the tunnel, the *pista* practically glowed, and I imagined loping through it on Baros's back, arms wrapped around his splotched neck, rocking with his gait.

Erich called down the line that the tigers were on their way, and the cats proceeded through the tunnel with due anxiety.

Females fought. Males sprayed territorially, causing the next male to think twice about waltzing through. One female in heat and all hell broke loose. Depending on each tiger's mood, one or two big cats went through at a time, and sliding metal partitions kept tunnel sections separate.

Stefano banged his long metal prod on the side of the tunnel, urging a Bengal on her way. The tiger scrunched her neck into her shoulders and twitched her upper lip to expose two-inch fangs.

"Keep her moving," Erich yelled from the zoo-end of the tunnel. "Close the divider as soon as she's through."

"During training, Giuseppe tempts them into the light with treats," Stefano explained as the tiger skulked past. "So even when there's music and noisy crowds—which should frighten the tiger—she still move toward the ring. And this," the partition clanged shut, "makes it impossible for her to turn back."

The tiger slunk into the spotlights. From center ring, Giuseppe's baby blue tuxedo shimmered as he coerced the animal to its mark.

Turning his gaze to the approaching tiger, Stefano asked, "Still thinking about Japan?"

"Sure I am." I leaned back against the bleacher scaffolding and twisted my clog in the dirt. "I just didn't think we'd still be here."

"We wouldn't be *here.*" The next tunnel guard closed the divider between the ring and us, and Stefano opened his to let two cats in. "We'd be *there.*"

One by one, twelve tigers took their places lying in a row until the ring became a carpet of cats. With a twist of his baton, Giuseppe instructed them to roll over. Shoulders touched. Ears flattened. Teeth flashed. Amid rumbling growls and spitting hisses, the cats rolled first one way and then the other in unison. Once on their feet, Giuseppe's Bengals, Siberians, and Sumatrans circled as smoothly as a merry-go-round. They played musical chairs on chrome pedestals and leapt through flaming hoops. Near the end of his performance, he had them all sitting on their hind legs in a row, pawing at the air, saluting the audience with a mighty roar. As the awestruck crowd looked on, the trainer bowed and then ordered each tiger, except his two most trusted, back through the tunnel.

For the finale, Giuseppe performed the signature act that had helped him win the circus equivalent of an Oscar, Monte-Carlo's Golden Clown Award. The trainer stepped out of the cage and returned piloting a motorcycle with a sidecar. One tiger leapt onto a platform behind Giuseppe's head, the other into the sidecar, and the three of them motored around the ring. The Bengal at his side looked more pussycat than predator as she rubbed cheeks with Giuseppe, bathing him in steamy breath and bringing the crowd to its feet. One day between cuddles, the cat punctured her fangs into Giuseppe's forearm. Without alerting the audience, the trainer raised his arm in a wave and coasted to a stop. Blood dribbled down the inside of his tuxedo sleeve and ran in red rivulets over his starched white shirt, but he kept waving to his crowd as he ushered the two remaining tigers out through the tunnel.

No tendons were ripped or bones crushed, at least that time around, and Giuseppe probably would have sewed up the holes himself if someone hadn't insisted on hauling him off to the emergency room. As with most complications, he took the attack in stride. Giuseppe knew perfectly well a tiger doesn't wake up one day wanting to leap through a ring of fire. Even if born into captivity, a 500-pound cat understands that performing is against her nature. Perhaps she even inherits memories of the wild, knows she should be free to roam and hunt and mate, to prowl at night and sleep in the sun. Circus animals may resist training at first, but at some level, whether it involves positive reinforcement, intimidation, or beatings, most succumb.

Circus life was never kind to tigers, especially the babies. Those born to siblings were often deformed and promptly disposed of. Others were born healthy only to be refused nourishment or, as if her instinct was to prevent her cubs from living in captivity, eaten by their mother. Even when healthy cubs survived, Stefano and I found it bittersweet. Their fate, at best, would be the same of their parents: thrust into the performance ring under threat of whips and prods and forced to live out their lives within an eight-by-eight-foot cage.

To watch a Bengal turn tricks is to witness her defeat.

I leaned against the wall of the phone booth and took a deep breath as I waited for the familiar ring of an American phone. My hand bulged with change next to the slot, poised to slip some in if she answered.

"Mom? Just a minute—" Coins jangled through the metal box. Calls home were rare, and her voice made Oregon feel only six miles away instead of 6,000. "How are you, Mom?"

"Fine, Kathleen, fine. Where are you?"

"Monfalcone. Northeast of Venice on the Yugoslavian border. By late May we'll be up near the Austrian border and then back to the East Coast around mid-July." The phone's meter clicked its way toward zero. "They say we'll spend the summer on the seaside entertaining tourists."

"Sounds hectic. Still riding the ostrich?"

"Now I'm a dancing girl."

"I thought you didn't like the dancing."

"I didn't have much of a choice—but it's okay. They're going to Japan next year, Mom, and they want me to ride the giraffe."

"The giraffe? Is that safe?"

"Of course, Mom."

"And Japan? Wow."

"Yeah . . ." I drummed my fingers on the wall of the booth,

took a deep breath, and emptied my pocketful of change into the phone. "Could you send me some of my things?"

"Does that mean you're staying?"

"For now." My practical side reminded me that I could always send the stuff back to Oregon.

As she listened to my wish list, I pictured my mother standing in her kitchen, surrounded by evidence of her busy life—students' papers on the dining table, waiting for her corrections; fresh baked bread on the counter, its aroma filling the room. I could almost taste her homemade preserves, both tart and sweet at the same time. I missed her.

"If there's room, could you add some blackberry jam?"

"I'll make it fit."

"Thanks. And, Mom?" I could see it perfectly—there on her kitchen shelf, its red and white spine long gone, ragged binding bare to the world and yellowed with old glue, pages stained and stuck together with remnants of my childhood pleasures. "Can you spare your Betty Crocker cookbook?"

CHAPTER TWENTY-TWO

SFIGATA

Zigzagging through the Veneto region in a series of three-day venues made the circus a flurry of setting up and taking down, reviving and razing. We barely finished assembling in one town before the time came to take it all apart and move to another. With all the huffing and puffing it took to get the animal tents up and down, I began to think of them as inflatable barns.

Every day, I dreamed of riding Baros. Finally, Giuseppe said the time had come for Dieter to break him. Giuseppe, Dieter, Stefano, and I congregated in the big top at nine a.m. and waited for Nino to finish practicing with the rhinoceros.

Bent-kneed, whip in hand, Nino stood on Joomba's four-foot haunches as she loped around the ring. This 4,000-pound armored beast posed the greatest risk of all circus animals — not for her tonnage, but because those two tons were steered by enormous stupidity. The most complex trick the rhino could grasp after years of training was climbing onto a squat stool in center ring. She was dense, and dense meant dangerous. The sedative needed to halt a rhinoceros emergency in the close confines of a circus tent was so potent that if the smallest amount of the drug touched the dart maker, he would drop dead. The circus didn't make any darts. If Joomba ever went ballistic, she would plow through spectators like a dump truck with one hell of a piercing horn.

After Joomba's practice finished, Nino steered her to her cage. Dieter strapped an acrobat's training harness around his chest and thighs and clipped a rope to his back. The other end of the rope looped around a pulley contraption on a track, allowing him to circle the ring safely suspended ten feet in the air. When Nino ushered Baros in a few minutes later, Stefano and Giuseppe hoisted the giraffe jockey up to the rafters.

Baros flicked his ears and studied the man suspended mid-tent. Dieter, his arms crossed over his chest, studied the giraffe. Besides the bony hump at his shoulders, the giraffe was one hazardous slope from head to tail. Dieter had a better chance of riding a greased pig.

"This is going to hurt," he said. "I know this is going to hurt."

While Nino distracted Baros with carrots, Giuseppe climbed an adjacent ladder and draped a wide belt over the animal's haunches. Giuseppe cinched the strap down one notch at a time. He clipped one end of a second rope to the giraffe's belt and tossed the other end to Dieter. A flick of Nino's long whip, and the animal skittered to the edge of the ring. Dangling Dieter used the rope to pull himself toward the giraffe. Baros bolted. The German pulled himself in again, but the animal scooted away. After a dozen attempts, the giraffe finally allowed Dieter to hover over him, and Nino called it a day.

The next morning, Baros refused to cooperate. Recapturing the previous day's accomplishment took the entire half-hour training session and consumed precious practice time in the big top, but Giuseppe gambled that if Baros allowed Dieter to hover, he would soon let him sit on his back. They tried in Portogruaro to no avail and then again in Scorzè. Days passed. Towns passed. Patience wore thin.

The circus pulled into Carnia, a remote area close to the Austrian border, through corridors of red-roofed buildings whose tall white facades mimicked the backdrop of snow-capped mountains. A devastating earthquake had rocked the region's foundations thirteen years earlier, and diligent locals had painstakingly rebuilt their communities. There in Tolmezzo, Giuseppe decided to try the painful approach to riding the giraffe.

During the next practice, when Nino gave the word, the German spread his legs and reeled himself in with the rope. Baros scrambled away, but Dieter insisted, reeling himself in again, hand over hand. The giraffe leapt forward, his neck see-sawing as he towed the German around the *pista*. Whenever Baros lowered his head, his bucking shoulders rammed Dieter's crotch. The pulley squealed. Dieter screamed. When he finally let go of the giraffe's rope, he hung from the rafters like a battered yo-yo.

Giuseppe and Nino cajoled Dieter into trying again. His hoarse screams soon filled the tent. Each time his butt connected with the giraffe's haunches, Dieter ricocheted back into the air only to land harder on the next blow. Finally, they pulled him up. The German slumped in the air, his hands cupped between his legs.

"Ancora?" Giuseppe called up to him. Could he take any more?

"No," Dieter squeaked. "No more."

I respected him for trying as hard as he did and couldn't blame him for giving up. To appreciate the gravity of the situation, one needs to understand Italy's candid relationship with what a good portion of the world considers their unmentionables. First off, Italian men touch their penises a lot. Publicly, privately—it makes no difference. Though not sexual, the touching goes beyond simple rearranging, as if the crotch were their comfort zone, and the act of confirming that all is well down there reassures that all is well with everything else that matters. Other uses abound. Most Italian men will not pass a graveyard or auto accident without cupping their jewels, as jabbing the air with the pinky and forefinger of one hand while clutching one's balls with the other hand wards off bad luck. (Americans clearly lost something in translation to end up knocking on wood.)

The way Italians treat their package, a casual observer might conclude that the Italian *cazzo* has attained a level of honor no other body part is worthy of. In Pompeii, erect penises grace the entries of 2,000-year-old villas to signify and welcome abundance—certainly a good thing. A modern Italian man using a two-finger lift to invoke protection only empowers the image. Yet that same man is just as likely to say *che cazzo* (what the dick) when pissed off or *grazie al cazzo* (thanks to the dick) when disappointed. And when someone does something meaningless or offensive, it is called a *cazzata*, suggesting that the penis is bad.

Buttocks, on the other hand, are always good. When things go well, one has *culo*, and the larger the luck, the larger the ass. Aced a test? *Che culo.* Found a good parking spot? *Che culone.* In short, Italians hope always to have very big bottoms. (For well-endowed women, it might ease the shock of a public fondling to consider it the Italian version of rubbing Buddha's belly.)

Despite the status of the generous derriere, no other body part exemplifies beauty and bounty like the *figa*. The English language lacks a term even remotely complimentary of Eve's Ornament, but Italian pays homage to her gift. While *figa* identifies only the actual organ or a gorgeous woman, a beautiful place or wonderful thing is notated with largesse, as in *figata* and *figona*. When fortune strikes, the magnitude of the figurative *figa* knows no boundaries, and her immensity encompasses all that is good with the world—which is why, in Italy, it's always wise to stay one step ahead of *sfiga* (the negative "s" meaning "without *figa*") and the bad luck that is sure to follow. And even if cradling a *cazzo* might deflect evil, your time is better spent developing the biggest *culo* you're willing to tote around. After all, size does matter.

But balls are still balls, and in the game of potential injury versus financial profit, ball safety trumps giraffe riding. Had it been Dieter's foot in danger that day in the tent, the trainer might have pushed the German to keep trying—or found someone else willing. Some things are not worth risking.

Later that day, sitting in the zoo making the animals' afternoon meal, I knew another dangling carrot had turned to mush. First the ostrich, then the giraffe . . . I still drifted through the microcosm of the circus without a place of my own.

When Baros leaned over his fence and wafted warm breath into my hair, I craned my neck back and reached up to caress him. Rasta bounded into my lap and arched up to lick the giraffe's billowing nostrils before bursting away.

At five months, Rasta's English-setter blood had turned his spotted puppy coat long and soft, as if he were a long-haired Dalmatian. Flattening his fluff against the bars, the dog wriggled into the antelope pen and continued into the llama's cage where he turned a few circles and curled up next to Mina. He'd befriended everyone—from third-class workers to circus elite—and refused food from no one—whether kielbasa, couscous, or curlicue pasta. Rasta even snacked on the tigers' rations. Once he'd deduced that the big cats were caged, he graduated from tiptoeing past their trailers to peeing on their wheels. Rasta lay in front of the cages each afternoon, waiting for Erich's blue wheelbarrow to deliver dripping chunks of raw meat. Amid the tigers' eating frenzy, scraps of flesh and bone inevitably slipped through the bars. Rasta hauled each morsel to the wide-open space in front of the cages where he'd lie in the dirt, slurping on their bones for hours, polishing off their dinners right under their noses. Rasta seemed more comfortable in these surroundings than I would ever be.

"These people sure love you when they need you, eh Baros?" When the giraffe stretched closer, I reached up to scratch his cheeks until fine white hairs showered down on me. "The rest of the time, they forget you're here."

A few years later, a careless worker allowed a plastic grocer's sack to work its way into Baros's cage, and the giraffe lapped it up. By the time the sack reached his throat, it was too late. My precious giraffe suffocated and died.

Five boxes of hippie heaven arrived in Montebelluna the same morning we did, ending a three-year pact with myself not to collect more than I could carry. I ignored my uneasiness as Stefano and I made our way, squeaky blue hand truck in tow, to the front office. Within minutes of bringing the boxes to our room, it looked as if they'd exploded all over the bed. I donned a tie-dye shirt and rubbed amber crystals between my wrists while Rasta sniffed through skirts and scarves, beads and birth control pills.

At first, Stefano seemed worried about the mess this new stuff would create. Then he found my music. "So much of this Grateful Dead," he said, piling his lap with cassettes.

I plucked the tape from his hand. "Kaiser Auditorium—Chinese New Year, '87. Good show," I said, popping open the tape deck.

"No, this one, this one—" Stefano slipped the Stones in instead. "Wait," he said, clicking off his dilapidated player to trade Mick for Paul. The Beatles crooned a few lines before Stefano switched to Ziggy Stardust.

Looking at my collection of beads, Stefano said, "Makes me think of when I worked leather."

"You did leather? What kind of leather?"

"Lighter cases. Tobacco pouches. Small stuffs to sell on the street," he said, "back when I tried to clean up my life." Stefano fingered the vials of tiny glass beads. "This guy I knew used to sell in street markets, and he offer me a place to live in exchange for helping with his leather work." He shook his head and continued rummaging. "We barely make any money—so I leave for Spain and find the circus, but I liked working with the leather. Maybe I try again someday—" Stefano gasped. "Who is Betty Crooked?"

Damn. I'd planned to tuck the book away before he noticed it. "Crocker," I said. "Betty Crocker. She cooks."

"Americans cook?" He grinned and scanned the index. "Why no recipes for pasta?"

"Try N. Back then, we called them noodles."

"Noo-doles?" Stefano flipped pages so joyously, I thought he might rip one out. "Ohhh—you going to be making me one of these?" He flashed me a frosted three-layer cake with pink and green filling.

I wondered what I'd been thinking when I'd asked for Betty. "Can't bake without an oven," I said, "and there's certainly no room for one in here."

By lunchtime, four chunks of wood blocked our bed up an extra foot, and I stuffed the things I couldn't place elsewhere back in their boxes and slid them underneath. After displaying the cookbook like a piece of art on our strip of counter, Stefano grabbed a couple of cassettes and headed for the elephant tent. Giada and I dug into my bead collection. Sifting through iridescent seed beads while listening to the Dead reminded me of colorful times gone by. Bead by bead, we strung glittering droplets of glass until we each had half a dozen bracelets on our wrists. Giada insisted on having clasps on hers.

"This way I wear only a little each day. Will last longer, no?"

"Probably."

"Why no clasps for you?" she asked.

A friend and I had come up with The Bracelet Theory years before. Strands of beads were pretty things to adorn our lives. Once made, the bond needed to be constant, but the nylon string fastening them was thin and fragile, destined to break. The fallen beads were never gathered; the exact same bracelet never made again. Enjoy its beauty while it existed; accept its demise as inevitable change. But how could I explain this in broken Italian, simple English, and hand signals? I held out my wrist so Giada could tie on another bracelet and said only, "Because nothing lasts forever."

We left the Veneto region and journeyed west along the Austrian border. As the yellow and blue convoy climbed into the lower reaches of the Alps, snowmelt streamed down toward warmer temperatures in the plains. The rest of Italy dove headfirst toward summer, but the area around Bolzano clung to winter. Frigid air blew down off snowy ridges to the north, and steam puffed from animals' lips.

Disillusioned by the giraffe number, I kept my sights on Japan. No one else seemed to be talking about it. Only by pressing Stefano for information did I find out that we'd probably travel in fall when the season slowed, and in light of the long ship ride over there, we'd stay six months to a year. Adding the return trip to Italy meant I had plans for the next two years.

May 31, 1989, Bolzano, Italy: Two years—the most long-term plan of my adult life.

By mid-June, we descended the mountains and traveled toward Italy's eastern shores. That's when Daniele, a waiter Stefano and I had met the previous winter in an after-hours bar near Naples, popped in for a few days to help celebrate Stefano's birthday. Everything about Daniele was pointed—his dark widow's peak, his abundant nose, his dimpled chin, his nonstop conversation. I loved when he came to visit.

The first time we met him, he had served us beer and *bruschette*—fire-toasted bread, rubbed with garlic and garnished like miniature works of art—some decorated with halved cherry tomatoes, others with cured meat, olives, grilled vegetables, or minced herbs. I'd devoured one of the meatless versions before he'd set down the tray. Later that night, as the bar's crowd thinned, Daniele pulled up a chair and immediately drew us into a conversation. His expression eased into a smile every few words as he explained that, when not waiting tables, he followed his artistic heart by painting canvases and composing operas. Stefano and I liked him immediately, and Daniele took a shine to us as well, promptly declaring that he was going to take care of us. And he often did—showing up at the circus with bags of groceries that he quickly turned into delectable meals.

That June, Daniele's visit left a permanent mark when he tattooed Shiva's profile onto Stefano's arm—a symbol of my lover's devotion to the elephants. I remember Daniele sketching the animal's likeness onto Stefano's skin, hunching over his bicep, and puncturing him with a thread-wrapped bundle of sewing needles, giving him a prison-style tattoo. Now, I wonder how I felt watching Daniele dip the needles into that broken vial of fountain-pen ink and poke Stefano again and again, permanently embedding the design. Surely I hadn't wanted my name blazoned into his skin, but did it have to be an elephant?

One thing's for sure—the tattoo far outlasted the black star and sterling silver bracelet I gave Stefano for his birthday.

Eager to help tourists spend their vacation budgets, Circo Moira Orfei arrived at the seaside in mid-July and opened in Cervia to packed crowds. The big top would be within minutes of the Adriatic for the next two months—sometimes even butted up against it. Within a week, I'd seen enough thick gold chains buried in hairy chests to last the entire season.

As the mercury rose, it grew hard to be in the circus, hard to roll out of cool cotton sheets to make the exotic troupe's morning meal. Though I was one of the lucky ones who usually managed a few mid-morning hours on a pebble-strewn beach, I was back on circus grounds for the afternoon performance, sweltering in a stiff white blouse and knee-length black skirt, ushering patrons into the show-tent-turned-steam-bath. No one above the age of ten looked as if he wanted to be there. Even the smells of dung and dust wanted to flee, but the sea breezes seemed to stop right at the entryway and push the heat back into the tent.

Nights were different. Streams of people waltzed through the door, commenting on the vastness of the big top and chattering with anticipation. Men tipped well as their dates in provocative dresses looked on, and children raced toward bleachers to find their seats.

Holidays did not exist in the circus, but we couldn't resist the crowd's summertime mood. Stefano and Giuseppe had developed a genuine friendship over the past months. The trainer's wife, one of the few English-speakers around, was not circus blood, and she and I became friends as well. Occasionally, on longer engagements in larger towns, Walter rewarded the whole circus with a Monday night off, and it became routine for Giuseppe, his wife, Stefano, and me to share a relaxing seafood dinner in a nice restaurant. Nights off were rare, though, so Stefano and I usually joined one of the after-show parties that popped up around the workers' quarters, swigged "wodka" with Russian performers, or hopped into town for a midnight snack. I savored those social times because Stefano and I were together physically and emotionally.

Late one night, as we strolled down the boardwalk in

Fano, Erich and Dieter waved us over to their table. Dieter slid across his bench to make room while Erich ordered a round of Hefeweizen.

"Same story every year," Dieter said when I brought up Japan. Swirling the bottle to loosen the sedimentary yeast, he emptied a fresh beer into his glass and squeezed lemon into the honey-toned brew. "Crowds thin after Christmas, so the directors discuss where we must go to earn money. Last year Russia; this year Japan. Then summer arrives. Tourists come. We start earning well again and all is forgotten." Dieter gulped his beer and wiped the foam from his blond mustache. "You'll see. We never go anywhere."

Giuseppe confirmed Dieter's prediction the following day. I felt tricked by the circus and angry with myself for allowing it. Stefano, trying to console me, suggested hiking up a nearby ridge after the late show.

As the sun sets behind the big top, it glows briefly before shadows from its peaks stretch across the lot like fingers reaching for tomorrow, fondling everything in their path. When Stefano and I reached the hilltop, the sun was long gone, the big top dark. We reclined against a crumbling stone foundation that overlooked the sea, and I snuggled into his arms, my head rising and falling with his chest as I stared at stars and listened to waves.

Though I lay still, my thoughts ran rampant. "We're through with this circus in September, right?" I blurted out. "We could spend a month traveling to Amsterdam, then go to America." I popped up. "I'll show you Oregon and Big Sur. We'll dance at Dead shows and visit national parks—"

Stefano was a different kind of excited. "Travel a month? America?" A stone he hurled cracked against other rocks as it tumbled toward the water. "Where we find all this money?"

"I have my ticket—we only need to save enough for yours."

"Money for ticket, money for Amsterdam, money for getting started in America—all in two months?" Stefano fumbled for his smokes. "We been here since January and we haven't saved anything yet."

"We'll start now. Every penny."

He touched his lighter to the tip of his cigarette. "What about tobacco or pizza or beer? Food for Rasta?"

"Please don't make it sound as if we're stuck here." I reached for his hand, but he pulled away. "Why won't you leave this place?"

"To be homeless on the street? Where your only friend is the high and you struggle to survive?" The glowing tip of his cigarette bounced with his hands as he spoke. "Is better a life that asks too much than one that asks too leetle."

"You're saying we should shackle ourselves to this circus and stay?"

"Not forever. Maybe it takes five months. Six. Sooner or later—"

"Every time I talk about leaving, you try to patch what's wrong. No more band-aids." I inched back into his arms. "The two of us alone up here feels so right, Stefano. We need to create a life that allows us time for each other."

"Seven elephants is a big responsibility. I have my workers to keep in line."

"For a man who resents authority, you sure love being in charge."

Beneath my hands, his chest turned to stone. "Is better than being told what to do all day. *Cazzo,* Kat'leen," he said, jerking away from me. "I can't run away."

Stefano drew heavily on his cigarette and extinguished the embers on a rock before saying, "In my days on the street,

I think I would never make anything of my life. I may work hard for Giuseppe, but he treats me with respect. I feel appreciated. Needed."

"Don't you see, Stefano?" I reached for his hands, hoping he would feel my words as firmly as my touch. "They're wooing you with the promises of those things like they wooed me with promises of travel and adventure."

He flung my hands from his. "What is this *woo* word?"

Far below us, the big top mimicked the sea, reflecting the moonlight and wavering with the wind. It pulsed like a living organism. Like a predator enticing workers into her fold, so she could consume them.

"If we don't fight back, this circus will swallow us."

"No, Kat'leen." He chuckled and pulled me toward him. "I am too rebellious to let this circus swallow me, and you are too strong."

Stefano believed his words; I did not. Delicate as cotton candy, wispy as an ostrich plume, the circus's web was almost intangible. Yet each day its hold grew stronger. We lived on the fringe of a micro society that damned Stefano and me as much as it cherished us for being different. This conformist and capricious world, as refined under the spotlights as it was ragged outside the ring, used barbed threads to sew its sparkling sequins into place.

Six months after Erich had warned me to be careful here, I finally understood the significance of his words. The circus had many claws. Eventually, she'd snag every one of us.

"You'll see, *amore*." Stefano stroked my hair and spoke softly into my ear as I snuggled into his embrace. "One day we going to be happy."

CHAPTER TWENTY-THREE

SWIMMING WITH SHARKS

Giada and I melted into the warm beach, just as we had most mornings over the past two months. Lounging under the sun's burning rays, I pretended I was on vacation. My skin had turned deep bronze, and the tips of my curls were bound for blonde. But August 15, a.k.a. *Ferragosto*, an old Pagan holiday marked by eating, drinking, and sexual excess that now symbolizes the climax of Italian summer holidays, had already passed. Tourists were heading for home. Tomorrow the circus would move on as well, traveling hundreds of miles west, away from the riviera, away from these lazy, lolling mornings. Eyes closed, mouth open, I soaked up the sun and savored our last day at the beach.

"Some of the girls complained again about you not wearing underwear in the costume trailer," Giada said.

"It's a dressing room for Chrissake." Sand shifted under my weight as I rolled onto one elbow. "I can lie topless on a public beach or shake my G-stringed booty twice a day for thousands of strangers, but sitting naked in the company of a handful of women is scandalous?"

Circus women often acted like X-rated nuns. Exhibitionists by day, they bared belly buttons and bottoms for appreciative crowds and paraded around in skin-tight dresses. Afterwards, they filled nearby eateries and *discoteche*, carrying on like stars. When not on display, however, they cloistered themselves in their campers, gossiping about another woman's too-short miniskirt or too-snug blouse, plotting ways to outshine each other.

Rivalry and hostility weren't limited to the women. This jealousy-infused petri dish infected everyone. Backstabbing, ass kissing, and bed sharing were well-worn rungs on the circus ladder. Hierarchy—whether in the ring, in management, or on the payroll—turned brother against brother, friends into enemies, and the circus into a soap opera.

Reclining onto the sandy beach, I sighed and urged the hot sun to melt the constraints of the circus from my life. *Soon.* In six weeks, my return ticket to America would expire, and I planned to fly home before it did. When I'd told Stefano the previous night, he'd snapped out of his dreary-eyed, late-night state.

"You are . . . coming back?" he'd asked.

I knelt next to the bed and pulled him into my arms. No matter how much I wanted to be away from the circus, I wanted him more. "I'll come back, Stefano, and I'll stay, for as long as it takes."

Stefano locked me in his embrace. We made love, intoxicating love, heady like the scent of jasmine, potent as Sicilian *vino nero*. Lying deep in his arms, I had believed I would return. But here on the beach, listening to waves pound rocks and gulls cry overhead, I hoped I was being honest about returning from America—honest with him and honest with myself.

Giada and I soon scampered away from the sounds of the sea. As we approached the circus, the cacophony of forklifts and trucks overpowered the harmony of waves and gulls until Circo Moira Orfei was all I could hear.

In the ninety-five-degree tin box of a dressing room, I stared at my reflection. Sweat seeped through my makeup and beaded along my lip, my nose, my brow. My skimpy silver costume lay on the counter, and the headpiece's pom-pom fringe looked anxious to suffocate me. When a dancer made a catty remark about me being bare-breasted, I decided she needed a better reason to bitch, so I slipped off my thong underwear and propped my feet on a stool. And I lingered there, enjoying her shock, fanning my face with a shoebox lid, wondering if I'd ever break out of these dance routines and out of this dressing room for good.

Three days later, I broke free.

The morning we arrived in Bergamo, an old stone fortress beckoned from a nearby hill, and I planned to ask Giada if she wanted to go exploring that afternoon. Instead, Stefano pounded up the steps of our room to tell me that Walter needed me.

After motioning us into the office, the circus boss fixed his gaze on me and spoke in Italian. "The woman who performed the shark number has left the circus. Will you take her place?"

"There's little chance of danger," Giuseppe threw in.

I should have contemplated Giuseppe's skewed impression of danger, or that I'd never plunked myself into any size fish tank, much less a 10,000-gallon *shark* tank, but the promise of adventure hooked me like a shiny silver lure.

Stefano mistook my silence for hesitation. "Tell them you'll think about it," he whispered in English.

Walter said, "My offer is 15,000 lire each day you perform."

"Twenty," I told him. A fourteen-dollar-a-day raise wasn't much when you figured I'd be diving into a shark tank as many as three times a day, but it would triple my current take for making the exotic troupe's food. If I somehow managed to stash that extra $400 per month away, it could snowball into the nest egg Stefano and I needed to get out of here. Besides, I had a few more demands up my sleeve. "Plus no more dancing *and* I'm taking October off to visit my family in America."

Walter bounced the tip of a pen off his desk a few times before answering. "Twenty thousand lire. No more dancing. October in America." Aiming his pen at me, he said, "But you perform tonight."

When I shook Walter's hand, Giuseppe patted Stefano's back saying he'd known all along that the *Americana* had balls.

Now, there are all types of balls. Wheelin' and dealin' with the circus authorities, I must have had some mix between meaty *I-Can-Do-Anything* balls and dipped-in-steel *You-Want-a-Piece-of-Me* balls. That afternoon, standing in front of the fifty-ton aquarium, my balls shrunk to *What-in-Christ's-Name-Did-I-Agree-To* raisinettes.

I studied the two sharks through walls of glass and felt very, very small. Traveling some 50,000 miles a year at twenty-five miles per hour, this six-axle truck had sloshed salt water from one end of Italy to the other. I had seen the show a handful of times over the past nine months, but I'd never imagined performing it. Only a hefty double-pane window separated the carnivores from me. Soon, there wouldn't even be that. A nearby jackhammer jangled my nerves, and regardless of the warm September air, I felt chilled.

Hans, the sharks' lanky German caretaker, said, "They explained that two layers of glass make them appear smaller than they are, didn't they?"

I shook my head.

"Don't worry. The female's only seven and a half feet long, the male barely nine."

Nine feet? My stomach flip-flopped. Minnows scare me, and these were real sharks—with real shark teeth.

"What are their names?" I asked.

Hans laughed and motioned for me to follow him. "Sharks don't have names." He unlocked the metal door at the back of the truck, reached inside, and passed me a weight belt. "Put this on. Not too loose or the lead will drag and scratch the bottom of the tank."

I took the canvas belt from his hand and wondered if I could still change my mind. Italians loved the circus, and this one most of all. With her early acting career and outrageous personality, Moira had become a media darling, and her exploits filled newspapers and gossip pages. This far-reaching fame meant journalists, local bigwigs, and important families would fill every box seat. No shark show on opening night of a nine-day run in a wealthy city was unacceptable.

Outside the tank, a few stray workers gathered. The brothers, Walter and Giuseppe, approached from the big top. Fleeing now would not only let them down, but it would sully the perception of American bravery. I'd grown up in awe of Dorothy Hamill and Wonder Woman, but when I tried to gather strength from memories of their triumphs, I knew that Dorothy would never have doused her perfect bob in shark-poop soup, and Lynda Carter's Wonder Breasts would have buoyed her away from the beasts.

I needed only to look to my mother. Long before meeting my father, Mom dove with the California State University dive team and swam in exhibitions with tiger sharks. But either I hadn't heard that story yet or I'd long forgotten my mother's valor, and I looked to my father for courage instead.

Easy as pie, his deep voice echoed in my head.

Growing up piss-ass poor with six brothers in a fatherless family couldn't have been easy for him, and my father expected his children to eat what life dished them. Being daddy's little girl did not save me from the crush of grand failure when I disappointed him. Even after he left us, his mantras stuck to my family as spoon-flicked hot cereal had stuck to our ceiling.

Easy as pie.

I buckled the weight belt over my swimsuit as Hans steered me into the tiny room at the back of the truck. The clammy air tasted of salt. Refrigerator-sized filters hummed to one side of a stainless steel deck; chemicals, nets, and buckets covered shelves to the other.

Hans patted a ladder leading to the crawl space above the water. "You'll find a wooden plank up there. Crawl out over the water and lower yourself in. The water will reach your neck. Go slow and the sharks will move out of your way."

"You're not coming in with me?" The flip-flops in my stomach grew stronger as I slipped out of my sweats.

"They're nervous when more than one person's in there—maybe they feel outnumbered."

"*They're* nervous?"

Picturing stars and stripes, I stilled my chattering teeth

and climbed the ladder to walk the plank. Broad gray blobs rippled under the water's surface, splotches of cartilage, muscle, and teeth. Three-hundred-pound hunting machines. Fear thrummed in my head, echoed in my bones, and pricked the arches of my feet.

Easy as pie.

I shivered as I slipped feet first into the warm water. By the time my toes touched the floor and water slapped my chin, the nameless sharks had slithered off to the far side of the tank, some forty feet away.

"You've used scuba gear before, right?"

I turned to see Hans, tank in hand, at the top of the ladder. "Noooooooooooo."

"All you need to do is breathe." Hans passed the tank into my outstretched hands. "Arms through the straps, latch the clip in front, and breathe."

When I nestled the mouthpiece between my lips and sucked, the rubber shuddered and squealed.

"Don't force air from the tank," Hans said. "Slow and natural."

Breathe. Don't force the air. Act natural and swim with sharks. Right.

After a few deep breaths, I said, "Okay. I can deal with the tank. Now what?"

"For the moment, watch your feet. Here comes the big one."

Oh shit. Sharks! My stomach cartwheeled.

"The mask, Hans. I can't see." I smacked the mask against my face and peered through as the shark stationed himself six inches from my ankle. His body seemed to stretch forever. "You sure he's only nine feet long?"

"Just over three meters. You probably feel him sucking water past your feet."

"Exactly." The shark sucked so hard I had to press my heel into the metal floor to keep it from lifting off. "Is that how he gets my scent?"

"That's how he feeds."

"Feeds?" Only fifteen sets of onlookers' eyes kept me from peeing my pants.

"Don't worry, they just ate. Won't feed them again for three days."

Water coursed past my ankles, over my feet, and into his gaping mouth. "I think he needs a snack. And look—" The female closed in. *What are my shiny red toenails doing in this fish bowl?*

"Move your foot a little. He'll go to the other end of the tank and she'll follow."

I scrunched my toes so tight my calves cringed, and then I pivoted one foot. The shark didn't budge. "Haaaans . . ." Fear glued my feet to the floor. Now or never.

I pushed my foot within an inch of the male's jaws. He twitched and they both bolted away. I bit down on the mouthpiece and sank into the salt water. Silence. Settling on the bottom of the tank, I couldn't remember experiencing such quiet since I'd joined the circus. My breath sounded like a windstorm as I inhaled. Then silence. Slow gurgles as I exhaled. Silence again. Almost silent enough to forget that I wasn't alone.

From twenty-five feet away, four wide-set, beady gray eyes studied my two green ones. Gray skin turned speckled and then white around jaws wide enough to feed on a foot. With each breath, their gills shuddered and their fang-like feelers quivered. Shuddered like my heart. Quivered like my hands.

Easy as pie.

My stomach's flip-flops became doubles and triples,

somersaults with quadruple twists and backspins thrown in. I hoped I wouldn't barf.

What are they thinking? Do sharks even think? Can they smell the stranger in their territory? What does fear smell like? Dinner?

Watching the sharks watch me, I wondered why the woman who used to do the number had left. What if she were bitten—or worse? From outside the tank, Hans's warped image waved me forward. Giuseppe assured me with a nod. Beside the trainer, I found Stefano. No amount of distortion could hide his concern.

I pushed off and glided along one side of the forty-foot tank. With a flick of their tails, the sharks slid through the water above me, heading for the end of the tank that I'd vacated. Again, we rested on opposite ends.

Breathe. I forced myself toward them. This time the sharks held their ground. My fingers pulled my body forward, inching along the floor. Closer. Closer. Curling my hand into a fist, I reached for the male as if he were a stray dog. He swished his tail and swam past me. The female followed.

I finger-crawled toward them again. *Breathe.* This time, the male let me stroke his grit-encrusted forehead before swimming away. I turned and thrust myself after the sharks, grabbing the male's dorsal fin as I'd once seen the last woman do. His sliver of cartilage felt slick in my grip, polished. He pulled me the entire length of the tank. Bubbles gurgled toward the surface as I tittered into my mouthpiece. *The little girl from the rundown motel in rural Oregon is swimming in a semi-truck full of salt water and sharks. In Italy.*

When the shark turned, I let go and watched him retreat to the opposite end. Hans knocked on the window, motioning me out. Behind Hans, Giuseppe gave me two thumbs up.

Stefano blew me a kiss and then faded into the haze beyond my field of vision as he returned to his duties.

The commotion of the circus jarred me when I popped my head above water.

"Time's up," Hans called. "We're putting a circus together out here, remember?"

I heaved the gear and then myself up onto the plank. "When can I get back in?"

"Tonight. Be here before the elephants end. You'll have to wait in the back of the truck for fifteen minutes while people file out of the big top. The ringmaster will be here to announce facts about the sharks and comment on your performance. He'll knock on the door when he arrives and expect you to jump right in."

When Hans turned to leave, I asked, "That other woman—she didn't get bitten, did she?"

"Oh yes she did—by the big boss man. Argued with Walter about something." Hans shrugged. "He gave her two hours to move off the lot before someone threw her off."

Over the last nine months in the circus, I'd learned that I could either be a spoke in the juggernaut's wheel or the dirt over which it travels. As the new "shark tamer," I'd become part of the wheel, adding to its strength. The circus may have been rolling me down some yellow brick road, but I was the one hunting for Oz and its promises of fulfillment.

Once outside the shark truck, I draped my shirt over my shoulders and stared in through its glass wall. The sharks didn't look quite so scary anymore. Only then, when no longer in danger, did I feel a twinge of remorse for the sharks. I regretted that they would be stuck in this tank for eternity instead of swimming free off the coast of their native Florida. At least they should have names. Comfy, southern names. I mulled the thought and then tapped on the glass. “Goodbye, Billy Bob. Goodbye, Jolene. See you tonight.”

I headed for our room but changed my mind and slipped out of the circus fence instead. At a pay phone across the street, I dialed his number.

“Hey, Dad. It’s Kath. Good morning . . . It has been a while . . . Everything’s good . . . Still in the circus. I have a new job—swimming in a shark tank . . . Yes, they’re real sharks . . . Yes, Daddy, I exercised caution and remained calm, cool, and collected at all times . . . No, it wasn’t difficult; it was easy. Easy as pie.”

CHAPTER TWENTY-FOUR

PRESENTING MISS KATHLEEN FROM CALIFORNIA

Outside the shark truck, the crowd buzzed. The ringmaster would introduce Miss Kathleen from California any minute. Though I'd spent most of my life in California and had lived there right before traveling to Europe, I considered Oregon home. Unfortunately, the world didn't equate the Great Northwest with bikinis and beaches.

I paced the metal deck in the back of the truck. "But what am I supposed to do in there, Hans?"

"Same as today. Pretend you're afraid."

"I wasn't pretending."

"Do whatever you want, just do it for three minutes."

"How will I know when three minutes are up?"

Hans looked at me as if I were a dimwit. "Count how long it takes you to swim from one end to the other, then figure out how many passes add up to three minutes. If it takes you thirty seconds, then it's six passes. Got it?"

I didn't feel as if I *got* anything, and the announcer was already rapping on the door.

Hans frowned when I dropped my robe. "I thought that suit was for practice."

I glanced down. I knew they wouldn't want me wearing long johns, but I figured the high-cut legs and low-cut front of my one-piece suit showed enough skin. "My two-piece is too skimpy."

"Well this one covers too much."

"So swimming with carnivorous beasts and counting to three minutes at the same time isn't enough—you want me to do it in a string bikini too?"

The announcer started speaking, and Hans pointed to the ladder.

Since the crowd couldn't see through the surface of the water, the show didn't officially start until I climbed in with the sharks. But evaporation had dropped the water level six inches, leaving a bare strip of window that allowed the closest onlookers to watch what happened above the tank. From crawling on a foot-wide board above the water, I had to get down into the tank without flashing any more of my derriere than already showed.

The row of halogens cooking my head made the water shimmer and the sharks hovering over their shadows in the corner look sinister. I twisted onto one hip, rolled onto my bottom, and dangled my feet in the warm water. The animals twitched but stayed on their side of the tank. Knees clamped together, I slid off the wood and hoped it wouldn't splinter. My rear end splashed into the water, and my feet thudded against the floor. Hans chuckled as he lowered the scuba tank onto my back. I strapped the mask in place, wedged the mouthpiece between my teeth, and sank to the floor.

From outside the window, a wall of distorted faces eyeballed me. *I am a sideshow freak.* Children pointed. Flashbulbs popped. *They're hoping I'll be eaten.* My heart thumped hard. If I didn't move now, Hans would have to pry me from the floor of the tank when my air ran out. I was no Mabel Stark, the legendary tiger wrestler, but I could do Miss Kathleen, couldn't I?

Pushing my fingertips hard enough against the metal floor to turn my knuckles white, I pulled myself toward the beasts. Jolene jetted away. Billy Bob followed, his white belly passing right over me. He was so big around that if I'd tried to embrace his girth, my fingers wouldn't have touched on the other side.

The sharks settled in the opposite corner. I approached again and stroked Billy Bob's forehead as if he were the one who needed calming. When he pushed off, I latched onto the firm ridge of his dorsal fin. Water rushed over me. My spirits soared as exhilaration replaced anxiety. I was neither graceful nor coordinated, but I was ecstatic as the two of us glided through the water. We turned at the other end, and I flicked my feet like a mermaid's tail as we streamed back toward the front of the tank. When he curved again, I let go, and he drifted away.

I glanced outside. *Looking at the circus from the inside out feels different.*

A sense of security welled up inside me, as if this womb-like vessel of water and glass could protect me from the circus. Or maybe it was just the opposite. Perhaps I felt secure because I'd earned membership in Moira's club on my own merits—even if those "merits" were the simple willingness to dive into a pool of tepid water that happened to have a couple of sharks in it. Perhaps I felt like I belonged.

Rasta snaked between my legs and around Stefano's, sniffing everything in the ex–shark tamer's seventeen-foot camp trailer.

"I think we should take it. Look how big the bed is." As if pretending he hadn't noticed it, Stefano kept his back to the one part of the camper that churned my stomach. Then he spun around and sucked in his breath with mock surprise. "Did you see, Kat'leen?" A well-placed hand at the small of my back urged me forward. "What a beautiful kitchen."

Kitchenette seemed more appropriate. The sink, a two-burner electric stove, and one linear foot of countertop could have fit in a dollhouse.

When I didn't budge, Stefano sidestepped around me and swung open a cupboard. "Perfect for deeshes." He pulled open a drawer. "Forks will go in here. Everything will have its own place." Stefano opened a few more drawers and doors before turning, eyes wide, to say, "Look—a real table. We can sit together. Eat without being in a cafeteria bursting with people. Giuseppe tells me that we earn more money if we don't eat cafeteria food. Don't you think is perfect?"

In the circus pyramid of power, swimming with the sharks had lifted me above the mid-level rank of a dancer. Since I only had to be crazy enough to jump into a tank with a couple of sharks rather than train for years and years, I hadn't reached the upper echelons of *artista* and would never merit an alcove in the pantheon of circus stars. Nonetheless, the status leap had earned Stefano and me an offer of our own camp trailer. It was certainly an improvement from our current sleeper, but I questioned his qualification of "perfect."

The camper's pink curtains fluttered in the breeze. I only liked pink in flowers and sunsets and the moist spot on an animal's nose. Tugging open the two doors across the aisle from the kitchen revealed a small closet and smaller bathroom—its sink barely large enough to hold my cupped hands. "There's no toilet and no shower."

"Was so bad using the workers' showers?"

"I prefer having our own."

Rasta hopped onto the bed and curled in a corner.

Stefano pointed. "Rasta says yes. What about Kat'leen?"

I plopped onto the mattress—five wonderfully wide feet compared to our current three and a half. "Kathleen likes the bed."

Stefano grinned. "Well," he stepped closer, "if we take the camper, we also get the bed." He toppled me onto the mattress. "No more squishing Kat'leen into the wall when Stefano rolls over." He nestled closer. "No more wondering if the worker next door is sitting only one foot away when we make love."

My face must have shown how I adored the way that word came out of his mouth.

"*Lloow-vah*," he said again.

Regardless of Stefano's presumption that I would use the kitchen, the camper would combat one of the circus's great deficiencies: privacy. Our own wheels could tuck us into the more . . . *fragrant* animal zones that others rejected.

When I finally agreed to take the camper, Stefano covered my face with kisses. "You do love me," he said.

I pushed him away. "You better know I love you, Stefano, whether or not I agree to move into this camper."

He pulled me close again. "You love me enough that you going to cook for me? Especially now you have your own kitchen?"

I couldn't roll away fast enough. "Who said the kitchen's mine?" I scrambled off the bed and toward the door. "You know I don't know how to cook."

"Yes." Stefano caught me by the hand and spun me back around. "I know."

"So there won't be any pressure to cook, right?"

He looked shocked that I would even ask.

Stefano studied the table. "You said you were cooking lunch. I don't see any cooking."

"I said if you'd eat dinners in the cafeteria, then I'd serve lunches." I pointed to the spread. "Bread, cheese, fruit, wine—lunch. You should be pleased, Stefano. It means fewer dishes for you to wash."

"Deeshes?"

"Yes. If I make food, you wash dishes."

Stefano's groan sounded like a muffled meow as he slouched onto one of the dinette's benches. "Is okay this hummingbird picnic sometimes, but we need more stuffs, like prosciutto and olives—those green Cerignola ones are the best. Maybe some grilled eggplants." He flopped a thick slice of soft cheese onto a hunk of bread and sighed.

To me, cooking meant reheating pizza or warming soup. Intricate culinary concoctions would simply not come out of my kitchen, yet part of me still wanted to please him.

Maybe I couldn't cook, but I could bake.

A couple of days later, my fingers slid along the perfect shine of new stainless steel. I twisted one of the oven's bright red knobs and smiled at my reflection in the pristine glass door. I'd splurged almost an entire week's pay, but this De'Longhi toaster oven was my second chance at an Easy Bake Oven.

My parents had given me an Easy Bake for my fourth

birthday. Disaster struck after my two brothers sneaked into my room and scarfed all the powdered mixes. My mother suggested we make our own chocolate cake mix, but it rose too much, and the batter flowed over the edges of the palm-sized pan, covering the oven's innards with an impossible-to-clean chocolate crust. I couldn't turn the oven on again without the whole house reeking. To a four-year-old, it equaled tragedy. This time, I vowed nothing would go wrong.

During my morning of shopping, I'd found a new swimsuit, bought socks for Stefano, the oven for me, and then searched for chocolate chip cookie ingredients. Shortening, sugar, eggs, vanilla, flour, soda, and salt were easy to find; chocolate chips were not. The "drops of chocolate" from the grocery store were only flecks, which disintegrated when stirred in, turning a perfect marriage of vanilla dough and chocolate chips into sludge.

I baked them anyway.

"What is this stink?" Stefano wanted to know.

I cranked open a window. "Cookies."

"Smells like burning plastic." Pointing to the oven, he asked, "Aren't you supposed to heat these things without food the first time?"

I shrugged. "The instructions are in Italian."

"You speak Italian."

"Speak," I told him. "Not *read*."

"Okay, first we get rid of the stink." He unplugged the oven and hauled it outside. "Next," Stefano sorted through his stash of Italian-brand *National Geographic*s and comic books, "you practice reading."

I glanced at the book he'd tossed on my side of the bed. "Donald Duck?"

"*Paperino* in Italian." Stefano rapped a burnt cookie against the table. "I wait next time to try your famous American *biscotti*." Then Stefano noticed the 3-pack of white terrycloth socks I'd purchased that morning. "*Grazie, amore,*" he said and reached for the black felt-tip marker that lived in his jeans pocket.

Stefano was a methodical man who needed order—order in his life, order in his elephant tent, order even in his sock drawer. Granted he owned only seven pairs of socks with these new additions, all the same color and brand, but they were at different stages of wear. Stefano didn't like mismatched pairs where one sock felt a millimeter cushier than the other. So he labeled them. Not simple labels such as 1, 2, 3 or A, B, C, but complicated codes.

Peeking over his shoulder, I watched him write ☆▲☆▲☆ on one pair and XXOXX on another. I knew I shouldn't poke fun at his quirks, but I couldn't help myself.

"What's the last pair going to be," I asked, "$e = mc^2$?"

Stefano grunted. I feared I'd gone too far until a smile crept across his face as he wrote *Fredo* on the next sock. When Stefano saw my questioning look, he mustered his best *Godfather* voice to say, "*Fredo*, you broke my heart."

Stefano displayed his new socks on the table, kissed me, and walked out. I could hear him laugh as he walked away, and I laughed with him. At least his antics had dulled my disappointment at turning my De'Longhi oven into more of a disaster than my Easy Bake. I had botched my first attempt at baking for Stefano, and I wasn't sure there'd be a next time, but with the afternoon show less than an hour away, I had no time to decide my new oven's fate.

Since I no longer danced, I stayed behind with a few other ushers to seat stragglers until the time came for me to don boots and jeans and warm Lara's stallion. Ninety minutes after covering my face with makeup, I returned to my trailer to exchange those boots and jeans for my new two-piece swimsuit.

In the mirror, I saw only skin, skin, skin. My big-boned stature looked a bowl or two of pasta thicker than it had the previous spring. I didn't feel that spreading 150 pounds over a five-foot-five frame necessarily qualified as fat, but if anything kick-starts a diet, it's displaying your body behind glass.

Hans hemmed and hawed when I arrived at the shark tank. He held out the weight belt saying, "Maybe this will cover things up."

I girdled my gut with the strap, but the weights slid to my hips. Yes, the gear would conceal things — the weights, hanging low on my hips, hid the bottom half of my swimsuit; the tank's straps covered most of the top.

"Can you even tell I have a swimsuit on from the side, Hans?"

"Let's go."

"But I look naked."

"Let's go."

I slipped on the mask and sank into the water. Face to face with Billy Bob and Jolene, I knew of only sharks, bubbles, and me. The sharks stalked me with their eyes. Their vise-like jaws could crush bones, rip flesh, turn my hands and feet into a bloody wave.

I shouldn't be in here.

But I am Here, right Now. Swimming with sharks.

This alliance of fear and courage simmering in my lungs would transform my role in the circus from sequined drudgery into an edgy and thrilling underwater adventure.

"What you mean you're on a diet?"

I set aside Donald Duck and sat up in bed. Not performing in the finale meant my day finished after the last intermission. Stefano still had to help with the tigers, feed the elephants, prepare their beds, close the tent up for the night, and complete any other tasks Giuseppe added.

"I need to lose weight."

"And I need to eat." Stefano draped his shirt and pants over a coat hook and rolled his underwear and socks into compact balls before dropping them into the wash bucket. "What the food of this diet is going to be?"

"Salads. Fruit."

"Rabbit food." He opened the refrigerator and drummed his hand on the door as he eyed empty wire shelves. "What a waste," he said, turning his attention to the cupboards.

I stifled a laugh as my naked Stefano scoured the empty kitchen for a midnight snack. "This kitchen isn't the only place you can be fed."

"I thought I was supposed to stop eating in the cafeteria so we could save money. How long do diets take?"

"Four weeks until I leave for America. We'll start with that."

"I starve so you can eat with your American friends?" The indignant shudder started in Stefano's shoulders, rippled down his chest, and sent parts of him wiggling that he certainly didn't want me laughing at.

I bit the insides of my cheeks to stop my smile. "You want me to diet on vacation?"

Stefano plodded to bed empty-handed. "I don't want you to diet at all." He flopped beside me and sighed long and deep. "Isn't worrying about seven elephants and three workers enough? Now I have to worry about diets too?"

"It's just a few pounds."

Turning me toward him, he said, "A skinny weemun doesn't enjoy food. How can she enjoy life if she doesn't enjoy food?" His hand slid across my back, dipped along my waist, and followed the curve of my bottom. "What if there's nothing left for me to hold on to?"

CHAPTER TWENTY-FIVE

THE HOMECOMING

September 9, 1989, Cremona, Italy: Anxious to be away from the circus, to get some fresh air flowing through my brain. Some time away from Stefano won't do me any harm, either—perhaps it will even help answer some of these questions rattling my mind.

As the circus rolled toward summer's end, I prepared to leave for America. Sharks or no sharks, I needed a vacation from the road trip that had turned into a job.

Stefano needed a vacation as well. The elephant crew did not aspire to Stefano's standards, and the resulting stress turned minor frictions into explosions. He was a straightforward man who treated others with dignity, and he requested the same in return—that people live their lives with honesty and integrity. He didn't realize how much he asked of the world. The day a coworker mouthed off to him and then disrespected an elephant by refusing to clean her bed, they settled it with their fists. I packed tissue in Stefano's bloody nose and ice on his swollen cheek, but I did not know how to heal his angst.

At first, I had welcomed the idea of taking a month off from Stefano's escalating anxieties, yet as my departure date grew close, I held his hand a little tighter, his embrace a little longer.

One night, Stefano studied me from his seat on the edge of our bed. His gaze trailed me as I fit Italian chocolates, favorite clothes, and my precious journal into my backpack. He whispered, "You sure you're coming back?"

My heart fluttered before settling into a secure place, as if Stefano held it safely in his hands. This man, who exuded strength as easily as sweat and handled four-ton elephants as if they were bunnies, didn't fear showing his vulnerability. I knelt before him, shushing his worries, promising that after two weeks with family in Oregon and two weeks with my friend Helene in San Francisco, I'd hightail it back to him.

When I'd bought my plane ticket for this Great European Adventure, the year had stretched infinitely before me. On that night, my time in Europe seemed shorter than the pinch of pages it filled in my journal, and my ten months with Stefano a mere introduction to love.

Traveling 6,000 miles from Italy to Oregon took me a million miles away from the circus. Instead of smelling musky tiger pee, smearing gloss on my lips, and living in a camp trailer, I inhaled the sharp scent of Douglas firs, felt rain on my cheeks, and slept in the motel I'd once called home.

My parents' small town still felt like the isolating place

I couldn't wait to leave six years earlier, but I soon discovered that I had changed. People poked fun at the accent I'd developed by repeating English words to Stefano in a way he could understand. And back when I'd cruised through Oregon on my way from San Francisco to Amsterdam the year before, I'd felt less conspicuous in my flowing paisley skirts and elk-hide moccasins. This time, more than one lumberjack paused mid-stride to note my slick Italian boots and snug black skirt.

My father wanted to hear all about Europe. Listening to stories of elephants and ostriches and sharks, he meshed his eyebrows into one long brown strip. In his low barbershop-bass timbre that I remembered so well, Daddy counseled his baby girl on the dangers of wild animals. But when I spoke of my travels before joining the circus, my father's eyes lit. His voice resonated with boyish excitement as he recounted his own European adventures back in the fifties. Comparing our impressions of Venice while sharing a bottle of red wine around the picnic table in his rustic kitchen, I felt like an adult in his eyes.

My mother lived a few miles away on a skinny piece of land that runs deep into the woods, the sort of property one passes by quickly. There is more to it than meets the eye. Hidden behind the first stand of trees sit four old motel rooms that were once part of downtown Eugene's Capistrano Motel.

Thirty years earlier, my parents had honeymooned in romantic San Juan Capistrano, but that rundown Oregon house had been no second honeymoon for them. California's Capistrano is a symbol of fidelity and dependability. Cliff swallows have nested in the mission for centuries, coming and going every year, their arrival so predictable, locals plan celebrations around it. According to legend, the birds took up residence in the mission to escape an innkeeper who kept destroying their mud and saliva nests, and the crumbling stone walls continue to provide safe harbor to hatch young before the birds fly south each fall. The swallows always come back.

My father never came back. By the time I visited from Italy, seven years had passed since he'd abandoned my mother. I still saw her as broken. One day, I would return, as the swallows had, to call these motel rooms my home, but only after I learned firsthand that holding a family together takes more courage than walking away.

In the autumn of 1989, my mother was sharing her home with my single-parent sister and her three children. The whirlwind of visiting my extended family kept me busy, but in every quiet moment, my thoughts shifted to Stefano. My acute loneliness extinguished any lingering doubts about returning to Italy, and I spent hours copying thirty pages of Pink Floyd lyrics longhand into a wire-bound book for Stefano. I would later learn that, thousands of miles away, he had listened to *Wish You Were Here* every day until I returned.

We'd spoken only once in two weeks. As cell phones were still uncommon in Italy, the circus tapped into the landlines in each town. And even though I could get the ever-changing number from Moira's headquarters in northern Italy, on-site management balked at traipsing the grounds to look for an elephant keeper. Contact depended on Stefano's calls from pay phones, and elephantine events half a world away dictated whether he could keep a pre-arranged appointment. Mispronounced messages left with one of my sister's children were incomplete at best. Late at night, sleepless in a strange bed, I longed to feel his warm belly against my back, his moist breath on my neck—to know he was there.

As each Oregon day inched toward the next, the sun seemed to make the same arc at the same slant over the motel's four front doors. Each night, the same trees rustled in the same moonlight outside the same window. I grew restless. Wasn't it time to pack up the animals, dismantle the tents, and move on?

I left Oregon with my mother's assurance that she would come visit me in Italy.

The day I arrived in San Francisco, my friend Helene and I cruised an hour north to toast our friendship and the promise of an Indian summer on Stinson Beach. When the earth shook, we felt only a tremor and didn't worry. Perhaps we'd had too much champagne.

Driving back to the city, I glanced across the darkened bay and asked, "Shouldn't I be able to see the city by now?"

"Oh my God." Riveting her violet eyes across the water, Helene kept the car on course with one hand and ejected Steely Dan from the tape deck with the other. *"Are those flames?"*

Stunned into silence, we listened to the reporter's voice that filled the car.

Bay Bridge collapses! Marina district crumbles! Gas leak explodes!

Five hours before the earthquake hit, Helene had picked me up from the Oakland Greyhound station only blocks from the two-level freeway that had since flattened into one. As horrific death and damage reports of the 1989 Loma Prieta quake circled the world, I realized how lucky we'd been, and it made the distance between my lover and me feel painfully wide.

When Stefano could not reach me by phone at Helene's number, he called his mother and pleaded with her not to stop dialing until she knew I was okay. But the calls wouldn't connect, so Angela decided to call my mother in Oregon. Later, I learned how she'd spoken the only understandable words she knew: *Mamma Stefano. Katreen OK? Katreen OK?* My mother responded with the same words: *Kathleen OK. Kathleen OK.* And those two words sufficed. Soon, a panicked Stefano knew that I'd survived crashing bridges, crushing freeways, and crumbling buildings unscathed, and Mom's limited-yet-emotional first contact with Angela would bond two mothers for years to come.

Two weeks later, I said goodbye to America. When I'd first left for Europe a year earlier, I'd been a naïve young woman, unsure of where I went or what I wanted. This time, my destination was clear: Stefano.

Angela and Angelo scooped me up from the airport in Milan and shuttled me west toward Asti, through a patchwork of verdant green fields stitched together with curvy country roads and over sun-streaked, vine-covered hills cloaked in cozy fall colors. When I finally saw Moira's yellow and blue enclave in the distance, it seemed endless. Dizzy with anticipation, I welcomed the sight.

Rasta's yipping, bouncing merrymaking paled in comparison to Stefano's welcome. He pulled me close, pressed his mouth against my neck, and inhaled. "Kat'leen," he said, lingering over me, touching my hair, and kissing my face. "Kat'leen." Gripping my hand as if he feared I'd disappear again, he thanked his parents for bringing me and shooed them back to Milan.

Having finagled the afternoon off, Stefano stuck a handwritten *Leave Us Alone* sign to the door, and we spent the next few hours drenching ourselves in each other. For years I had drifted, anchorless and isolated. No longer. In the back corner of an unfamiliar gravel lot, where the air smelled of caged animals and the wind carried raised voices, I felt more sense of place wrapped in Stefano's arms than I ever had—anywhere.

I felt home.

CHAPTER TWENTY-SIX

PRESSURE

Torino, home to the Holy Fiat and the Holy Shroud, is surrounded on three sides by snow-covered Alps. The grand cupolas and lofty spires that dot this heavenly skyline are the threshold to an empire of ice—at least my travel guide said something to that effect. I'd also read about the city's elegant squares and Baroque architecture, as well as how these northern industrialists and well-heeled university students sustained some of the finest shopping in Italy. Turin's wealth would keep the big top packed for weeks, and we'd stay long past my twenty-fourth birthday, just twelve days away. I couldn't think of a better place for Stefano to find me the perfect present.

The morning after we arrived, Stefano asked, "Is this a day we are going to eat rabbit food, or is it a day you are going to cook?"

I glanced at my De'Longhi oven. Any attempts at cooking since we'd moved into this camper hadn't matured beyond salad, picnic food, steamed veggies, and pesto sauce from a jar. On that particular day, I felt more inclined to explore *Torino*'s arcade-lined streets with Giada than make a hot lunch capable of keeping an alpine chill at bay, but Stefano looked as hopeful as a hitchhiker.

"Good," he said when I agreed to cook something simple, "because I invite someone to eat with us."

"A guest? But I said something simple. There are barely any groceries—"

Stefano shrugged as he retreated out the door. "Is already invited."

"Thanks for the notice," I called after him.

What would I cook? What *could* I cook? Whom would Stefano have invited? Someone he'd befriended while I traveled in America? I had just enough time to run to the corner store, but for what? I liberated my Betty Crocker cookbook from beneath a stack of comic books in the closet. Welsh rarebit. *No.* Texas hash. *No.* Eggs goldenrod. *Come on, Betty.* Grilled cheese. Chicken pot pie. *Jesus. Is this what Americans feed guests?*

Of course. I slammed the book shut. *Tuna casserole.*

So what if I'd never made it before. How difficult could binding broccoli, pasta, and tuna in white sauce be? I didn't need to shop, and I didn't need Betty Crocker.

"Mmm." Stefano tromped into the trailer. "Smells good in here." A head full of dark curls bobbed in behind him. "Kat'leen, you know Giorgio?"

Handsome face, muscular body, brooding manner—yes, I knew the spandex Adonis. We'd never formally met, but for the six months I'd danced, I noticed him backstage. Giada had told me all about Giorgio the Gigolo—the big-shot trapeze artist who thought every woman swooned for him. *Yeah, right,* I responded at the time. *Who needs another Valentino?*

But when Giorgio's eyes met mine, I felt flustered. Wiping my sweaty palms on a towel, I wondered what triggered my reaction to this man. He was as handsome as a Roman god, but that didn't matter. His body was as perfect as a miniature David, but I wasn't going to do anything about it. His eyes, however, zoomed in on me like scopes, burning into me, making me feel both exposed and special.

Giorgio reached past Stefano to take my hand in his callused palm. He said, "The shark show wasn't nearly as interesting without you."

"No? I heard Dieter looked great in his Speedo."

I backed against the closet as Stefano stepped through the two-foot-wide "hallway" separating our bed from the table. Giorgio grinned playfully as he eased past me slower than necessary. Closer than necessary. While he and Stefano made small talk, I busied myself scraping glued-on bits of pasta off the bottom of a pot and then piled it with the pans I'd used for white sauce and broccoli. The trapeze artist kept his ears tuned to Stefano, his eyes turned on me. I responded to his efforts to include me in the conversation, but then I felt awkward, as if I'd encouraged his attention.

The next time I checked the casserole, the Parmesan cheese topping had turned a perfect golden brown. Giorgio's gaze followed me as I cut the cake pan's steaming contents into four pieces, then he cast his attention downward to study the casserole.

Far less discreet, Stefano pried his portion apart with his fork. "No pasta?"

"There's a quarter kilo of *fusili* in there."

Stefano stole a glance at the droopy corkscrew Giorgio held between the tines of his fork, cleared his throat, and extracted a broccoli stem bared of its florets. He said, "Is broccoli, isn't it?"

"You don't like it."

"Well, is . . . um . . . not . . ."

"*Al dente.*" Giorgio finished.

Stefano took a deep breath. "In Italy," he explained, "we stop cooking our pasta before *disintegrazione.*"

Stefano and Giorgio tiptoed through their servings, picking out what they recognized, leaving the rest.

Stefano stood first. "Time for coffee," he said, pecking my cheek on his way to the door.

Giorgio wedged past me to follow Stefano.

"You're coming back to do dishes, right?"

"Deeshes?" Stefano spun around. "What you want me to do to them?"

"Come on, Stefano. Why do we have to discuss this every time I cook? I'm not your maid." I slid from my stool onto one of the cushioned benches. "If I do one job, you do the other. That's the deal."

"No weemun ever tells me this deal before you."

"No *Italian* woman, maybe."

"Because American mens wash deeshes?"

"Yes. All of them." At least my mother had always made my brothers take turns cleaning.

Stefano opened the door. "Work waits for me in the elephant tent. Two shows today, Kat'leen." He poked the air with his fingers. "*Two.*"

"Go," I called after him, "but you'll come back if you want me to cook again."

It was a flimsy threat. The casserole didn't even come close to what an Italian palate considered edible, so something else must have convinced Stefano to return. I met him at the door with open arms, but he swerved around my embrace and stomped toward the sink.

"Three pots, Kat'leen? You need three pots to boil pasta?"

Stefano spewed dish soap into the sink he filled with cold water. Schooling him about the benefits of first heating the water on the stove would only exacerbate the situation, so I pulled on my beige fishnets, zipped my black skirt, and prepared for the afternoon show.

Stefano had never washed dishes as a child. In fact, he'd never had any real chores at all. His one responsibility beyond making his bed was to clear toys from the floor before his father came home from soccer—either that or his dad might fulfill his threat to dump them down the trash chute. While Stefano played football in courtyards or tossed firecrackers into churches, my siblings and I had washed dishes, planted gardens, and trolled the yard for dog bombs. Mom labored right beside us. Perhaps pooling efforts for a common goal would have deepened Stefano's relationship with his parents. Perhaps pooling ours would deepen my relationship with him. At the very least, it would clarify that meals in our home were a task for two.

I peeked over my makeup mirror to watch Stefano clamp a pasta bowl between two fingers and pet it with the yellow sponge. Suds floofed onto the counter and his shirt, the wall and the floor. Dirty pans soiled seat cushions. Unwashed plates tainted washed plates. The tidiest man in the world was making one hell of a mess.

Stefano slammed the stack of bowls on the counter. "How is possible to wash deeshes if they don't fit in the sink?"

Washing human-sized dishes in our doll-sized sink was a frustrating endeavor, but it was also hilarious. I wanted to laugh with Stefano about it, not fight with him, but I feared the slightest chuckle would convince Stefano that I was laughing at him.

He continued his tantrum, fussing and flinging things around, turning our trailer into a pressure cooker. Backing away from the mess, he said, "I can't do it. I can't. Why am I the only man in this country who has to wash deeshes?"

His anxiety cornered me. Scratching my way into the open, I yelled, "You know I don't want to cook. You know I *can't* cook. Did I thank you for bringing an audience yet?" I scooped bobby pins, earrings, and lipstick into my black beret, grabbed my blazer and kicked the door out of my way. "Either join the fun or quit dragging me kicking and screaming into the kitchen."

I slipped the satin blazer over my shoulders and wished I'd grabbed a real coat. Mid-fall in northern Italy was too cold for me to linger outside, but the first show wouldn't start for a couple of hours, and the empty big top would still be frigid. I needed somewhere to hide.

Humid air rushed out when I opened the back door to the shark tank. Slipping inside, I shut out the cold, shut out Stefano. I kicked off my black pumps, and they clattered against the floor as I padded up the metal ladder in stockinged feet. Seeing Billy Bob and Jolene side by side in their favorite corner lifted my spirits. I inhaled deeply. The warmth rising from the water caressed my face, and the meditative hum of the filters soothed my nerves. When I left the shark truck, I would feel the cold outside even more.

CHAPTER TWENTY-SEVEN

RIDING THE PAINTED PONIES

The circus is full of Lifers, people who devote their lives to The-Almighty-Show-That-Must-Go-On, clownfish who live under the protection of an anemone, darting out for supplies and hurrying back before the current whisks them away. Lifers live both in front of and behind the spotlights. Some need tents, sequins, animals, and applause to feel truly alive. Others latch onto the liberation from electric bills and car payments, resting assured that a hard day's work guarantees room and board. Many are there because they have no other place in the world to call home.

Lifers were performing families such as Giada's, eight people from three generations undeterred from this livelihood by injury, infidelity, or old age. Or they were people such as the head mechanic, ruler of an eleven-man auto shop and responsible for keeping a mile-long train of circus trucks rolling down the road. I remember hearing about how he chose to stay when his family left, even though it meant staying alone. And I remember an aging seamstress who seemed to hunch closer to the ground with every passing day. She stared out from the window of her cramped camper and called out to passersby, hoping to spark a conversation, asking for something to mend, a task to complete, proof of her worth.

With all the seasons they'd seen blow through the back lot, Lifers probably didn't notice how cold the air turned in *Torino* as November faded toward December. Probably didn't flinch over the deep cracks the wintry weather grooved into our hands, or care that ice formed on the inside walls of the big top overnight and then dribbled off in rivulets as the heaters rumbled to life each afternoon.

I was acutely aware of the sinking mercury. Frost crunched under my black pumps as I hurried toward the big top, and I clasped the stiff collar of my sequined jacket around my neck to keep out the cold.

"Where's your lipstick?" Moira barked from the doorway of her seventy-foot villa-on-wheels as I passed through the gangway.

I glanced up to see her glowering face haloed by wispy black tufts—all that remained of her famed tresses. Queen Moira regularly lashed out at her subjects with little provocation and turned macho minions into cowering shadows with a few well-chosen words. I tapped my jacket pocket and kept walking.

Moira wagged a red-tipped finger. "Time to diet, young lady," she shouted. "You're lucky I let you keep the shark number looking like you do." When I continued walking, she screeched, "Are you listening?"

I faced Moira's scowl. Until then, I'd been proud of the additional eight pounds I'd lost and figured that She Who Sees Everything would have noticed. The Queen of the

Elephants clutched the decorative handrail that bordered her veranda, lifted her fur-cloaked shoulders, and looked down on me. She had to be approaching 65, an age Italians called *anziana*, ancient. Sans wig and makeup, Moira looked like a washed-out photo of her former self. I wondered if the fear that fame would slip away with youth is what sometimes compelled her to act like the Wicked Witch of the West. Perhaps bitterness, rather than age, had stolen Moira's splendor. Her puffy cheeks and lips reminded me of the silicone rumors. Years later, magazines would show Moira's face as inflated as a Macy's balloon, and I would feel sorry for her. At twenty-four, however, I saw only a woman frantically grabbing at vanishing youth. Warping her maturing beauty to cheat time didn't become the Queen of the Elephants in my opinion; it compromised her legend.

"I've got my lipstick, Moira, and I'm trying to diet. Isn't that enough?"

The woman seemed to worship plastic surgery. Through the years, she'd funded boob jobs and nose jobs for performers and extended family. Watching her stare me down, I couldn't help but wonder if she had some nip-tuck suggestion up her frilly sleeve for me.

Moira poked one of her long nails at me and said, "I'm watching you."

I continued on to the big top, ignoring the snickering dancing girls sipping espresso at the circus bar. "Diet, diet, diet, diet," I said in puffs of steam that kept time with my footsteps. "Diet, diet, diet, diet."

When I returned to our camper after ushering, I glanced at the secondhand washing machine that Erich, the master tiger-tender, had deposited on the tongue of our trailer a few days earlier. I hated washing by hand and appreciated him giving us his old washer when he bought a new one. And yet, when Stefano and Erich had bolted it into place, I'd felt as if they'd bolted me down as well. *Cook, clean, and look real pretty when yer asked, you hear?*

I was surprised to find Stefano inside the trailer.

"Is your birthday," he said, pulling a stuffed elephant in a pink tutu from behind his back. Pudgy cheeks nearly swallowed the smile sewn onto the animal's face.

"I thought you forgot."

"Giuseppe's wife reminds me an hour ago. Is Monday. Stores are closed. A bar down the street . . . Was all I could find." Stefano raked his teeth over his bottom lip and studied the toy. Then he jammed it into my hands so quickly it was as if the elephant had singed his skin.

Compared to the previous year—waking up hungover and alone in a Spanish bar after Colin and my other bus-mates had ditched me—the elephant ballerina was a vast improvement, even if it didn't feel that way at the time. I thanked Stefano and set it next to the present Giuseppe's wife had brought over earlier in the day—a set of bowls, each hand painted with a simple pasta recipe.

"Is time to . . . The elephants need . . ." Stefano shuffled backwards out the door.

Later that day, Giada gave me a tiny brass box inlaid with a stone yin-yang symbol. A gift that didn't scream *circus* or *cooking*, a gift that sang *me.* Over the past eight months, Giada's friendship had become essential, a friendship that would remain dear to me long after her sister's marital problems with Nino, and therefore Moira, would force her family to flee to another circus at the end of our stay in *Torino*.

Two weeks later, I waited at the table in our camper. I had survived on salads and sit-ups since my scene with Moira, but I would break my diet to celebrate my one-year anniversary with Stefano. Fresh bread, the prosciutto he loved, and a slab of his favorite taleggio cheese decorated a cutting board. Roast chicken from a nearby rotisserie warmed in the oven. I'd hidden my preparations and figured Stefano had some sort of a surprise planned for me as well. He hadn't remembered my birthday, but surely he wouldn't forget ours.

Our 12:30 lunchtime came and went; Stefano never showed. After another fifteen minutes passed, I went to find him. A mechanical whine filled the elephant tent. Through a white haze, I saw Stefano kneeling in front of Shiva. Fine white powder covered his face, making him look more elephant than man.

When I approached, Stefano nodded without taking his gaze from the elephant foot Giuseppe steadied on a stainless steel stool. I fanned the pungent dust away and stayed put. Stefano glanced up. Then he glanced again. Finally, he turned off the tool, removed his safety glasses, and cocked his head. If I weren't feeling so dejected, I would have laughed at the owlish mask of sweaty pink circles the glasses had left around his eyes.

"What are you doing?"

"Fixing Shiva's nails," he said, poising the glasses in front of his eyes as if to ask if I was finished interrupting.

"You're giving her a pedicure? With an angle grinder?"

"Is solid, like bone." The glasses crept along his nose. "Is like horses, Kat'leen. Elephant feets have to be filed down sometimes."

"But why now? Why today?"

"Will be Christmas soon. Is time to prepare."

"Well, sure. Christmas *is* right around the corner if today is the *FIFTH OF DECEMBER.*"

Stefano hunkered down, studying the sole of a foot that outsized his head before pushing his glasses into place and resuming his work.

"What about our lunch?" I yelled over the grinder's whine.

"Giuseppe's wife already brings me a sandwich," Stefano said, honing one of Shiva's mottled, half-moon nails to a pristine white.

I suppose I could have told him what this day meant to me, could have explained how I wanted to come first in his life every day but might settle for just this one. At the time, however, it only occurred to me to run away. I wanted to run fast and run far, but our trailer was only fifty feet from the elephants, so I scuttled along in my clogs, dodging guy wires and tent stakes, and tripped up the steps into our camper.

Hunkered in a corner of our bed, I recalled that first evening in Spain when I'd sauntered onto the circus grounds hoping to expand my adventure in new and interesting ways. I hadn't bargained for the life that would engulf me one year later: a circus queen eyeing my waistline and my eyeliner, princess ballerinas cackling over my every move, and the exasperating ritual of a man preoccupied with food. Unless, of course, his elephants took priority.

Bright lights. Loud music. Beautiful animals. Constant movement. I found it easy to forget that this whirling circus carousel wasn't really going anywhere. Easy to overlook how alone I really felt. But Stefano would always be just ahead of me or just behind me, never completely within reach. Sometimes, I believed that he could become a Lifer, but riding the painted ponies wasn't enough for me. If he wouldn't leave, I had to find the strength to go alone.

"Alone," I said to the mirror as I turned the contents of a bottle of beige foundation into my circus mask.

December 5, 1989, Torino, Italy: Alone. After a year of "together," that word sounds so . . . lonely.

That afternoon, I rushed up and down the bleachers, hurrying spectators to their seats as if it would hurry me to the one place in Moira's circus that I belonged. I tapped my foot faster than the beat of the big bass drum, urging the band to hasten its numbers. The moment I climbed on the white stallion's back, I taunted him into a lope. When Dieter frowned at the steam surging from the horse's nostrils, I shrugged as if the animal had instigated the run.

Finally inside the shark truck, I lay on the plank above the water and let the mystical steam calm me. Outside, workers assembled safety barriers and yelled commands in preparation for intermission. When the announcer's microphone clicked on, I lowered myself beneath the salty surface, and all the noise disappeared.

In the tank's depths, no one existed but Billy Bob, Jolene, and me. Toes pointed, arms against my sides, propelling myself through the water, touching neither walls nor floor, I became more mermaid than woman. Billy Bob swam my way, and I met him in the middle, belly-up. His white tummy nearly tickled my own as we breezed past each other. I tucked and rolled half a somersault forward and then stretched in the opposite direction, trailing the shark, holding onto his fin, curving my body when he curved his, arching my back when he arched his. Because in mimicking Billy Bob's movements, in this game of follow the leader, I became one of them.

In the warm, amniotic depths of the shark tank, 10,000 gallons of salt water blurred the world around us. Within my glass-walled refuge, nearly naked under bright lights, I hid in plain sight.

Funny how I believed I could escape the circus by sinking deeper within.

CHAPTER TWENTY-EIGHT

L'ARTISTA NAPOLITANO

"We need you," Giuseppe said, tossing me a set of keys the night before leaving *Torino* for Naples. "We're short on drivers."

From Italy's bootstraps to its ankle, we rode on trucks, trailers, railcars, and vans, and the 800-mile trip took its toll on man, woman, and beast alike. Stefano traveled with the elephants. I regretted ever telling Giuseppe that I'd acquired an international driver's license while in America and begged Rasta into the Bedford van so I wouldn't have to drive alone. The camper I towed had its own idea of where it wanted to go, so I crept along Italy's major north-south artery eyeing my trailer through the rearview mirror, hoping it was as willing as I to play follow the leader. Bookended between the schoolroom and the cafeteria, Rasta and I soon slipped into long-haul gear. The familiar chug of a tired engine lulled me into a comfort zone as I recalled the 40,000 miles I'd driven over America's blue highways in my VW bus following the Grateful Dead. Forty thousand miles . . . nearly twice the earth's circumference, and I still hadn't "arrived" at my destination. Still wasn't sure where, or what, that destination was.

Somewhere south of Florence, Giuseppe crammed the whole circus into a too-small parking lot as if he were stowing a toy train in a suitcase. After Stefano fed and watered the elephants and scraped the dung out of their trucks, Giorgio joined us for dinner in a nearby pizzeria. Early the next day, we resumed our southbound saunter, rolling past churches, bars, stone bridges, and red-roofed farmhouses. Mostly, I saw the square yellow and blue butt of the trailer in front of me.

In Naples, road rules of engagement do not apply. To navigate a one-way street in the wrong direction, Neapolitans simply shift into reverse and drive backwards. When the circus convoy entered that high-speed, traffic-packed driver's nightmare, I snapped out of my yellow and blue daze. Dinged and dented cars hurtled past like ants on amphetamines. Screaming horns and screeching brakes assaulted my ears. When I finally spied circus trucks parked in the distance, I rolled toward the positioning line and eased my grip on the steering wheel.

Warm weather, palm trees, and Naples' vibrant heartbeat invigorated me. I perused a nearby street market each day, absorbing the merchants' lively serenades. One morning, I listened to a man chant *Tre limoni mille lire* from behind a wooden crate topped with three brilliant yellow lemons. At the stall beyond him, translucent pink octopus tentacles writhed over the rim of a blue plastic bucket. *Fresco fresco,* the merchant called. *Fresco fresco.* I repositioned the sack of fragrant clementines in my hand, wedged my quarter loaf of rustic bread under one arm, and continued maneuvering through the crowd. The way the locals cooed and cawed in dialect made most of their animated chatter indecipherable, and the illusion that I strolled an exotic bazaar in some unfamiliar country kept a spring in my step long after I left the market.

Daniele, our friend who had tattooed the elephant on Stefano's arm, came calling nearly every day, and I recruited him to help me scour his hometown for a Christmas gift for Stefano. I considered rubber boots or heavy-duty jeans, perhaps a few pairs of leather work gloves, but I decided that I didn't want to give him something that had to do with the circus any more than I wanted to receive a stuffed elephant. Remembering how Stefano had reminisced about his leather crafting days when my beads had arrived from America, Daniele and I searched downtown *Napoli* for some basic tools and a few pieces of hide, a starter-kit of sorts and a reminder for Stefano that life existed beyond these circus walls.

Christmas Day was a three-show blur. From noon to midnight, the circus worked us like animals. I barely saw Stefano. I'd anticipated giving him his leather tools for days, but in the end, I practically threw them at him in passing.

Stefano's mother took the train down from Milan to visit after Christmas. As in Spain, she stayed only a couple of nights in a nearby pension. Stefano didn't find much time to spend with her, so Angela and I visited the *Museo Archeologico* and shopped *Via Vittorio* on our own. I remember her gift of green lace lingerie—something to please both Stefano and me. I also remember her shocked look when she saw that Stefano's curls had tangled into dreadlocks.

To be stylish in Italy, one follows the trends. Matted locks were a rarity, an affront to Italian grooming standards that earned looks of repulsed curiosity. Not one to follow trendy philosophies or fashions, Stefano embraced his latest rebellion. Still, I had instigated the hairstyle. With my tomboy clothes and unkempt hair, an earthy approach to life and distaste for convention, I must have been as different as different could be in Angela's eyes. Yet her contact with her son had grown significantly since my arrival in his life, and criticizing my influence on him would have alienated both her son and me.

Years later, I came to understand the tightrope Angela must have walked while welcoming me into her family.

The circus caravan camped in Neapolitan suburbia through late January. Americans may make lemonade when life gives them lemons, but Neapolitans make *limoncello*—grain alcohol turned palatable by the addition of lemons, sugar, and water. The locals we met were friendly, passionate, and as hot as their *peperoncino*-infused food. Life pulsed with Sophia Loren–style sensuality. I felt camaraderie and community there, and I felt close to the man I loved.

Daniele often showed up at midnight, as we finished our day's work. Scrubbed clean of dander and dung, of blush and brine, Stefano and I eagerly passed the wee hours with him at the bar where we'd first met. Hand-to-mouth delicacies and robust northern-European beer flowed as easily as our conversations.

During these times, when Stefano and I talked and laughed

and circus stress didn't overshadow our bond, I thought we might actually make it. During these times, I forgot about the "other woman" who demanded so much of him. Though Daniele's company of friends at Pub Amsterdam often questioned us about circus life, our bar-banter responses elicited hazy images that left the pressures and constraints unfelt, the noise and gossip unheard, the conflicts and hostility unseen.

The circus left Naples by the end of January, but we lingered nearby for the next month, performing from the rocky cliffs of the Amalfi Coast to the hillside vineyards of Benevento. Daniele borrowed a car and appeared at our trailer door one sunny afternoon in Salerno looking like a grocer's delivery boy.

"What is all this?" I asked, peeking into his bags and bundles as I welcomed him.

"Now? Just ingredients. In a few hours it will be *la Parmigiana.*"

"Eggplant Parmesan? Yummm. No diet today."

"Stefano?" He lifted an eyebrow and looked toward the elephant tent.

"On a hay run, won't be back for two hours."

Daniele held up a paper-wrapped parcel. "I have a present for the two of you, but we'll wait until Stefano returns. In the meantime, we'll do a slow cook on the sauce. When is dinnertime?"

"Stefano eats in the cafeteria when he finds a few minutes. I nibble between shows."

"No, no." Daniele scoured drawers for kitchen tools. "There must be a dinnertime."

"Either between the two shows or after the last one — seven p.m. or *mezzanotte*."

"Midnight is much too late for a heavy *Parmigiana*. Dinner will be ready at seven o'clock. Did you get yourself a big sauce pot yet?"

I shook my head.

"These two small ones will do. How about a casserole dish?" When I shrugged, he selected the two cake pans I used for cookie sheets.

Daniele swirled olive oil into the pots and then sautéed onions, carrots, and celery in bubbling oil. He dumped a large can of San Marzano tomatoes into each pot and lowered the flames until blue flickers circled each burner like tiny flower petals.

"What's the salt for?" I asked when he sprinkled the eggplant he'd just sliced.

"Helps them shed their bitter water," he said, shifting between gurgling pots of sauce, dozens of purple-rimmed eggplant slices he'd fanned across the table, and the plates of grated Parmesan that dotted the bed. Daniele's artistry extended to his cooking, and the whole trailer had become his canvas.

"Who taught you how to cook?"

"My mother and my grandmother, I suppose, but they didn't teach me by saying, 'first do this, and then do that.' I was a hungry boy, and I spent so much time in the kitchen that I absorbed the ability to cook."

I leaned over the pot he stirred. "You think I'm absorbing anything right now?"

"It is not enough just to be here. You have to love the food, Kathleen. You have to love it when you're hauling it home from the grocery store," Daniele said, gathering eggplants and stacking them on a plate. After sponging liquid from the table, he knelt down to sop up what had dribbled onto the floor. "You have to love it when it's weeping bitter water off the edge of your table." He chuckled. "Love it when the steam from your cooking pots makes sweat drip down your neck." Daniele gave the sauce another stir and laid the eggplant on paper towels to dry. "Then you can love your food when it's beautiful on your plate and delicious in your mouth."

Daniele cracked four eggs onto a plate and blended in a pinch of salt. Leaving his saucepots percolating on the stove, he dusted the sliced eggplant with flour, dipped each slice into the egg mixture, and slipped them into popping oil. When Stefano arrived an hour later, a pile of golden eggplant decorated the table, and the aroma of simmering tomatoes filled the trailer.

"Dani—what a surprise." Stefano bounded through the door and embraced his friend. "When I smell cooking coming from our trailer, I think I am dreaming." Without taking his eyes from the food, Stefano leaned toward me for a quick kiss.

"He brought us a present," I said, handing him the package.

Stefano flicked open his pocketknife and sliced through string. Layers of brown paper revealed a painting of an elephant's head swathed in horizontal bands of deep blue, lush rose, and lime green. That day in Salerno, looking at Daniele's art from a few feet away, I saw colors, both contradictory and complementary, struggling for prominence. When I look at that painting today, I see so much more. The blue, rose, and green form the contour of a human eye; the orange elephant's head an iris. The elephant seems in exodus from the eye, leaving behind the human vision that held it captive. In the process, the elephant's trunk pushes on part of the lower lid, reshaping, perhaps, the perspective that kept the creature confined. Simple colors, simple lines, and big ideas, as straightforward as they are complicated.

"*Bellissimo*," Stefano said. "*Grazie.* We find the perfect place." Stefano turned in a circle, holding Daniele's artwork up to trailer walls either too small or too full of doors and windows to fit the canvas. "Humph," he said, spinning a second circle. Finally, Stefano scooped condiments away from the table's far end and leaned the painting against the window. Satisfied, he stuffed a piece of fried eggplant into his mouth and asked how soon we'd eat.

"It's a slow cooking sauce." I spoke as if I knew all about these things. "The rest is on hold until the tomatoes condense, so we'll eat at seven."

"Then I have to run to the elephant tent."

"Sure you do," I said, following him to the door.

"I have to make sure they did the morning work right, Kat'leen. You two come with me. In a couple of minutes, we all come back together, open some wine."

Daniele followed Stefano; I stayed behind.

"He'll be back as soon as he can," Daniele explained when he returned alone. "The elephants—"

"The elephants this . . . The elephants that . . ." I finished blackening my lashes and tossed my makeup bag into the bathroom. "I've heard every excuse a hundred times. Hay, washing, fixing—a crew that can't do anything right without him . . ." Tugging my black beret over my curls, I tromped out saying, "Stefano believes the elephants need him, Daniele. He *needs* the elephants to need him."

Ninety minutes later, between warming Lara's horse and the shark show, I returned to the trailer. Daniele stood over two cake pans, bonding layers of fried eggplant with tomato sauce and cheese. I plucked a sliver of *Parmigiano* from the table and popped it in my mouth. Under gentle pressure from my tongue, the cheese disintegrated, filling my mouth with tangy crystals. Reaching for another piece, I asked, "Is there enough?"

"Plenty."

The cheese melted in my mouth while Daniele scattered fresh basil leaves over a layer of sauce, as if creating a work of art. I loved the way crescents of eggplant pierced the top and how pale Parmesan contrasted the red, red sauce. Daniele had spoken the truth: He loved the food at every stage of its creation—which must be why he'd toil away most of a day for a single meal.

"So many hours of work," I said, wiping away makeup.

"So many hours of pleasure. Now they just have to spend enough time in the oven to meld the layers and enough time out of the oven to cool to the perfect tasting temperature. Too hot and your tongue cannot fully enjoy itself."

"I'll be back in thirty minutes."

"Come hungry."

I didn't wait for the intermission crowd to disperse before slipping out of the shark truck. Back at the trailer, one *Parmigiana* cooled in the middle of the table, another bubbled in the oven, and Daniele held an open bottle of red wine.

"Wow. It looks as if somebody's mamma lives here."

Daniele passed me a glass. "You don't have to be a mamma to cook, Kathleen."

"I'll drink to that." Stefano vaulted through the door, slid onto one of the benches, and raised the remaining glass. "To Daniele and all the cookers of the world."

Daniele stacked our plates with eggplant. Tomato sauce flecked with cheese and basil oozed from between layers as I plunged into the *Parmigiana*. Flavors fused to perfection in my mouth as the browned crust of cheese gave way to soft eggplant and delicate sauce. The three of us ate, and we ate, until we could eat no more.

"When the day will come that you cook that way for me?" Stefano asked me that night as we lay in bed.

I looked beyond him at our home, past the bare counters to where Rasta snored under the table. Daniele had cleaned everything during the second show. If I couldn't smell the bouquet of sweet basil he'd left in a jar in the sink, see the elephant painting resting on the table, and feel the pressure of my still-full belly, I might have doubted he'd been here.

It seemed impossible for me to turn our kitchen into a gourmet gallery as he had that day, and the thought saddened me. "I can't," I whispered. "I don't love the food like Daniele does. I want to, but I don't."

"You don't have to love the food," Stefano scoffed. "You only have to love me."

My melancholic moment vanished. "What is wrong with you?" I demanded, staring him down. "How can you confuse my cooking with my love?"

"Wrong with me?" Stefano pulled away, his head wavering as if off balance. "What is wrong with you? All my life my grandmother, aunts, cousins, friends, lovers, all the weemuns ask me, 'Stefano, what can I do for you? Stefano, what can I cook for you? Stefano, is there anything you need?'"

"You've told me a hundred times that your mother never had time for you."

"She is the only one who doesn't have time for Stefano. Somehow, I think you are going to be different. You are the one that is supposed to love me the most, but I never hear you ask what you could do for me. Never."

When I didn't respond, he said, "What? Nothing to say?"

"I'm trying to remember," I told him, turning from his sneer to face the wall, "the last time you asked what you could do for me."

CHAPTER TWENTY-NINE

MARILENA

Marilena Galletta cackled her way into my life.

Through our camper's sheer pink curtains, I observed Carmine, her beanpole Neapolitan husband with a big crooked nose, park their thirty-foot trailer on the edge of the circus lot. While he detached camper from car, Marilena flicked shoulder-length cinnamon hair from her face and unloaded wine bottles, wash buckets, and winter blankets from the rundown blue hatchback. She smoked one cigarette after another, joked with her husband and son, and made me giggle right along with her rough-hewn laugh. I would soon learn that Marilena was her husband's chef, maid, and nanny—everything Italians expected a woman to be. Everything I refused to be.

The next day, in a nearby supermarket, Marilena checked out in front of me. She looped her fingers through the handles of four bulging yellow sacks and hefted them from the counter. On the way back to the circus, she struggled with her load and shifted all the weight into one hand so she could stretch the other.

"I could help you carry those," I called in Italian.

Marilena turned, her light brown eyes studying me from under straight-cut bangs. "You don't have bags of your own?"

I raised my one plastic sack, half filled with bananas, lettuce, tomatoes, and yogurt.

"You must eat in the cafeteria."

"No, I just don't cook."

That made her giggle. "What do you eat if you don't cook?"

I shrugged. "I get by."

Marilena laughed harder. "Then here, carry some of my groceries." She passed me a bag brimming with cans of peeled tomatoes and Styrofoam packages of zucchini and carrots. "But only if you come over for a glass of sangria."

When I showed up on Marilena's doorstep, she popped her head out the window and motioned to a folding picnic table. "Have a seat. I'll be right out."

Instead of arriving with a bottle and a couple of glasses, Marilena carried a bag of fruit, two knives, and a cutting board. She chuckled at my confusion. "Where did you think it would come from if we didn't make it?"

I felt silly and American for having expected bottled sangria, but Marilena seemed to laugh with me, not at me.

"Cut the fruit into bite-size chunks," she said. "Peel the bananas and apples, not the oranges and lemons. I'll get the wine and a can opener for the peaches."

"You're not circus, are you?" I asked when Marilena returned.

She shook her head. "I worked in another circus for a year,

but I wasn't born into it. My husband used to run a photo store—that's how he knows Pippo, the photographer here."

"I know who Pippo is. Can't say I'd work for him."

"We made good money taking pictures for him during Christmas," Marilena told me. "That's hard to do in *Napoli*, and I have to think about raising my child."

I should have spoken up about Pippo's ghastly treatment of animals, but I had grown complacent. Marilena's need to support a family seemed to justify her job, and I kept my mouth shut as my new friend uncorked a magnum of Lambrusco.

Sloshing all but the last few inches of wine into a bowl, Marilena covered my mound of apples and bananas. She funneled four spoonfuls of sugar and one of cinnamon into the wine bottle and swirled until its warm smell floated in the air. I eased orange and lemon wedges into the bowl as she poured the spiced wine over the fruit.

"I heard an American worked here. You speak Italian well—been here long?"

"One year." My gaze traveled over the patch of weeds that separated her camper from ours and on to the elephant tent. "One long year."

Marilena blended the fruit, wine, sugar, and spice with a big wooden spoon. "It's different," she said, "living in the circus."

"It's my boyfriend who wants to stay—for the elephants." I fiddled with the curled apple peels around the cutting board, stacking them one on top of the other. "If it were up to me, we'd search the world over to find a place of our own." Looking up at Marilena, I said, "It's been a long time since I called one place home."

She stepped into her trailer and returned with two glasses and a ladle. "Fruit's supposed to chill with the wine for a couple of hours before it's any good." Marilena filled the glasses and sat next to me. We sipped in silence before she said, "I imagine it's hard to compete with elephants."

Yes. Stefano's fight to improve these imprisoned elephants' lives was beyond admirable. But that aspiration was only part of what drove his devotion to his job. Stefano's true fight was against himself. He'd told me in many ways—back in Venice when he urged me to try Moira's circus, and up on the hilltop when I begged him to leave this place. It took a long time for me to see through his words, but I finally understood: He was a free spirit who had faltered and lost his way, lost faith in himself. In the circus, where survival depended on precision, Stefano had found the perfect place to keep his life in order. Everything in tiny boxes. No room for error. No room for me.

His salvation had become his cage, and the claustrophobia wore blisters into our hearts.

I gulped my wine and said, "I'm selfish, Marilena, but if Stefano would put half the effort he puts into this circus toward taking care of our relationship . . ."

"Ahhh, but he's Italian," Marilena said. "He's been taught that you are going to take care of him."

"That's not going to happen." I shook my head. "So something else needs to give. Whether him, or me, or this situation, something has to change."

"So change it."

I tilted my head back and emptied my glass. "I've been here a whole year. Nothing ever changes."

"Things have changed since this morning. See that bowl of sangria?"

"What about it?"

"You just learned how to cook something."

Marilena and I became quick friends. I loved her genuine and playful manner that easily strayed into wild behavior. We shopped together, drank together, and laughed together, and we took every chance we could to break free of the circus. Marilena had lived all her life in Naples and knew the surrounding area well. With her five-year-old son in tow, we slurped down creamy *scamorza* fresh from a cheese vendor in Nola, shopped for leather in Avellino's craft markets, picked out miniskirts and snug shirts to flatter my slimmer figure in Sora, and whooped and hollered over a soccer match in a crowded bar in Battipaglia. Giorgio, who'd found a home away from home in Marilena's dining room, occasionally joined us for our jaunts through town. Even when Marilena couldn't get away, I found it easier and easier to step out of my rut, whether exploring the magnificence of Pompeii with Daniele or splurging on lime green designer jeans in Avezzano.

Those first months of 1990 were a rejuvenation of sorts that made the Orfeis' dictatorship seem less absolute, the dancing girls' antics less intolerable, and Stefano's absence less weighty. A few months after Giada's family had spirited her away to Germany, Marilena took my young friend's place as comrade and confidante.

Stefano hung his long red show-shirt over its hook and watched me dab concealer under my eyes and coat my lips with Cocoa Sheen lipstick. He stared with either frustration or concern. Lately, I'd had a hard time telling the difference. "Since when you wear makeup to go out?"

"Shhh. Half the circus can hear you." I tried to soften his mood with a caress. "Does it look so bad?"

"I want to see your pink lips and your green eyes, not colors from sticks and bottles."

"But you won't see anything because you're not coming out to eat with Marilena and me, are you? L'Aquila is supposed to be a beautiful town. You should come."

"Is midnight, Kat'leen. If food was right here right now, I would eat with you. But is already not enough hours left for sleep tonight. Tomorrow has two big shows. The *veterinario* is coming because Katia has a cold. Giuseppe says we must unload a truck of bar supplies into his concession stand and is telling me to clean the walls of the tent for over a week now. And somehow, I must find the time to go purchase 500 kilos of oats. Is too much, Kat'leen. Too much."

I agreed. It was too much. But Stefano had wanted the responsibilities of head elephant caretaker as badly as I had wanted the ostrich gig, which made it his turn to "pedal the bicycle."

"You're not expecting me to feel sorry for you, are you?"

While I waited for his response, Stefano stripped off his underwear and folded them over and over on themselves until they could have fit in a matchbox. He placed his underclothes into the laundry bag and stood there in his birthday suit, brushing his teeth with more-than-usual precision, scrubbing each individual tooth with the tip of his brush. Top row. Bottom row. Inside. Outside. Still I waited. When he finally sat his naked body on the edge of the bed and spoke, his voice sounded raw.

"Why, Kat'leen? Why you are changing on me?"

"I haven't changed. You've just forgotten who I am."

"Who is that skinny weemun in the mirror with the makeup and fancy clothes? You look like every other circus girl." He huffed and slapped his bare thigh. *"Have not changed."*

I glanced at the door and then back at Stefano, who had reclined onto the covers. "Marilena's waiting. I take it there's no goodnight kiss coming."

"Not on brown lips that I never seen before." He raised himself on one elbow and slid my veil of curls aside. "Here," he said. "I kiss you here, where I still see the real you." His lips brushed the hollow of my neck. With his cheek still against my skin, he whispered, "Be safe."

Stefano's stark fluctuations between tempest and tenderness made my head reel. I touched my cocoa lips to his forehead, glanced in the mirror, and left. Maybe if I'd really looked at myself, I would have seen the changes the way Stefano saw them. Maybe I would have noticed how the circus had slowly painted me with her colors. But she'd been layering her identity on top of my own so subtly for so long, that my eyes did not distinguish her presence. The woman I saw in the mirror had stretched the seams of the circus until it fit her needs. She had used this world of makeup and montage, of illumination and illusion, to reinvent herself, and I embraced this new me as evidence of change in a world that always seemed to stay the same.

Two hours later, tired and tipsy, I came home to a darkened trailer and slipped into bed. Stefano wrapped his arms around me and pulled me close, spooning his warm body against mine. His soft breath on my neck reminded me of peaceful times, when love outweighed our difficulties, before accusations and anger burdened our affection.

I fell asleep wondering whether the pleasures or the challenges of our relationship would determine its future.

CHAPTER THIRTY

MAMMA MIA

We spent the morning in a harrowing journey over the steep roads of southern Umbria. The old cargo van I'd driven since the *Torino-Napoli* trip strained and struggled up every hill. I leaned forward and held my breath each time, as if doing so might help push the van, the trailer, the dog, and me to the top. Once at the crest, the rig seemed to float like a gull finding its bearing on the wind. I managed only a few deep breaths and a glimpse of a lush panorama, majestic waterfall, or stone villa before the weight of our load thrust us into the decline, leaving my stomach in knots.

I arrived in Spoleto at midday, exhausted and anxious. High above our *piazza*, a massive pale church crowned a hill. The ashen city seemed to flow from it, down a brilliant hillside turned lime green with spring grass. I considered finding public transportation to the old city, but after performing in eighty-one ornate Italian towns, would yet another renaissance arcade or Roman ruin offer anything new?

Far below the domes and bell towers of Spoleto, Moira's 5,000-foot-long convoy of thirty-five trucks, forty tractor-trailers, and fifty campers morphed back into a metropolis. To shake off the stress of the trip, I took Rasta meandering through some nearby fields. Staring up at the city, I wished I had someone to share the vista with, but Rasta wasn't one to wax poetically over a panorama, no matter how stunning. We ended up in a coffee bar a few kilometers away where the dog scavenged crumbs while I sipped a cappuccino and contemplated using the orange pay phone tucked in a corner of the bar.

By the time Rasta and I returned to the circus, Stefano and his crew had moved from raising the elephant tent to cleaning cannonballs of dung out of the elephant trucks. I found him hauling a load to the manure pile.

"I called home. My mother is coming to visit."

Stefano nearly steered his wheelbarrow into the side of a truck.

"This summer," I continued, watching him ratchet his grip on the soiled handles of his *carriola*. "I thought I'd pick her up in Milan and introduce her to your family. Then we'd sightsee for a week or two before coming back."

"Two weeks? She should just stay here in the circus with us."

"Stefanoooooo." I drew the end of his name out long. "I want to take her to Florence and Venice. I want her to experience Rome."

Stefano stopped beside the mound of manure that would soon become a mountain. He grunted and hefted his wheelbarrow on end to dump its contents. Elephant poop rolled onto the pile, dwarfing horse nuggets and making the llama turds practically disappear.

"Is not safe in those places for two foreigner weemuns." Stefano righted his cart and spun toward the trucks.

"Stop making excuses." I scurried behind him. "You'll be too busy to notice I'm gone."

"What about your sharks and the exotic food? Why would Walter give you time off?" Aggravation clipped Stefano's voice and scrunched his shoulders as he hastened toward the elephant trucks.

I barged after him. "Dieter can do the sharks like when I was in America. The Moroccan workers can handle making the exotic troupe's food. And the ushers will welcome splitting the extra tips. If you'd think for a second, you'd see my plan makes perfect sense."

"You leaving to spend time with some other person makes no sense."

In light of his detachment to his own mother, I realized it must have been difficult for him to fathom the bond I shared with mine, but tears of frustration still stung my eyes. "She's my mother."

"So now you going to cry?" Stefano's shrill words bounced off the truck's walls as he leapt onto its bed. "Are all Americans actresses like you?"

I stared in disbelief. "How can you be so vicious?"

Stefano cursed and tossed his shovel aside. "No. Not vicious." He jumped down from the truck. "Every day there is more work, more responsibility." The way he raised and lowered his arms reminded me of a bird with clipped wings struggling to take flight, frustrated by his inability to get off the ground. "We're doing good here, right? Sometimes I— I—"

I lunged into his arms. Stefano clutched me against his body, and we molded our curves together as if doing so might energize our union, but it would take more than a hug to heal us.

"The circus is stopping!" Stefano rushed into the trailer. "You hear what I say? The circus is stopping!"

I didn't believe him. Movement equals life for a circus. Stagnancy equals death. Just as it would for a wild elephant. I stuffed the beaded bracelet I wove for Stefano's birthday under my leg and said, "The circus never stops."

"It does when the world football championship is played in Italy."

"We're on the road 365 days a year. We don't stop for Christmas or Easter. We don't stop when the big top is flooded. We wouldn't stop if somebody *died*, but we'll stop for a soccer game?"

"Is not a soccer game, Kat'leen, is the *Mondiale*. What Italians will go see a circus when the World Cup is right here?"

Under the table, I fingered the bracelet's smooth bands of red, green, and black converging on a yellow peace symbol. Peyote stitch—a web of glass and nylon fibers—is a strong weave, even if one of its elements is easily capable of destroying the other. In my hand, it felt both supple and solid.

I shrugged off Stefano's announcement, picked up the decoy bracelet I'd planted on the table, and slipped a droplet of red glass onto a needle. With neither a television nor evenings off to follow games, I'd barely acquired an interest in Italy's national pastime. Stefano, as a result of his father's tunnel vision, rejected the sport. Yet there he stood in the trailer's doorway, beaming.

"It means one month with no shows," he said. "They're

going to rotate the animal workers—give each of us two weeks vacation."

I dared to believe him. In the fifteen months since we'd joined Moira's circus, only a few dozen nights had passed that I hadn't heard trumpets and a ringmaster amplified into the night. I reached for Stefano and snuggled my forehead into the warm skin below his ear. We needed this vacation. We needed remote areas and romantic nights far away from his elephant obligations, long stretches of empty beach and plenty of moonlight.

"Greece," I whispered. "Let's go to Greece."

"Ruins . . . seafood . . ." Stefano leaned his head back and licked his lips as if already savoring Aegean delicacies. He said, "We need a motorcycle."

Stefano wasted no time. He found the secondhand silver Moto Guzzi 1000 SP in the town of Ascoli Piceno in early May. Giuseppe convinced Walter to let Stefano withdraw most of his retainer from the Bank of Moira—a risky and unusual concession, but no one questioned Stefano's loyalty to the circus.

With the new motorcycle, free time materialized. Stefano no longer needed an afternoon nap to get him through his workday; a ride on his *moto* would do instead. At first, I felt jealous that he found time for a machine of chrome and steel and speed when he couldn't find time for me. Then it occurred to me that maybe Stefano's daily naps had given him more than rest. No matter how much he loved his elephants, he was stumbling under the weight of his commitment. The Poles had their vodka; I had my sharks. Perhaps sleep—and now his Guzzi—helped Stefano shut the circus out.

I seized the chance to sit on a seventy-horsepower vibrator and wrap my arms and thighs around a man who rarely held still long enough for me to do so outside of the bedroom. Bolting away from the circus at eighty miles an hour, we slowed only for hairpin curves and hilltop castles. I remember the night we went out at midnight in search of the best gelato in town, how Giorgio had tagged along on his buzzing moped and the Guzzi's 1000cc rumble seemed to poke fun at his two-stroke whine.

The motorcycle made the weeks until Greece pass quickly, even if Moira's dark eyes stalked us from every publicity poster we passed. As the vacation rumor flourished, I kept expecting someone to take it back, like the tour to Japan. When the circus veered toward its headquarters in San Donà di Piave in mid-May, I finally started to believe that Stefano and I would leave for paradise in four weeks.

Even Dieter believed. "Good for you," he said when Stefano and I told him about Greece. "In fact—" Dieter pulled an old hardbound atlas out of his room. "I want you to have it," he insisted, pushing the frayed blue book of maps into our hands. "I'm never going anywhere . . ."

"It's working out perfectly," I announced.

Stefano stopped spreading straw to listen.

"I just spoke with my mother. She flies into Milan the day after we return from Greece. I'll take her on a whirlwind tour, and then we'll meet the circus in the first *piazza*."

Stefano gouged the tines of his pitchfork into the dirt and pitched it back and forth, widening the punctures with every move.

"Come with us if you don't want to be alone," I said.

"You know I can't."

The other workers peered over their pitchforks, but I'd heard Stefano's voice this frustrated so often lately, it sounded normal to me. These days, our relationship felt slicker than wet marble, and the slightest dispute sent us sprawling. If I didn't drop this conversation right now, it would end in a fight, but I lacked the finesse and the desire to tiptoe around his moods.

"Stop acting like a one-man band, Stefano."

Stefano charged back into his work, scraping the elephant's deck with such force it sounded as if he carved grooves into the wood. "Go," he said. "You will never understand and you do what you want anyway, so just go."

I tramped out of the tent and ran for the zoo. When I barged around the corner and popped open his gate, Baros scrambled halfway up before he saw me and eased his belly back to the dirt.

In the distance, Stefano's Moto Guzzi revved into action and tore out of the circus. I pictured his fist clutching the throttle, twisting the gas wide open before cinching it down tight; I felt his tension emanate from the motorcycle's distant whine.

The giraffe arched his neck down to nuzzle my arms with his floppy lips. "Oh, Baros," I said, scratching him until the full weight of his head rested on my shoulder.

Some seek comfort in a lover, others in a friend. When torn between wanting everything and questioning whether it was worth the struggle, I turned to a knobby-headed giraffe.

CHAPTER THIRTY-ONE

LA DOLCE VITA

Ancient ruins, Venetian castles, water so blue it glowed, and enough grilled seafood to pamper Poseidon—the beauty of Greece enthralled us, and Aphrodite summoned us into her arms. Dionysus danced over rocky hillsides, intoxicating all who dared, and the air pulsed with civilizations long lost. Romping through the Peloponnesian countryside with my curls bouncing behind me, my arms encircling Stefano, and the motorcycle's throaty laugh vibrating beneath us, I felt free. We played like children while building a rambling sand castle on an isolated beach, and we surrendered to romance while viewing a room we might rent—the bed's massive wooden headboard reaching for the high ceiling, its crisp white sheets begging us to rumple them.

I wanted Greece to last forever.

On the day we explored an abandoned hilltop castle, wind whispered through the fallen fortress like voices from its past.

Scrubby weeds filled the courtyard, scenting the hot air with sage. Pigeons cooed. Fragments of arches rose proudly toward the sky, attesting to past grandeur. I meandered among piles of white rock, the remnants of someone's home, and dragged my palm over the rough edge of a half-fallen wall. What had prompted this castle's demise? An attack by enemy forces? Poor upkeep? Or had it simply succumbed to the passage of time? Turning full circle, I drank it all in—crumbling mortar, fractured terraces, pillars turned to rubble, stone steps leading nowhere.

From a nearby lookout, Stefano called, "Come see the vista."

He drew his arm across the panorama, then rested it on my shoulders as I arrived. We stood in front of a circular opening in the castle's foot-thick wall and leaned out. Below us, the rocky knoll fell hundreds of feet, giving way to a patchwork of pine trees, olive groves, and dusty fields that stretched for miles.

In Greece, we had no condemning fights, no nervous outbursts, no stress over the world around us. Neither of us sidestepped the other as if negotiating an obstacle between ourselves and our happiness. I turned to Stefano and noticed how golden his hazel eyes looked against his tan, how easily he smiled when not on edge. Overwhelmed with attraction, I pulled him close and whispered, "There's not a soul in sight."

I brushed his collarbone with my lips, tasted his salty skin. He lifted me onto the wide rock-ledge, and I leaned back over the expanse. His strong hands gripped the small of my back, steadying me. Heat emanated from the stones beneath me, from the man above me. Sleep did not call my lover away, nor did Giuseppe. No workers loitered nearby. No performances drew near. No duties called. Under the guidance of Grecian gods, our lovemaking seemed to take as long as it took stonemasons to build this castle. I arched toward the sky. Felt the sun's warmth on my face. Wanted all the promise of here and now.

The passion of two lovers caught between sleek sky and rough terrain dared me to hope.

CHAPTER THIRTY-TWO

IN THE QUIET OF THE NIGHT

"You're still going, aren't you?"

I gripped the ferry's cool metal railing and stared down into the swirling whitecaps. "We haven't even docked yet," I said, turning toward the bench where Stefano sat.

With his bare feet spread wide and the cotton pants we purchased on the slopes of the Acropolis rolled above his tanned ankles, Stefano still appeared to be on vacation. It was his voice that had changed.

"But when we do," he said, carving his name into the wooden plank and flicking curls of wood away with the tip of his pocketknife, "we go back to the circus, and then you will go away."

"My mother is about to board her plane in Oregon. You want me to cancel now?"

Stefano rubbed the scruffy ears of a ship hand's lonesome brown dog we'd found on this lower deck. "Left alone," he mumbled, "like this poor dog. Nobody around to love him."

Stefano tried to look serious, but soon cracked half a smile. Appropriate for a man only half kidding.

The 250-mile ride back to the circus on a trash-strewn freeway thick with barreling trucks and speeding Alfa Romeos seemed longer than the 800 miles Stefano and I had covered circling the Peloponnese. I missed the Grecian villages growing up from the rock beneath them. I missed the adventure, the laughter, the romance of being surrounded by a herd of goats while lost on a forgotten mountain road.

With half of the workers on vacation and all the artists gone, Circo Moira Orfei seemed deserted. Nothing about returning to the shell of the circus was good. Stefano was in such a funk, he slipped under the side wall of the elephant tent and dove into cleaning Banana's deck without greeting her. He commanded her to lift her foot while nudging her leg with the handle of his pitchfork. Banana didn't realize which mere mortal dare touch her unannounced. She swung her trunk. For an elephant, it was a relatively polite swat, but Stefano still flew eight feet and slammed into the tent's back wall.

Stefano screamed her name. Realizing whom she'd attacked, the elephant dropped to her knees, as if begging forgiveness. Stefano knew he'd erred and never considered reprimanding Banana. Instead, he hobbled to the trailer to cram tissue into his bleeding nose. He paused to watch me repack my bag before grabbing an apple for the elephant and returning to the tent. Before long, he'd immersed himself in his duties, and I was ready to leave.

"You sure is okay you go to the train station alone?" Stefano paused at the fence delineating the circus grounds.

"It's fine," I said, noticing how the red, gold, and green beads of the bracelet I'd woven him shone against his bronzed forearm. He'd latched it on the moment I'd given it to him in Greece and hadn't taken it off since. "I'll be in Milan before dark," I told him. "Your parents and I will pick up my mom at the airport in the morning."

"If you ask, I bet Angelo would drive you two straight back here." He slid my bag off his shoulder and passed it to me.

"It's only ten days, Stefano."

Our kiss was a little too short and a little too light.

Stefano's mother rushed to meet me as I climbed down from the train. She kissed both my cheeks and welcomed me into her arms. Angela's green eyes sparkled as she pressed her face into mine, and she held me in a way I imagined she would hold her own daughter, if she'd had one.

"Come, come." She looped her arm around mine as we descended the great white staircase of Milan's *stazione centrale*. "I've been waiting to meet your mother for so long, and now it will happen tomorrow morning." Italian words bubbled out of Angela like uncorked spumante. "Stefano's grandmother will stay with Angelo and me so you and your mother can have her apartment. I've changed the sheets and brought fresh flowers. There's milk in the refrigerator for your *caffellatte,* biscotti for your breakfasts. There's red wine and white wine and . . ." Angela paused. "Do you understand?"

"*Sì, sì*. Every word. Gramma's apartment. Milk. Cookies. Flowers. My Italian is even better than when you came to Naples last Christmas."

In front of the station, Angelo waited in the no parking

zone along with twenty other cars. "*Ciao*, Katreen. *Ciao*," he called, waving his arms.

"What did Stefano think about staying at the circus without you?" Angela asked as we zipped through Milan's traffic toward their apartment.

"*Mamma mia.*" I shook my head. "He tried to convince me not to leave at least fifteen times. Wouldn't give up, even in San Donà as I left for the train station."

"The same as when he was a child." Angela's stunted laugh sounded forced.

Stefano's stories of his childhood tumbled into my mind. His father lived and breathed soccer, but rheumatic fever had kept Stefano off the field. According to Stefano, by the time he'd recuperated enough to pursue his father's passion, Angelo had deemed it too late to make a worthy player out of his own son and instead spent his days making top-notch players out of other little boys. Stefano's mother worked afternoons, so she'd pick him up from school, hurry him through lunch, and then shuffle him off to Nonna's house. Women were not necessarily liberated in 1970s Italy, and most stayed home to care for their children. Stefano had not understood why his own mother could not, establishing his fear of abandonment long before I showed up.

"*Pronto?* Katreen?" Angelo's voice brought me back to the car. "I asked about Greece," he said. "How was your trip?"

"Greece? Beautiful. Romantic."

I didn't tell them how in recent months their son's unrelenting passion for everything from elephants to food had threatened our relationship. Did Stefano's parents know how intense their son could be?

Of course they did.

Stefano had also told me his version of the bad years. With

Harry Chapin's "Cat's in the Cradle" acting as soundtrack, I heard stories of an adolescent questioning why he should listen to two people he felt hadn't had the time to raise him, of a teenager experimenting with self-rule and self-indulgence. The constant clashes as their relationship spiraled into chaos. Parents commanding with an iron hand, demanding he live by their ideals. A son choosing to live on the sordid streets of an industrial city because he felt more at peace there than he had at home.

Stefano once said that he and his mother were too alike to get along—as if his own intensity was not enough; double it and flames were inevitable. The few times Angela had visited us in the circus, the two of them couldn't spend an hour together without sparring. My presence eased that volatility; I had become the grease that allowed them to maneuver around the past with less friction.

Perhaps Angela held onto me the way she did because she couldn't hold her only child.

Seeing my mother across the crowded airport warmed my heart. The natural face, pastel clothing, tennis shoes, and trim body of a true California Girl stood out among the masses of chic black-clad Europeans. I plowed into her embrace.

"Look at you, Kathleen." She unraveled me from her arms. "You've lost weight. And you're wearing a miniskirt."

"It's been eight months, Mom."

She looked around. "Where's the man who swept my baby girl off her feet?"

"Stefano's working. We won't see him for a week and a half, but his parents are anxious to meet you."

Angelo and Angela kissed my mother's cheeks. Grabbing onto Mom's hands, Angela told me I had her curls and her wide green eyes and then babbled on at my mother, unconcerned that Mom couldn't understand a single word.

"Pleasure to meet you," Mom squeezed in between Angela's chatter. Then to me, "Which one of their names means Angel?"

"Both. The family story goes that the two angels got married and made a little devil."

"Stefano? Tell me it's a joke, Kathleen."

"Of course it is, Mom."

For the two days we spent in Milan, Angelo was our tour guide. Together we explored Castello Sforzesco, climbed to the roof of the Duomo, and peered in the windows of the *alta moda* stores on Via Monte Napoleone. Meanwhile, Angela shopped for our favorite foods, delivered fresh milk to our apartment each morning, and cooked our evening meals. She drew our baths, aired our sheets, and asked to wash our laundry.

"But we have barely any dirty clothes," I said, tugging my travel bag from her hands.

Angela assured me she had nothing else to do, but I knew differently. She cooked for her husband, helped her ill sister-in-law, doted on her aging mother, volunteered at a hospital three mornings a week, and worked every afternoon as a receptionist in a doctor's office. Angela didn't have a spare moment in her day, but she still offered to take care of our every need. Perhaps she had changed over the years, though I doubted it. And yet, Stefano believed Angela hadn't been there for him, as if all that physical mothering had left little energy for emotional mothering.

The day Stefano's parents saw Mom and me off at the train station, there were hugs, kisses, and tears. I wonder if the irony of growing closer to Stefano's family while my relationship with him was faltering occurred to me at the time.

"*Ciao,* Katreen, *ciao*. I'll come to visit you in the circus soon." Angela held me close. "And tell your mother I'll meet her in this exact spot to take her to the airport when she returns." She squeezed me once more. "Be safe," she said. "And tell my son that I . . . I say hello."

The Padanian plains disappeared behind us as my mom and I sped southward for a whirlwind excursion. We picnicked at the Forum, and we pondered which statues depicted which rivers in Piazza Navona while the fountain's mist cooled the hot Roman night. In Florence, we toured leather markets, traipsed back and forth over Ponte Vecchio, and waited hours to see *David*. We giggled like sisters when we noticed that from a particular angle *David* appeared to be giving himself a good pelvic scratch. Wine, bread, and cheese had once again become a celebrated meal, and I cherished our harmony. Yet even with the circus far away, and the only burden of our days choosing which ancient treasures to see, I stayed on edge. It saddened me that after months of chasing peace with Stefano, I had forgotten how to unwind.

But in the quiet of the night, I still missed him.

On our last night in Florence, hunched over bed pillows in our room, my mother and I spread out all the souvenirs we'd take back to the circus with us in the morning. Mom eyed the collection of silver conchos I'd bought for Stefano in a leather supply shop.

"They're nice," she said. "He'll like them."

"He might." Then again, he might not. Lately, I'd put the leather tools I'd given him the previous Christmas to more use than he had.

Metal clinked against metal as I separated the silver elephants from the rest of the trinkets and lined them up in a train. Sometimes, things were so good between Stefano and me, I believed that leaving him would mean losing the one great love of my life. Other times, we created so much tension, I couldn't imagine being around him another minute. He was just too much. I loved knowing that at the end of the day he would be there, warming our bed, holding me close no matter how we'd argued or how tired he was, but I couldn't pinpoint whether I loved companionship or *his* companionship, a warm bed or *his* warmth. I loved him, but I questioned whether wanting him in my life trumped everything else I wanted.

I considered asking my mother if her good years with my father were worth the later heartache.

My mother had grown up blonde, beautiful, and privileged. She was one of the first female lifeguards certified at Huntington State Park and a career-minded college freshman with a destiny limited only by her dreams. No one ever thought she'd dream of marrying my father. They met on the ice rink, where she trained to dance on ice. He was the rowdy rink guard who drove fast cars and rolled cigarette packets in his shirtsleeve. His father was a family deserter, hers the deputy chief of police. Ignoring her family's objections, my mother twirled open-armed into her infatuation with my father's rebellious rough-and-tumble good looks, and their ice circles wound into one. Only photographs prove their love once existed.

I feared becoming my mother. Not the woman who allowed me the freedom to choose my lifestyle without passing judgment; not the teacher who encouraged her students to discover themselves and the world; not the homemaker who supported her family mentally, physically, and financially until scarcely anything remained for herself. I feared becoming a woman who'd bound herself to the wrong man for far too many years.

Maybe if she talked to me, told me how it turned bad, *why* it turned bad, I could avoid making the same mistake. But she'd never opened up, and I'd always been afraid to ask. Eight years after he'd left her, my mother's wounds still seemed raw.

I quit fiddling with the elephants and reached for a pillow. Smoothing the casing over its stuffing, I asked my mother, "Can wanting to be loved by a certain person turn into merely wanting to be loved? Can that happen?"

My mother set down the lacy espresso cup she'd been examining and nodded. We both knew people fell out of love as easily as they fell into love. What I wanted to know was if it had happened to me.

"Look." I pointed out the window. "The moon is rising from behind the dome."

We leaned into the cool glass in our T-shirts and underwear, watching the full moon illuminate Brunelleschi's great cupola. The graceful bands of light stone that ran from the top of the dome down to the bottom shone like great white ribs, yet the masses of brick between them remained dark. In the dome's image, I saw my relationship with Stefano. Strips of light, the peaks of our happiness, surrounded by dull swaths, the daily effort just to get along. The bright stone seemed to hold the whole cupola in place, but I'd learned something about its construction that day. The bands of white were frosting on the cake. Beautiful, yet insignificant, unless adorning something meaningful. Four million unlit, interlocking bricks had sustained the dome for 500 years. Bricks. Day to day life. The passionate, the painful, the mediocre.

Side by side, my mother and I stood at the window as the moon began her solitary path through the darkened sky.

CHAPTER THIRTY-THREE

THE BALANCING ACT

Circo Moira Orfei amazed my mother. She hadn't expected the grounds to be so big or the show so professional. American circus performers aren't celebrities, so she wasn't prepared for Moira's stardom or Giuseppe's charisma.

Stefano's dimples and Italian good looks charmed my mother, and his lyrical speech captivated her. Even if neither of us always understood what he said, we still loved the way he said it. But watching the two of them together reminded me of a Who's on First act: Stefano not understanding something Mom said and responding with *"what-ah?"* only to have Mom ask Stefano if he needed a glass of water. *What-ah?* Water? *What-ah?* Water? Over and over.

Late bloomer that I was, it must have been interesting for my mother to finally meet a man that I had allowed myself to love. One thing Mom remembers about their first encounter is that she thought he was shy. I've never thought of Stefano as shy, and I can't help but wonder if her perception echoed Stefano's cool relationship with his own mother.

During my mornings off, I became a circus tourist, calling Mom out of the vacant workers' room she slept in so we could gawk at tigers, dodge llama spit, and feed entire heads of lettuce to Baros while he drooled down our arms.

The elephants enchanted her. Inside their tent, I found the perfect equilibrium between entertaining my mother and assuring Stefano that I both wanted and needed him. Under his supervision, Mom worked her way down the elephant line, dropping morsels of bread into upturned trunks, laughing out loud as the elephants tossed the treats into their mouths and flipped up their trunks to ask for more. Stefano, from a few paces behind, showered her with elephant lore and stories of his experiences.

During my absence, the successful birth of three tigers had inspired Giuseppe. He wanted his new cubs to ride elephants, he told me one day. "But I'd have a much better chance convincing an elephant to let a familiar animal onto her back first, wouldn't you say?"

Rasta pranced into the big top looking content to be the center of attention in a previously forbidden place. When Giuseppe urged him onto the kneeling elephant's back, Rasta didn't hesitate. Claws splayed and eyes wide, he cleared the stool that Stefano had prepared for him and scrambled onto Katia. The elephant slapped her trunk so hard against the rubber base of the ring, it sounded as if lightning cracked. My heart froze when she swatted at the dog. With a quick flick of his bull hook, Giuseppe halted Katia's attack. The trainer murmured into the startled elephant's ears, taking her attention off the now-terrified speckled mutt straddling her spine. Tongue flailing and eyes darting, the poor dog clutched the elephant's haunches as if her back were the obvious place to hide from her wrath. The elephant rumbled and the dog whimpered. Both looked torn between pleasing their masters and running for their lives.

When it came time for the following day's practice, Rasta had disappeared. He finally crept out of hiding at lunchtime, and Giuseppe ordered an impromptu practice. A trainer, his elephant, a dog, its parents, and one curious American mom filed into the tent hoping for success, but each time Stefano heaved Rasta onto the shimmying, swatting elephant, the dog skittered off like a frightened bug. I didn't know which animal I sympathized with more. One, in his search for attention, was lobbed on the back of a fearsome beast that could squash him with a single swipe. The other, while trying only to do her job, felt the weight of another's expectations heaped on her shoulders. Neither was where they wanted to be. The impossibility of the two working together soon became clear, and Giuseppe abandoned the idea, ending Rasta's stint in center-ring.

Readjusting to the circus after a month of vacation was grueling. Midsummer's muggy heat made it hell. From half an hour away, the cool breezes of Venice beckoned. One afternoon when Stefano sat down in the trailer for lunch, I explained that Giuseppe had given me permission to miss the following afternoon's shark show so Mom and I could take a day trip.

"Anyone going to ask if I want to go to *Venezia*?" His arms locked over his chest.

"Great. Come to Venice."

Stefano scrunched his mouth into a wad. "A vet is coming tomorrow. I have to be here."

"We'll go the next day."

"A load of hay has to be picked up. I must drive halfway to Treviso."

"The day after."

Stefano stared at the table. "Where is lunch? I don't smell food cooking."

"I thought we'd wait for my mother," I said, pulling a rainbow of sliced melons, kiwis, peaches, and cherries from the refrigerator.

"Lunch, Kat'leen. Not a snack."

"It's too hot for anything else." The only thing less appealing to me than eating a warm meal was cooking it. "Mom thought it was a good idea."

"Because is what your *mother* wants?" Stefano pounded his palms on the table. "How come nobody cares what Stefano wants?"

Not three weeks had passed since our return from Greece, yet the tenderness we'd found there was fading faster than my tan. Stefano was agitated and irritable, confronting me over everything, inciting fights over nothing. Edgy and taut. A spring about to be sprung. Disagreements marbled each day, and hiding them from my mother meant keeping her away from him, which only aggravated the situation. Like tectonic plates fighting for dominance, the pressure built.

Preserving the peace exhausted me.

My mother tapped on the side of the camper. "Hello?"

"Hello, Elizabeth." Stefano stood as she leaned through the doorway. "Goodbye, Elizabeth." He whisked past her and down the steps.

"How about some fruit salad, Mom?" I said, glancing past her troubled eyes to see Stefano disappear into the circus.

When my mother prepared to return to Oregon, I recalled the last night we'd spent in Florence and how I'd lain awake wondering if confiding in her had skewed her opinion of my relationship with Stefano before she had a chance to come to her own conclusions.

The day she left the circus for home, I watched her stilted goodbye to Stefano, eyed her tenuous smile. I needn't have worried about saying too much. My mother had heard our fights, seen us fail to make amends, felt the fractures in our relationship crack wide open. She'd observed our instability first hand. Surely my mother had recognized the signs, knew what would follow.

Eight years earlier, back in Oregon, I had witnessed her learn the hard way.

The moment is etched in my mind. I see my mother just inside our old motel-home front door, crumpled against the wall of coats. Her hands cupped her eyes, as if keeping her tears from falling could keep her heart from breaking. Her face, that California face, which always seemed tanned no matter how many hours she spent in the classroom, paled against the bright wools and plaids, the scarves and hats. The full lips that had encouraged each of my accomplishments and soothed so many of my worries collapsed into a thin red line of hurt.

My mother, who had always been my rock and my ladder, who had made her children's path softer at the expense of her own needs, withered before my teenage eyes. Seeing her so frail, so vulnerable, so *exposed*, frightened me. I dropped my schoolbooks and stepped to her, lifted her shoulders as if it could ease her pain.

"Your father," she said, slipping through my arms as she slumped to the painted plywood floor, "he's gone."

My father had already been gone for some time, first emotionally, soon after breaking his back, and then physically, a couple of years after moving to Oregon. That day in the motel, I believe my mother accepted he was gone forever. It was the first time I had registered that depth of emotional pain, and it was the genesis of a concept: Never allow anyone close enough to cut so deeply.

The credo had since ripened and matured in my mind. By the time my mother visited the circus, I had spent eight years so afraid of following her footsteps that I would follow my father's path instead and inflict the same awful pain onto the person I had professed to love.

CHAPTER THIRTY-FOUR

BREAKING THE ELEPHANT'S BACK

"*Cazzo*, Kat'leen." Stefano paced the four-foot length of our camper's hallway. "You're not even dressed yet."

"Relax for once," I said, dabbing brown shadow on my lids. "We're supposed to be going to a party."

"Only because is the first time this fucking circus offers me something to eat besides cafeteria garbage." He jostled a crooked drawer that hadn't slid all the way in, had never slid all the way in. When that didn't work, he rammed it with the heel of his palm. "I don't give a shit about Nino's birthday."

"Stop concentrating on how angry you are with life."

"I am angry with you," he barked.

"Why, Stefano? Why are you always angry with me?"

When he didn't answer, I answered for him. "For a year and a half, I've shared you with your elephants, with Giuseppe, with this whole circus. You never shared me with anything until my mother came. Look how you reacted the first time you couldn't have all of me."

Stefano spun around. "I never had all of you, Kat'leen. Either you are too selfish or too afraid—"

"Just because I don't fit into one of your neat little boxes?" I stood to face him. "You're angry because I catered to someone else like you wish I'd cater to you. You don't like anyone or anything anymore, Stefano. Do you even remember how to have fun?"

"Fun? *Fun?* They teach you in America that life is supposed to be fun?" Some half chortle, half screech charged out of his throat. Leaning closer, he sneered and said, "Life is one shit job after another. There is no fun."

His words stung as if he'd slapped me. Then they oozed over me, through me, saturating me with their weight as they puddled at my feet in a dark, viscous stain.

"You don't mean that. You know I hate this place, but we've had fun riding the motorcycle, haven't we? Fun visiting with Daniele? In Greece?"

"There is no fun."

"But—what about you and me? Please, Stefano. You're making it sound as if we've wasted a year and a half together."

He stared at me with a face of stone.

When I heard my voice, the words seemed to come from far away. *"Don't I mean anything to you?"*

Stefano shrugged and stormed out, slamming the door behind him.

A wave of emptiness buckled my knees. As if caving in on myself, I crumpled onto the bed and rolled into a ball. Stefano and I hadn't shared a minute of peace in the weeks since my mother left. Both weary and vulnerable, I reached for him one moment and ran from him the next. And I felt as if I were losing my way.

When I looked in my mirror, a jaded woman stared back.

Who is she?

In a frenzy, I darkened my sulking lips and masked my swelling lids.

A year ago I hated makeup. Now I hide behind it.

The clock ticked ten minutes away. My cotton minidress looked more like pajamas than a party dress, but I didn't care. The one man I wanted to attract was too enraged to notice.

The door flew open. Stefano burst in, his curses flooding our small space. Rasta scuttled under the table as Stefano pummeled the counter and slammed his fist into the crooked drawer. The trailer heaved and dishes chattered. I flinched with each crash.

"How could he?" Stefano screamed the words again and again as he paced back and forth, seething and wheezing, clenching and unclenching his reddening fists. *"Come si permette?"*

"Who?"

Stefano yanked the cushion off the dinette bench and seized his red backpack from storage beneath it. "Can't count on you. Can't count on them."

"Tell me what happened!"

Stefano ripped cupboards open and slammed them shut. "That bastard, Nino." He stuffed two T-shirts and a pair of jeans into his pack. "Personally invites me to his fucking party. Soon I walk in, he sends Dieter and me to the kitchen to haul food trays to *his guests*." Stefano grabbed a handful of cassette tapes. "Am I his fucking servant?" Underwear. Socks. "I won't shovel their shit without their respect." His camera, his razor. "Enough. You wanted to go? Now we go."

I bit my lip to stop its quivering. Stefano, consumed by

anger, looked like a stranger to me. He charged from one end of the camper to the other, grabbing his things. Though his feet and arms moved like a cartoon on fast forward, Stefano's torso stayed strangely rigid, as if bending even a little would break him in half. "Slow down," I pleaded. "What if you misunderstood?"

"Nino's Italian. I'm Italian. What is to misunderstand? When I say I didn't come to serve his guests, he yells. Treats me like shit. If Dieter didn't stop me, I would have smashed in his face. Who cares if he is Moira's son? They pay me shit. Always more work. Fucking people. *I will not work for people who do not respect me.*"

Stefano cinched his bag shut and looked up. "Pack, Kat'leen. *Forza.*"

"Pack what? You, me, and the dog? All on the motorcycle? You're out of your mind."

"You going to offend me too?"

"Will you please stop and think?"

Stefano's eyes flashed from me to the dog to his bag. "Rasta. I forgot Rasta." He scrunched his eyes into slits. "Try to understand. I have to leave. Now."

Tears crept down my face.

"Don't cry." Stefano knelt in front of the bed, pulled me toward him. "Was wrong what I said before—I want to be with you. Is the circus I am leaving."

Stefano brushed away tear after tear, but I couldn't stop crying. Couldn't stop feeling isolated. Couldn't stop coming to the obvious conclusion.

Stefano grabbed his bag. He said, "I'll sleep a couple of hours at Nonna's, then come for you and Rasta with Angelo's car. Please don't cry. I am not leaving you." He scooped up his helmet and kissed my cheek. "I am not leaving you."

The Moto Guzzi roared out of the lot and faded into the night.

When things were good between us, I would have followed Stefano to the ends of the earth. But not now. Not like this. Not when he'd told me our years together had brought him no joy. Not when he was in the midst of demonstrating that he could leave his beloved elephants to spite Nino. I huddled in the corner of the bed until the pounding in my ribcage hushed and my tears ran dry. Then I picked up my journal and wrote:

July 25, 1990, Lido di Jesolo, Italy: I cried, Stefano, not because I believed you were leaving me, but because I knew I was leaving you.

"Don't come." I clasped my hand over the telephone's mouthpiece and sobbed into the early morning light.

"Not yet," Stefano said through a yawn. "A couple more hours sleep and I come for you—will be two o'clock, maybe three."

I dug my fingernails into my palm and struggled not to cry. "I don't want to leave with you."

Heavy breathing. Murmurs of confusion.

"We can't be together anymore."

"What you are saying, Kat'leen?!"

I yanked the receiver away from my ear. "Why do you have to yell?"

"What's going on? What they do to convince you to stay?"

"I need time," I said. "Give me a few days. I'll call again."

Later that morning, I answered a knock on my camper to find Giuseppe in sullied work pants and a perspiration-drenched shirt. He looked as if he'd spent the entire morning traipsing after the elephant crew. Over the last eighteen months, the animal trainer had become a mentor and a friend, and he certainly felt betrayed by Stefano's escape.

Flicking bits of straw off his shirt, Giuseppe asked, "What about you—staying or leaving?"

I squinted into the blazing sun. The naked reality of waking up alone had deadened the previous night's convictions. Stefano wasn't only fifty feet away in the elephant tent. He wouldn't be coming with morning kisses. Nor would he be coming to bellow over some petty nuisance.

"You should know," Giuseppe said, "we're leaving for Yugoslavia in two weeks. It's definite this time."

I had to go somewhere. Oregon? *Too far away.* Hitchhike more of Europe? *I feel too fragile.* Yugoslavia? *Might be exactly what I need to clear my head.*

I was still rolling the idea around when Dieter popped in an hour later with a Neil Diamond cassette. Since the day I arrived at this circus, Dieter had always been there, offering advice and encouraging smiles, but this playlist—"Song Sung Blue," "Solitary Man," and "You Don't Bring Me Flowers"—promised to drown me in my own tears. I tried to give it back, but Dieter smiled his crooked grin and backed away, assuring me that Neil had helped him through plenty of rough times.

I tossed the cassette onto the shelf with what remained from Stefano's and my tape collection. *Funny what's left when a relationship ends.* I didn't know which tapes were missing, although I was keenly aware of the vacant space where they'd been. He'd taken few clothes, yet our cabinets sounded hollow.

Taken away our opportunities to squabble with each other, but left me feeling empty.

Marilena showed up after lunch, a pitcher of sangria in hand. I dove into my drink the moment she poured it, slurping *vino* and sucking on a wine-laden peach until the tang of cinnamon swirled in my mouth.

When she asked what I was going to do, I pressed the cool glass against my temple, dragged it across my forehead, and said, "I'm tired, Marilena, and I'm numb, and I don't know anything anymore."

"You eat today?"

"No."

"You're starting to look too thin," Marilena told me. "You need food."

I raised my sangria. "Fruit is food, isn't it?"

"You come to my trailer and eat lunch this whole week. No excuses. Giorgio's already made himself at home—what's one more mouth to feed?"

That evening, heavy footsteps strode up to the shark truck and stopped in front of me.

"He's a fool for leaving you." Erich tucked his plump hands between his belly roll and hipbones and shook his head. Too emotionally spent to fend another vulture off the carrion of my relationship, I lowered my eyes, wishing the intermission would start so he would stop. "Zeese vomen, parading like virgin primadonnas by day, then skulking around after zee show, thinking no one knows vat they do. I see everything. Hear everyone." Erich leaned toward me. "You're different. You were good to that man, and he abandoned you."

"Mind your own business, will you? Will everyone just mind their own fucking business?"

Years later, when I heard a rumor that a tragic auto accident had stolen Erich's wife and young daughter from him, I remembered how I'd lashed out at him that day. My words sting me now. Whether or not the rumor was true, there must have been something that kept him so far from his country and whatever family he had left. The tiger handler would jab a bitten-off finger in your face or flash his scarred chest without much provocation, but perhaps he kept his deepest wounds hidden. Looking back, I wonder if Erich had been reaching out to me that day. I wonder if it pained him to see me grieve a love that didn't have to be lost.

I stood in the dark and stared at the dimly lit pay phone. Two days since Stefano had left. If I didn't call, he'd soon be in front of me, demanding answers. He deserved an explanation. Lifting the slip of paper I clutched up to the light, I read my words again. *When two people are no longer willing to make the time or the effort to show their love for each other, then they shouldn't be together.*

I wadded the lousy excuse of an excuse into a ball, shoved it in my pocket, and dialed his grandmother's number.

"*Ciao.*" I spoke softly into the phone.

"You tricked me. You know I wouldn't leave if you tell me you don't come." He waited. I didn't speak. "Why, Kat'leen? Why you are not with me?"

The note in my pocket crumpled under my fingers. "When two people—" I choked.

"I love you."

Tears pasted the plastic phone to my cheek. "I haven't stopped loving you, Stefano."

"Come to *Milano*. Nonna moved in with my parents. We'll have our own place. Please, Kat'leen. We make it work. I promise."

I clenched my bottom lip between my teeth. "The circus is leaving for Yugoslavia in ten days. I'm going too."

"Yugoslavia? *Where in Yugoslavia?* No yelling. Sorry. Sorry. No more yelling."

I pressed the phone to my ear and listened to him breathe.

"How long?"

"Four months."

"Don't go." His voice cracked.

I stifled my sobs with my hand.

"Kat'leen." From the other end of the phone line, Stefano whimpered. "Why you leave me if it makes you cry?"

"I have to go. I'll call when we leave Italy."

"Ten days?" His voice blasted out of the receiver. *"You won't call for ten days?"*

I hung up the phone and walked away.

As if it would extinguish my doubts, I separated myself from Stefano as oil separates from vinegar. Parts of me rushed to the surface, desperately seeking release. I made animal food, ushered guests, and swam with the sharks as usual, but there were no fights, no tense mealtimes, no harsh words. Feeling more at ease than I had in months, I savored this newfound space to breathe.

Other habits were harder to let go. Some mornings I waited in bed as if he'd arrive any moment to cover me in good-morning kisses. Once I stood immobile in a supermarket checkout line staring at the items I'd just unloaded from my basket—Nutella, the chocolate cream Stefano would shovel into his mouth until he'd scraped the jar clean; a four-pack of Pilsner that only he liked; two tins of Simmenthal canned beef; packaged prosciutto; bright green Cerignola olives. I backed away from the groceries. When the cashier looked at me, I turned and hurried from the store.

As the days passed, the separation between Stefano and me became more defined. The circus left the town of Lido di Jesolo for a new *piazza.* A new beginning, but part of me still reflected on the ending. One morning, dicing a pile of green apples, I wondered if people who chop away pieces of their lives eventually end up with nothing.

A man twice my age from the management team whom I rarely saw stopped me on my way through the circus one afternoon. He started with a wave. Next thing I knew, his arm clutched my shoulders, and his face sailed toward mine.

"Not getting lonely, are we?"

"Excuse me." I twisted away.

He assured me that he was only trying to let me know I had a phone call waiting.

I glanced toward the office. Ignoring Stefano's last few calls had not kept him from calling back.

Oscar's freckled cheeks rose when I crossed his threshold. He looked so pleasant and accommodating, I almost reached out to tousle his dark curls. His official title was secretary, but Oscar was much more than Walter Nones's assistant. Besides the daily paperwork for hundreds of employees, he handled payroll and phone calls, hirings and firings. He dealt not only with the dozen embassies governing Moira's foreign workers, but also with the Italian agencies that regulated the employment of those workers. From the day Stefano and I had walked onto the circus grounds in Rome and asked him for a job, Oscar had always shown us kindness and respect. He was the one manager besides Giuseppe whom I considered a friend.

Oscar said, "Giuseppe asked me to explain about Stefano's security *cauzione.*"

"He must know he lost whatever was left after buying the motorcycle."

Oscar nodded. "It's a retainer. If a worker leaves without Walter's permission, the circus retains the money."

When I asked if anyone ever earned his retainer back, Oscar declared the information confidential. His grimace told me that I shouldn't count on getting my *cauzione* back, either.

The secretary pointed to the flashing button on the phone. "Want me to step out?"

I shook my head. The call wouldn't last long. I inhaled and picked up the handset, expecting Stefano. Instead, Daniele's warm Neapolitan accent gurgled through the line.

"Yugoslavia is supposed to be beautiful," he said when I told him of our imminent departure. "I'd love to come along."

"Sure you can come to Yugoslavia." I looked over at Oscar, who shrugged and then nodded. I paused before asking Daniele, "Have you spoken with Stefano?"

"Not yet. Put him on."

"He's not here." My words caught in my throat as I broke the news to Daniele. I pressed my lips tight, stretching the phone cord to the floor as I slid off the chair and wedged myself into the corner between Oscar's desk and the wall.

Oscar glanced up from his paperwork. The secretary

handed me a cellophane packet of tissues from his coat pocket on his way out.

"I shouldn't come," Daniele said. "You need to figure things out without me in your way."

"Please come. I need a friend a hell of a lot more than I need space."

"So he left and you stayed."

I looked across the van's front seat to Daniele and then returned my gaze to the jumble of yellow and blue vehicles massed at the border. So far, this day had amounted to nothing but false starts and full stops. "Who would have thought?"

"Not me," Daniele said. "And certainly not Stefano."

"You talked to him?" I shifted my weight from one numbed cheek to the other.

"At some point, he would have known that I came on this trip. I couldn't have him think we had something secretive going on. He said he misses you. That he wants to see you."

"I told him I'd call before we left Italy." Craning my neck out the window, I looked fifty yards back to the last Italian coffee bar I'd see until November and the bright orange phone booth off to its side. Ahead, at the line dividing Italy from Yugoslavia, Walter, Oscar, and the rest of the management team still thronged the customs kiosk. "Come on, Rasta. Last chance to pee on Italian soil."

As Daniele and I entered the bar, the circus crowd quieted.

"She didn't waste much time," someone said from the far side of the room.

I gritted my teeth, bought a dozen phone tokens from the cashier, and left. Snickers followed me out. A frenzy of gossip would certainly follow my appearance with my new boyfriend, as Daniele had quickly been labeled.

"Sorry my being here caused that," Daniele said when he arrived a few minutes later with coffees.

Listening to the phone ring and ring at Nonna's house, I told Daniele, "Don't be. With or without you here, the stories would still fly."

Daniele shook his head and let out a squawk of a laugh.

"What?" I asked, hanging up the receiver.

"I'm confused why you chose this over Stefano."

"Because it's easier than digging myself out of the hole Stefano and I fell into."

We drifted toward my van as Rasta sniffed alongside of the road, peeing on every other weed.

Daniele said, "Stefano still has hope."

It took the rest of the afternoon to get over 200 laborers, thirty performers and their families, a troupe of Russians, a stable of horses, twelve tigers, seven elephants, five zebras, five antelope, three camels, two sharks, one giraffe, one rhinoceros, an American buffalo, a llama, an ostrich, an emu, and one aging circus queen through customs.

The weary circus rolled another forty miles into Yugoslavia. At first, vehicles traveling to and from Italy congested the two-lane road, but traffic grew light as we left Italian soil farther behind, and the cars grew noticeably older, shabbier. We swooped through wooded areas surrounded by mountains, around steep curves, and past white rock bluffs. Closer to the sea, shrub-covered hills dappled with red-roofed villages sloped toward the jagged coastline. Boats bobbed in the distance, and their shimmering lights grew brighter as daylight faded.

The town of Rijeka, Croatian for river, is sliced in two by a swift-flowing waterway. It is there, at the mouth of the Rječina river, that the Adriatic makes its deepest incision into the European continent, and there that I would make my home for the next three weeks. When I pulled onto a large lot flanking the sea, Giuseppe directed me to an area he called the quietest spot in town. Beyond Giuseppe's plush living quarters, in an empty area with the sea on one side and some small docks on the other, I shut off the van and waited for the engine to stop rattling.

Morning sun illuminated the camper's windows. I drew open a curtain to see the rough wooden docks holding rowboats by their leashes as they rocked in the current. Looking out another window, I saw that a small white camper had blocked my view of the sea.

Giorgio.

I left Daniele sleeping in the dining nook and went to prepare the animal food. Baros's head and neck jutted out from the open doors of his truck like a stick pony. He leaned down to nuzzle my hair as I passed, as if to hurry me along, but the workers weren't even close to having the animal pens ready, so I fed the giraffe a few lettuce leaves and snuck away to explore the boulder-strewn coastline.

I didn't make it very far. Still within the boundaries of the circus, I sat down, slipped off my sandals, and dipped my feet into the cool, crystalline Adriatic. Three hundred and sixty degrees of unfamiliar territory surrounded me. The hills rising behind me held secrets of ancient Celtic settlements and historic Roman fortresses. Before me, myriad islands dotted the far-reaching watery domain of maritime Venice. History, beauty, and the unknown. *I'm soaking my toes in Marco Polo's playground, for Chrissake.* Yet I couldn't even muster the motivation to wander a few hundred feet up the coastline.

Stefano still has hope.

Daniele's words echoed within me. Despite the pain of adjusting to being one instead of two, I'd grown more certain each day since Stefano left that we had to let go. All that remained was for him to accept it as well.

The deep rumble was unmistakable. From the camper door, I saw the silver Moto Guzzi veer around Giuseppe's truck. The cutting board slipped from my hand and clattered to the floor. Stefano's gaze locked on the trailer. Our eyes met. *He came for me.* In that one moment, everything I loved about this man surged through me and bubbled to the surface, tickling me with its effervescence.

Kickstand down. Helmet off. Long strides. *"Kat'leen."*

I wanted to hold onto this buoyancy. To hold onto him.

Stefano's hands, reaching for my face. Palms on my cheeks, pulling me toward him. His mouth on mine.

But the flood of fears still came. What would happen the day I did something he considered gravely disrespectful? Something irrevocable? Would he leave me just as he'd left his elephants?

"No." I pulled back.

Stefano held on. Pain tweaked his features. "Please . . ."

I stepped aside and motioned him into the trailer. "We were about to eat."

"We?" Stefano's gaze shot past the plates of cheese and bread. "Cook flagged me down on my way in, told me you found yourself a new lover."

"Since when do you believe circus gossip, Stefano? This is Daniele. Your friend. He told you himself he was coming."

Stefano grunted and tromped through the door. We sat in silence. I nudged my plate toward Stefano, but he looked away.

Wrapping a sandwich in a paper towel, Daniele said, "I'll be by the docks," and walked out. The trailer door swung on its hinges and then stilled, leaving us in silence.

Stefano toyed with a piece of bread and then chucked it aside. "We belong together."

"No, Stefano. I'm too tired."

He opened and closed his mouth a few times before finally whispering, "Tired of me?"

"Of trying to make it work. Of being in love while watching it fall apart. Christ, Stefano—love shouldn't be this hard."

He reached for me. "You love challenges. Hitchhiking Europe. Riding elephants. Building cabinets. Ostriches. Giraffes. Sharks. Nothing too difficult. Nothing too dangerous." Stefano wiped his eyes with the backs of his hands. "Why you give up on me?"

I stood and touched the wet smudge on his cheek. "I'm sorry, Stefano. It hurts and I miss you, but it's over."

He raised his hands, but no words came out. And I didn't know how to fill the empty space between us.

Turning for the door, I said, "Your things are in the closet."

I half ran, half staggered to the shoreline. So much love. So much pain. As hard as I'd tried to keep both feelings at bay, they kept flowing back to me. I closed my eyes and listened to the tide until my mind felt as clear as the water. And like water, I would choose the path of least resistance.

When I returned to the trailer, Daniele looked up from packing his bag to tell me Stefano had gone to see the elephants.

"I thought you were staying longer."

"So did I." He pushed the last of his things into his bag and zipped it shut. "Why would the cook stop Stefano on his way in to insinuate that we were sleeping together? And that bar at the border?"

I followed him outside and watched him strap his bag to Stefano's motorcycle. "You're an outsider. They just—"

"Are you defending them?"

"Explaining."

"Defending. One week, and I already feel this circus on me like a leech."

"It's different once you're here for a while."

He clutched my shoulder. "You need to do what you need to do, but if you ask me, you've been here too long."

Too long.

By August 1990, I'd pushed against those circus walls for so long and so hard, holding onto them comforted me. Steadied me. Two constants consumed my life, Stefano and the circus. One would slip through my fingers, the other I would cling to.

Stefano waited in the doorway of the elephant tent, his helmet slung over an elbow. He watched me approach, then turned back to the animals.

I stood at his side. My first love. My only love. Conceived, consummated, and now collapsing, all within the walls of an elephant tent.

Stefano squeezed my fingers in his. He brushed his lips against my forehead and searched my eyes one last time. "Will you call?"

I nodded, but knew that I wouldn't. "Goodbye, Stefano."

CHAPTER THIRTY-FIVE

IF YOU DON'T FEED LOVE, IT STARVES

Everyone was curious. Everyone was talking.

I wanted nothing to do with it and had purposely sat away from the other ushers while waiting for the gates to open. From far below my perch on the bleachers, Giorgio looked my way. I acknowledged him with the barest flicker of my mouth. Moments later, he plopped down next to me.

Reaching out as if to console me, he said, "He left you again."

I shrugged off his touch. "Stefano had every intention of picking me up the day after his fight with Nino."

"But he didn't. And four days ago, he left you again."

"I was the one who said no."

Giorgio toyed with the zipper tab on his sweat jacket, biding his time. "You must have had reasons," he finally said.

"Everybody has reasons."

He waited again, his gaze resting on a group of Polish

workers straightening the rows of red plastic chairs circling the ring.

I had a hundred reasons, and I had none, but I had no desire to discuss it with Giorgio. "Shouldn't you be stretching or something?"

Walter marched into the tent, glanced around the hollow big top, and gave the five-minute warning. I stood and smoothed my black skirt into a straight line above my knees.

Giorgio trailed me down the bleachers. His voice softened as he asked, "What went wrong?"

"It's simple," I said, leveling my eyes on his. "If you don't feed love, it starves."

Chitchat hushed as we approached the ushers, and they greeted me with inflated grins that verged on condescension. Alessio, the six-foot, second-tier, gay contortionist with a doo-wop hairdo, leaned against the bleachers and looked down his long straight nose at me. Walter had allowed Alessio to perform since Giada's sister departed. For some reason, pressing his gangly frame into a glass box so tiny his privates smushed against the panes like soft-boiled eggs filled Alessio with hoity-toity airs. These days he was as much of a primadonna as the worst of the girls—which was probably why Walter had assigned him the job of overseeing us.

"Well, well, well," Alessio finally said after Giorgio sauntered out. "You've made a friend."

"We ought to take one of those boats out tonight after the show."

I followed Giorgio's gaze to the rowboats rocking in the tide. In this remote *piazza,* where there seemed nothing much for performers to do outside of show time, he and I and a handful of others had spent the last few days sunbathing on the stretch of shoreline between his camper and the sea. Once upon a time, I would have been the one to suggest pirating a boat for a moonlight ride, but that wild-haired girl now dawdled, unhappy and uninspired, in circus limbo.

That night after the show, I arrived at the dock with Dieter in tow.

"He insisted on chaperoning," I told Giorgio when his eyes narrowed on Dieter.

"Wouldn't want those pesky stories starting up so soon, would we?" offered Dieter.

Giorgio shrugged and led us toward a twelve-foot green vessel. Water lapped against its wooden sides; anchor, benches, and nets filled its belly.

"Big, isn't it?" Dieter asked.

"Not for three." Giorgio balanced himself with my arm. Boards creaked underfoot as he eased into the boat. Standing one of the oars beside him, he said, "It's twice as tall as I am," and held the oar out to Dieter. "Looks like you're rowing."

Boating became our ritual, and the three of us rendezvoused at the dock after most late shows. Cool breezes. Warm emotions. Sensuous words spoken into the night. Oars caressed moonlit ripples, their music mingling with the silken sounds of the tide as we slid past the darkened big top. From the shadows where I dwelled, Giorgio seemed fresh, youthful, and alive. Caring and carefree. And he made me feel desirable. As the weeks passed, his voice prodded me like a preacher, soft, loud, then soft again, as he summoned me toward his embrace.

Dieter rowed us along the coast like a gondolier piloting two romantics around the canals of Venice. At the time, I'd wondered if Dieter had tagged along so he'd be next in line if nothing came of Giorgio's attempts. Looking back, I see that the trapeze gigolo's chameleon ways were as revealing as his spandex tights, and I wonder if Dieter intended to look out for me in the quiet way a kid brother might have. But settling into my solitary shoes was a lonely process, and even if Dieter had bellowed *danger* louder than an elephant, I still would have allowed Giorgio to romance me.

One night, after Dieter had already wandered off, I stayed to listen to the end of a story. When Giorgio finished, he reached for my hand and said, "Don't sleep alone again."

I hesitated. "It's too soon." But four weeks had passed since Stefano left. How empty my own trailer felt.

Giorgio reeled my face into his. His boyish grin made him look both bashful and warm as he explained that he was not asking for sex. "I just want to be near you," he said, "to wake up next to you." He hooked a finger around one of mine and tugged me toward his trailer.

I pulled back. "The dog."

"We'll bring him too."

Morning found me still in Giorgio's bed, his partially covered body resting not far from my own. My gaze followed his contoured abdomen to where it disappeared under the white cotton sheet. He'd stayed true to his word: offering only a glass of wine, a clean towel, and half of his bed; asking only for my presence.

If I weren't in the middle of my period, would I be the one to ask for more?

I'd almost dozed off when a sea breeze swept a distinctly dancing-girl voice through the curtained window.

"Oh look. *Rasta* is sleeping under *Giorgio's* trailer."

Another voice more penetrating than the first said, "Isn't that *Kathleen's* dog?"

Mind your own fucking business, I wanted to yell through the thin metal shell of his camper. Giorgio and I would have to deal with the whole goddamned circus acknowledging our tryst, but not now, not yet.

Studying the way Giorgio's russet curls sprawled over the curves of his shoulders, I flashed on how betrayed Stefano would feel if he knew where I lay.

It's over, Kathleen. Time to move on.

I wanted the sweetness of gliding through moonlit water. I wanted the fulfillment of Giorgio's undivided attention. I wanted to feel wanted.

Move on.

Giorgio stirred. When he stretched his powerful arm across my back, I let him draw me in until our heads shared the same pillow. The tip of his finger traced my jaw line, the dimple in my chin. He pressed his body into mine.

"No." I pulled back. "We can't."

"You sure?"

"I . . . um . . . No. I mean yes. I'm sure. I have my period. *Le mie cose.*"

Giorgio's head fell back onto his pillow. He turned to press his erection into the mattress and groaned. "How long do I have to wait?" came a muffled voice. "One day? Two?"

"Maybe three."

He groaned again. "Don't worry about me. It will go away eventually."

"There's a sea of cool water right outside your door."

"That's what I want. A cold swim."

That night at the show, the secretary pulled me aside and handed me three slips of paper, *Please call* written on each one.

"You're dancing on thin ice," Dieter said one night on the docks while waiting for Giorgio.

I looked up. "What's that supposed to mean?"

"It's English, isn't it? Figure it out."

"I understand the words, Dieter, but not what you mean."

"Loverboy over there." Dieter motioned toward the approaching silhouette. Said, "He's got other interests," and he refused to say more.

August 24, 1990, Rijeka, Yugoslavia: Dieter's words sticking with me. Head says they hold truth, body says not to listen.

The door of the shark truck opened. Giorgio slipped in and shut it behind him. Flipping up one finger at a time, he counted off the three days that had passed since that morning in his trailer. We never made it to the boat dock.

Urgency. Passion. Romance. How I'd wanted it all. But the only desire I felt that night was a man's hunger to appease his own need.

CHAPTER THIRTY-SIX

BOILING WATER

Summer is not a season for reservations or regrets.

The circus traveled west to Istria's resort towns where turquoise water and tranquil beaches filled my days, ritzy casinos and beat-thumping clubs my nights. The after-hours circus crowd ate well, played long, and partied hard. My drink of choice was vodka and *sok od naranče*, orange juice, and I chose to drink a lot. Having had my fill of conflict and confrontation, I vowed to have fun. Perhaps that's why I pretended it didn't bother me when Giorgio flirted with every woman that crossed his path. Like a squirrel that forgets within half an hour where he's buried his nuts, Giorgio the Gigolo already rummaged for his next meal.

> *September 1, 1990, Pula, Yugoslavia: When one dances on thin ice, eventually the ice will break. Do I run back to shore while it's still possible? Or continue dancing merrily along?*

September 5, 1990, Rovign, Yugoslavia: Dancing merrily along.

"You ever telling me what those other interests of his are?"

Dieter shook his head and handed me my stallion's reins. "If a certain someone found out I knew and didn't tell, I'd be thrown out of this circus in seconds."

"Stop being an enigma, Dieter." I flipped the stirrup around and hoisted myself onto the horse.

Trotting alongside on the big black stallion, he said, "I've given this circus too many years. I decide when it's time for me to go."

I yanked my horse to a halt. "Who dammit? Who's he screwing?"

Dieter pulled his stallion to a stop and peered over his shoulder. "All you need to know is she's married. Very married. Giorgio's the one screwing her, but I'll be judged just as guilty, because I knew."

September 10, 1990, Portorož, Yugoslavia: I'm swimming. Fortunately, the water isn't as cold as I'd imagined. Now that I'm drenched, let's hope I head for shore.

"Whose wife are you sleeping with?"

A flicker of surprise crossed Giorgio's face. "Doesn't matter," he said with a shrug. "She needed a shoulder. I offered mine."

"Apparently you offered a lot more than that."

"I give women only what they ask for."

Giorgio reached for me, but I twisted away.

"Fine," he said. "But once I go, I don't come back."

And for ten days, he didn't, yet I saw him hovering. While I showed patrons to their seats, he watched from the bleachers. While I performed in the shark tank, he mingled with the crowd. Still, he didn't attempt direct contact. Only later did I understand that he'd found easier prey. Why bother with a hotheaded American when an eager troupe of English nightclub dancers wanted to sample what lay beneath Giorgio's tights?

But once we left the smorgasbord of Istria's beach towns behind, his appetite returned.

"Giorgio's upset," Marilena said.

"He's upset?" I creased my brow at her as we cruised into Banja Luka's closest grocery store.

A woman sitting beside a bolted-down cash box tucked a strand of graying hair back under her dark scarf as we passed. When I smiled, she nodded and lowered her eyes.

The room was Third-World bleak. Nearly bare shelving lined two walls, and a handful of rough wooden crates at the far end made up the scant produce section. Emptiness filled the rest of the store. Marilena and I each picked up a cardboard box and headed for the crates.

Kneeling for a closer look, she said, "Same stuff we picked through three days ago," and scooped up a few clumps of garlic. Then Marilena chuckled. "I don't think women usually tell Giorgio to get lost."

"Maybe that's why he can't figure out what it means,"

I said, searching through a dozen red apples for one that wasn't soft.

"He says he isn't sleeping with her anymore." Marilena worked her way through a pile of eggplant and asked, "Think I can make two good *melanzane* out of three bad ones?"

"How would I know?" I nudged an orange dappled with mushy spots and left to find the canned fruit.

Marilena followed. "You miss him?"

Giorgio couldn't fill Stefano's shoes or his bed, but even if our liaison amounted to only small talk and sex, I noticed when he wasn't around. "Between you and me, I guess we had some fun." I held up a tin for her to look at. "You think that's a peach or an apricot?"

"Isn't that the same one you got last time?"

"I couldn't tell what I was eating—it was just orange and soft." I set two of the cans into my box. "I wish I would have listened to you and brought more stuff from Italy. I can't live on canned fruit and iced coffee."

"Your legs look skinny as sticks."

My weight had dropped considerably from the 150-pound high I'd hit the previous fall. Before we left Italy, I'd weighed around 130. I hadn't seen a scale since then, but the leather belt I'd made myself soon after arriving in Yugoslavia already needed more holes.

"I can't afford to eat out, Marilena. Walter won't let us ask for tips because Yugoslavians don't have the money to spare. Yesterday I heard that if he has to cut ticket prices to fill the tent, he'll cut workers' pay too."

"Here's an idea: Eggplant is cheap and simple. Why don't you learn how to prepare it?"

I hadn't lit my stove except to make coffee for weeks. *Hell no* tickled the tip of my tongue, yet without anyone demanding that I cook, the idea didn't seem so horrific.

An hour later in Marilena's camper, I watched her carve brown spots out of an eggplant and quarter the rest. "Remove the seeds," she said, slicing off the pithy center. "Pasta sauce calls for only the meatier outside. Cut what's left into pinky-sized strips." She held the knife out to me. "You've used a knife before, haven't you?"

"Ha, ha, Marilena." I took over slicing eggplant. "What about the skin?"

"Leave it. Once they're cut, lay them on an oven rack and—"

"Sprinkle them with salt so they shed their bitter water."

Marilena looked up.

"Learned that from Daniele," I said, recalling the *Parmigiana* Daniele had made in Salerno, almost eight months earlier.

"It takes half an hour." Marilena doused the bottom of a cooking pan with olive oil. "So we'll start our tomatoes in the meantime—you know it's always extra virgin in sauce, right?"

"Always extra virgin in sauce," I repeated, certain that I hadn't known.

"Chop a quarter of that onion and add it to the olive oil."

"Small pieces? Large?"

"It's an onion. Just chop it." The can opener creaked as Marilena twisted it around a large can of tomatoes. "Always—"

"San Marzano," I said before she could.

The mixture of olive and onion sizzled when Marilena dumped in the tomatoes, and her trailer smelled of sun-kissed vegetables. "When you're short on time, don't add their juice, but since we have to wait on the eggplant . . ."

Once the eggplant had rested for long enough, Marilena pulled out another frying pan.

"Not olive oil?" I asked, watching the pale yellow stream she poured into it.

"Too heavy. Use sunflower, and use plenty. Adding more later will cool your fry. The hotter your oil, the less your vegetables absorb."

Crowding over her small stove, I mashed and stirred simmering tomatoes while Marilena filled a pasta pot with water and tossed in a handful of rock salt. On a third burner, eggplant strips crackled in foaming oil.

Marilena grumbled as she pulled a jar of dried basil from her cupboard. "Who can expect fresh basil when we rarely find fresh milk?" Rubbing a hefty pinch into her palm, she said, "To release the flavor from dried herbs," and added it to the sauce. "We want this to reduce until it's thick enough to coat the pasta. When the olive oil pools on top, your tomatoes are done."

Rub dried herbs to release flavor. Olive oil pools on cooked sauce. San Marzano. Extra virgin. Rock salt. Bits of information, some old, some new, revolved in my head. Wedges of golden eggplant filled a plate, fragrant tomato sauce bubbled away excess moisture, and steam rattled the pasta pot.

"Water's boiling."

Marilena nodded and leaned out the doorway. "Carmineeeeee."

I remembered how each time I'd heard her noontime call, my mouth had watered like one of Pavlov's dogs. Standing there beside my friend, I thought, *I'll have my own table someday. An overflowing table that fills guests with anticipation and*—I caught myself in the middle of my thought and laughed.

"What's so funny?" Marilena asked.

"I'm cooking," I said, "and I'm enjoying it."

"I told you it's easy." She dumped half a kilo of *penne rigate* into the boiling water, explaining how the ridges on the pasta help the tomato adhere. Glancing into the saucepan, she said, "Add the eggplant and turn off the flame. When the pasta's *al dente*, we'll toss everything together, add *Parmigiano*, and we're done."

Carmine ducked his tall skinny frame through the doorway, his son in tow. Stopping short, Carmine said, "Kathleen's cooking?" Edging closer, he chuckled knowingly and whispered, "So you miss our little friend Giorgio, do you?"

"Marilena!"

"I had to tell him—he's my husband," she said, positioning her son's booster seat on one side of the U-shaped bench.

I grabbed the grater and cheese and slid to the far end of the bench.

Carmine leaned over the table. "In a minute, you'll be able to miss him in person. Set another place, Marilena. Giorgio's hungry too."

I stopped mid-grate. "He's coming?"

"Not coming." Marilena's eyes flickered toward the door. "Here."

Giorgio strolled in without meeting my eyes and sat down. The bench shuddered as he scooted toward me. I concentrated on metal swishing over *Parmigiano* until Giorgio's knuckles grazed my bare leg. The contact almost seemed accidental, but my hand still lurched, spewing tendrils of Parmesan confetti across the table. Ignoring the goose-pimpled trail his touch left, I pulled away. Giorgio's hand inched along the seat. *Think cheese.* Fingers brushing against me. *I'm grating cheese.* Faint pressure on my skin. *Wisps of cheese, tumbling down . . .*

"—is when the pasta resists your bite."

I looked up at Marilena. "Huh?"

"*Al dente*, I was saying, is when the pasta resists your bite." She held out a single penne tube on the tine of a fork.

I bounced up, distancing myself from Giorgio. The noodle felt plump and solid in my mouth yet gave way as I bit into it.

Marilena placed the steaming pot on the table and handed me a large spoon. "You serve," she said. "Cook's honor."

After mounding our bowls with pasta, I lined them up in front of me. *I cooked.* Angled pasta tubes entwined with bronze eggplant and draped with crimson sauce jutted from the bowls. I dusted each one with tiny curls of *Parmigiano.*

I actually cooked.

"Can we eat now?" Carmine pulled a bowl toward him. *"Buon appetito,"* he said, and the rest of us echoed his words.

Giorgio sat so close, I could feel his heat. Heat that tingled my scalp and curled my toes. *Ten days since I confronted him about his married woman.* Flesh is sensitive; it weakens the mind. *Marilena says he isn't sleeping with her anymore.*

During those last days of summer, I resumed my midnight mambo with Giorgio.

On September 23, a call from Stefano interrupted my dance. That time, I stood right outside the office and couldn't ignore his call. So many thoughts in my head; so few came out of my mouth.

"Don't forget me so easily," he said.

I hung up the phone without having the balls to tell the man I'd loved for almost two years that I'd exchanged him for a playboy.

Sometime during that period, I received another call. Stefano's mother wanted only to check in, she said, to see if I was all right. Make sure I knew that Stefano missed me. I do not recall every word she spoke, but I am certain of one thing:

regardless of their clashes over the years, Angela cared deeply for her son.

September 24, 1990, Doboj, Yugoslavia: I'm late, I'm late, for a very important date!

I bought a pregnancy test at a nearby pharmacy for twelve dollars, two dollars less than a day's pay for diving into the shark tank, but I feared that little white stick far more than I feared the sharks.

September 30, 1990, Zenica, Yugoslavia: The test stick says that I'm only late—but almost two weeks? To tell or not to tell, that is the question.

"Did Giorgio find out from you that I missed my period?"

Marilena opened a can of tuna and dumped its oily contents into a bowl. "Strain and rinse two spoonfuls of capers, then stir them into this tuna."

"Marilena?"

She stopped rummaging through her refrigerator and looked up. "I didn't mean for him to hear. Carmine and I were talking, and he was outside the window. I'm sorry." She rinsed a bunch of parsley and then set it in front of me. "Can you believe I found fresh parsley? This canned-food diet is getting to me. Sarajevo has to be better, doesn't it?"

"Don't change the subject." My paring knife crunched

through crisp green leaves, and their pungent smell tickled my nose. "Can't you be more discreet?"

Marilena half shrugged, half nodded. "So? You obviously talked to him too. What did he think?"

"Who knows? He barely said a damn thing besides that he knew I was late—like he wanted to prove that I can't have secrets from him."

When I finished mincing the parsley, I jotted down the ingredients we'd used so far in a leather-covered notebook I'd stitched together to hold Marilena's recipes.

"Make sure you write down that this sauce takes at least half a cup of oil," Marilena said, pointing to the pan of simmering garlic.

"Isn't that a lot?"

"Not when it's the only liquid in the sauce." Marilena added the parsley, tuna, and capers. "A bowl of pasta swimming in sauce is bad, but too dry is worse. Aren't you on the pill?"

"I was. And then I stopped. I started again when . . . but maybe they don't work right away. Christ, Marilena. I wasn't planning on sleeping with anybody."

Marilena looked at me. "You think you are? Pregnant?"

Reaching down, I slid my hands over a belly flattened by diets and begged it to stay that way. "I am not ready to say that word yet," I told my friend. "What's next with this sauce?"

"We're done. Once the spaghetti is *al dente*, we toss it with the sauce and we eat."

"Should I grate some cheese?"

"No cheese. Never on fish."

"I know that," I said, scribbling a reminder in the back of the notebook.

"Sure you do, Kathleen. You also know you should have an idea what you'll do if you're pregnant."

"I've got other things to worry about, Marilena. Like . . . like my washing machine. I've never owned one before. How could I know the pump burns if you don't clean the damn filter?"

Marilena burst into laughter, nearly dropping the spaghetti bound for boiling water.

"It's not funny, Marilena."

"Yes it is," she said, smirking in a way that made me feel she simultaneously laughed with me and at me. "But don't worry. First the kitchen—then we'll work on the rest of your home."

When we left Zenica, my washing machine stayed behind, unbolted from the tongue of my trailer and abandoned in the *piazza*. I contemplated it through my rearview mirror as I drove away and saw it as a silent testament that what we do not care for ends up cast off, broken, and alone.

CHAPTER THIRTY-SEVEN

THREE WEEKS IN OCTOBER

October 8, 1990, Sarajevo, Yugoslavia: Disconnected, fleeting thoughts. Stefano. Friends from home. My tummy trouble. Feeling as though my feet have been dragging . . . and I haven't the strength to pick them up.

"What do you think of Sarajevo?"

Striking blue eyes stared at me through thick black-rimmed glasses as I stepped out of the changing room at the back of the shark truck. Salt water dribbled from the tips of my curls onto my sweat suit.

"I haven't seen Sarajevo yet," I said to the young man. "We only pulled in yesterday."

The young woman beside him focused her serious brown eyes on me. Stepping closer, she said, "We know. We watched from up there." I followed her finger. "They're dorms. We're students."

Blue Eyes stuck out his hand. "I'm Miros. This is my friend Ilia."

"Nice to meet you. I'm—"

"Miss Kathleen from California." Miros pointed to the sign beside the shark tank.

"I usually just go by Kathleen."

The zoo lights flickered, beckoning the audience back for the second half of the show. I caught Giorgio's jealous glare from across the zoo, where he helped Erich with the tigers. His scowl seemed more aggressive than the irate cat he prodded through the tunnel.

"Sarajevo has 5,000 years of history." Miros's arms flew wide, as if to encompass his entire city as he retreated toward the show tent. "From ancient Illyrians and Romans through the Ottoman Empire. You can even visit the street corner where Gavrilo Princip fired the gunshots that started World War One."

"I'm sure I'll see one or two things before we leave."

"Six years ago Sarajevo was the center of the universe."

"Sure." I nodded, toweling my hair as I followed them. "For the Olympics."

"Yes." Miros's eyes flickered. "Not so much anymore."

Two days later, I ran into Miros and Ilia in the small square separating their dorms from the circus entrance. When I admitted that I still hadn't seen Sarajevo, they insisted I let them be my guides.

For three weeks in October, they escorted me through their city. Mosques, museums, minarets, and markets, they presented each place not only with pride, but also with necessity, as if they predicted the coming horrors. A year and a half later, the same buildings would be pockmarked with bullet holes, their glass shattered, their walls blown apart.

For three weeks in October, I rolled in and out of Giorgio's bed. We did not talk about the elephants in our living room—not my possible pregnancy, not what he and I were doing together, not the other man I was trying so hard to cut out of my life.

In a way, it was still summer for all of us. Cold winds blowing off Sarajevo's mountains hinted of winter, but the sun still shone on Miros and Ilia's city. I considered strolling through markets and lunching in cafés proof that my fall was still far, far away. Yugoslavia, as a single entity, was unsure of who it was or to whom its heart belonged. Though a trivial predicament compared to this city's, I also stumbled toward a chasm of chaos and change.

One night after the late show, Giorgio strutted into my camper as I prepared to leave.

"It's midnight," he said. "Where are you going?"

"Out with those students."

Giorgio tugged on my elbow. "Stay here with me."

"I made plans."

"To do what?" His voice grew loud.

"You're hurting my arm." I pulled from his grasp. "We're going out for pizza and then listening to music in Ilia's room. I guess you can come if you want."

"You *guess* I can come?" Giorgio's contempt caught me off guard. "Who gives a shit about Third-World students and their music?"

My answer should have been, *Why would Third-World students give a shit about this cavalier snot of a man?* Better yet, *Why did I?*

"Enough," I said. "Don't wait up for me. Don't come knocking on my trailer."

Giorgio laughed. "For how long this time? One week? Two? You know you won't stay away," he insisted. "You want me. You *need* me."

Late that night, I leaned against Ilia's ninth-floor dormitory window and stared down at the circus. My gaze traveled past the entryway and over the blackened big top. Rings of white campers circled it like a wagon train. The animal cages looked pieced together from an erector set. For nearly two years, I'd corralled my life within Moira's crooked blue fence.

"It's all so small," I said to no one in particular.

"How did you end up in the circus?" Ilia asked. "Are you from an American circus family?"

Imagining my mother and father performing in spandex and sequins made me chuckle. "No, I was traveling—"

"With your family?"

"I started out alone."

She seemed surprised. "Americans can do that?"

"You mean Yugoslavians can't?"

"Well, there are our families to care for. Land to cultivate. College if we're lucky."

Staring down at the circus, I traced the outlines of the animal pens on the glass and said, "Something will always keep us still if we let it."

"Our reality is different than yours." Miros stood beside me at the window. "I do not understand why you would leave your family."

"Adventure," I said. "I left in search of adventure."

Miros nodded. "Did you find it?"

I listened to the empty end of a cassette wind through the tape deck. Static, then nothing.

"I thought the circus was my adventure. I'm not so sure anymore."

Ilia flipped the cassette tape, and melancholy notes filled the room. The man's voice, almost a whisper, drew me into his tune. "What is this music?"

"*Galija,*" Ilia said from behind me. "The song is 'Da li si Spavala.'"

"It's beautiful."

"It is a sad song. He says, 'Did you suffer when you realized you lost me?'"

Did you suffer when you realized you lost me?

Miros looked at my reflection in the glass. "You're crying."

"This song. It makes me think of someone."

"The man from the trapeze. You mentioned him the other day."

"No. He means nothing to me. Another man in Italy. I left him when the circus came to Yugoslavia."

"And you hurt him when you left him," Ilia said.

"I hurt both of us."

"You still love him."

I nodded.

"I do not understand this way of being." Ilia shook her head. "Leaving your family for years at a time. Leaving the man you love for one that means nothing to you. Why?"

I looked at Ilia's face, pale and questioning in the dim light of her dorm room, and waited for words to come. But I had no answers for Ilia.

In 1990, Sarajevo was destined for despair. Little over a year later, social and religious upheaval would push her to the brink of destruction. Shells. Snipers. Bunkers. Bombs. The news would report over 200,000 people murdered in Bosnia, another 200,000 injured. Half of the homes and schools would be destroyed, a third of the hospitals. The lucky survivors would hole-up in dank, gray basements, sleep ten to a room, and forage for food and firewood under the crosshairs of a sniper's rifle. Others were not so fortunate. From behind barbed wire, emaciated men and ravaged women would plead to the world for help. The signs may have already surrounded me—students' hushed conversations, the way an inter-ethnic couple clung to each other, and one man's urgency to prove the existence of his city to me, as if an outsider's memories would make the coming devastation less complete.

In spite of our efforts to make it last, summer had slipped away as I'd followed my friends through the bustling streets of Sarajevo. Shadowed by apartment buildings aligned like dominoes waiting to fall, I could not hang onto the lightness of our time together. Brilliant red and yellow leaves, the last displays of color, abandoned their branches to swirl around our feet before tumbling out of reach. Three weeks in October ended, and we all had to acknowledge that autumn had arrived.

CHAPTER THIRTY-EIGHT

FALL

Blaming others for the routes we choose is far easier than owning our mistakes. By the fall of 1990, the miles of missteps separating Stefano from me seemed inevitable . . . If only my father had loved and honored my mother as he'd promised . . . If only Stefano's parents had nurtured a lonely child . . . Lost childhoods and absent parents, deserted lovers and fallen heroes. Youthful grudges keeping two adults from loving one another.

At some point, we must forgive our parents for seeking their own happiness. We must accept responsibility if we have not found ours. My turn came a few days after we left Sarajevo for Mostar, in the middle of one of Marilena's recipes.

"*Bucatini*, Marilena-style," she said.

I spread my notebook of recipes on the table in my camper and began to write.

"One kilo fresh San Marzano tomatoes, peeled raw. Chop into four pieces and heat without adding anything, no oil, no water . . ." Marilena playfully drummed her fingers on my paper. "How far did you get?"

"Bucatini."

"How long has it been?"

"I should have started again last week. That's two I've missed."

"Being pregnant isn't the worst thing in the world, Kathleen."

"Having a baby worries me, Marilena. Having Giorgio's scares me to death."

"You thought about why?"

"Have I thought about it?" I slammed the notebook against the table. A pregnancy made Giorgio more than a mistake. Having his baby obliterated any chance I still had with Stefano. "I think about it all day, Marilena. Every day."

"Then talk to me about it."

"I don't want to talk. I just want it to go away." I opened my notebook and waited. "Come on. Finish the recipe."

Marilena stared a moment, then started over. "*Bucatini*, Marilena-style. One kilo fresh San Marzano tomatoes . . ."

My thoughts returned to Stefano. Whichever way I looked, he was there.

Did you suffer when you realized you lost me?

When bidding Ilia goodbye in Sarajevo, she presented me with the tape of the song I loved so much. Since then, I'd played it over and over, louder and louder, until its haunting lyrics vibrated the walls around me and the walls inside of me.

Did you suffer when you realized you lost me?

Three months earlier, I would have thought the song had been written for Stefano. That day in my camper, I knew it could have been written for me.

For years I'd blamed my father for destroying my girlhood

image of love, yet I'd worn those immature expectations of devotion like a tiara my first time out to the ball, draping my dreams in Cinderella scenarios, envisioning a prince committed to waltz through life with me and woo me into the sugarcoated sunset of ever after. But fairytales aren't forever. If she hadn't run off, how sweet would Cinderella have found the palace the morning after? The year after? How dedicated and charming is a two-dimensional prince when Cindy hits sixty and sports sagging breasts and woman-whiskers?

Stefano wore no shining armor. He was a real man, full of real compassion, real integrity, real problems, and, yes, real mamma-issues. And he really loved me. When our relationship teetered on the edge of failure, Stefano had come to Rijeka and reached out for me, but I'd shown him my coldest, most selfish side, and then I turned my back. It hadn't deterred him. This man knew my greatest faults and my deepest fears, and he still wanted me.

Pregnant or not, I had thrown so much away.

Instead of writing Marilena's recipe, I scribbled and scratched out and wrote again until I ended up with: *True love isn't a vow to live happily ever after, but a promise to overcome the challenges of entwining two lives and two hearts, two pasts and two futures. True love understands its own worth.*

I wanted Stefano's forgiveness, but how could I ask for it if I still hadn't forgiven my father for turning his back on my mother? My father had the right to be happy whether or not that road included the rest of us. Yes, his abandonment devastated our family, but I also believe that it caused him pain as well. Despite his methods, I had to respect my father for having the strength and determination to mend his life.

Fall descended on the circus in earnest. I willed time to stop inside of me, as if ignoring the passing days would keep Stefano and me from growing further apart, as if it would keep a baby from growing within me. Only nature proved that one day lapsed into the next. Rain battered the big top. Waterfalls gushed off tents, pounded the earth, and washed topsoil away in dark, moody rivers. In my golden blazer and plastic rain boots, I trudged to and from shows, keeping to myself, pummeled by my thoughts. I dove in and out of the shark tank, barely registering that I performed a show.

Dieter tried to lift me out of my funk and keep me on my figurative toes by pulling practical jokes while I swam with sharks. Sometimes he flipped off the lights, leaving me bumping noses with Billy Bob in the dark. Other times he'd save the three-day-old water used to defrost their fish fillets and dump it in during a show. Though I could never smell the festering fish juice, Billy Bob and Jolene scoured the tank in famished fits. With a good tail-whomping far more likely than one of them sucking me into their jaws, the novelty soon wore off. That's when Dieter kicked it up a notch and pulled both stunts at once. Dodging 300-pound torpedoes in the dark gave me a physical thrill I hadn't felt since the first time I dove into the tank, one year earlier. I imagined I was running with the bulls of Pamplona, sans horns, though I'm sure it felt more dangerous than it actually was, and Dieter's intentions were never anything but playful.

Nothing pierced my emotional fog until the day Dieter delivered a German magazine to my camper. The cover photo sent waves of nostalgia surging through me. I flipped through page after slick page to find more snapshots of American Deadheads on the band's European tour. I hadn't even known the Dead were in Europe, but one arena was only a long day's drive away. Studying photos of girls in cotton calico shifts, their expressions warm and honest and uncluttered with makeup, I thought of fun times, free times, and the girl I used to be.

That night as I lay in bed, I looked around my darkened camper. Everything about the place was temporary, its use, its placement, its tenants. I'd grown to loathe its inherent transience. A month earlier, when I'd left Rasta here alone while I spent the night with Giorgio, the dog had torn a hole in the siding trying to claw his way out. I'd never fixed the damage. Hadn't even cleaned the camper for weeks. But my detachment didn't keep its four walls from weighing me down, from fooling me into thinking I'd found stability in this circus. That I'd found home.

Hours later, I awoke with a jolt. Still dark. I pulled on sweats, crept out of my trailer and across the circus. Outside the elephant tent, I paused until I heard the night guardian snoring from his cot in the corner, and then I unlaced the door. Humid air drifted out between layers of canvas. Soiled straw and sweet hay, pungent animal scent.

So familiar, so distant.

I slipped off my clogs and stepped into the darkened tent. Seven elephants slowly took shape. Four lay on their decks, fast asleep. Katia, Babati, and Banana stood—shadowy figures, swaying endlessly, as if they could rock their way to freedom.

I can almost touch him.

My bare feet shuffled through the cool dirt; my arm stretched before me, reaching. Watching Banana shift her weight back and forth, I began to sway, mimicking her movements, moving with the elephant. Chains binding her ankles to the planks beneath her jangled in the dark.

If she understood that her own weight kept her captive, would she have the power to break free?

Two years ago, there was another line of elephants, another early morning. I may have left those elephants a thousand miles away in Spain, but Stefano's words stayed with me.

For some is possible to change, Kat'leen. For some is not.

For as long as I could remember, I'd believed my father's desertion had doomed my mother. Yet she'd finished raising her four children and helped my sister raise three more. Mom not only made it on her own, she thrived — making the dean's list while earning her master's in education. She made a lifelong best friend who helped her cast off my father's shadow and realize her own worth. Years later, my mother even found the courage to love again, marrying a man my future husband would call The Last American Gentleman.

I had spent my adult life aiming to be different — cavorting with the Grateful Dead, hitchhiking across Europe, running away with the circus — but no matter how hard I'd tried, I was just like my mother and just like everyone else: trying to figure out who I am, whom I love, and where I go from here.

CHAPTER THIRTY-NINE

BURIED TREASURE

Spalato, "little palace," is what Italians call the town of Split. In this beautiful city on the Dalmatian coast, millions of time-smoothed limestone blocks blend seamlessly into slick white buildings. Deep within Split's curved facade lies a jewel, the remnants of Diocletian's fourth-century retirement villa, the little palace. I remember wandering under the city's towering colonnades and massive portals on the day we arrived, and I know their ability to weather time and troubles comforted me. I did not expect to find treasure there.

I spent our first full day in *Spalato* as I did in many towns: situating my camper, locating nearby stores and cafes, learning the lay of the land. One of the stores I'd wandered into was a perfumery. The clerk spoke English well, and I so enjoyed the distraction of speaking with someone who wasn't from the circus that I stayed for an hour, buying a sack of lipsticks and liners I didn't need. For that hour, the worry of being pregnant with a child I didn't want from a man I didn't love while longing for the man I'd lost faded under the normalcy of shopping for makeup.

After the show that night, Marilena left her husband and son to fend for themselves and dragged me from my camper, demanding that I come out to eat and drink. She said I'd lost more weight and looked rough around the edges. I'd argued, but Marilena had argued harder, and now here I was, walking out of the restaurant, belly full and head soft.

"Asshole," Marilena muttered, sidestepping the midnight blue Mercedes that blocked our pathway back to the circus.

Sixty feet away, beyond the gravel alley separating the restaurant from the circus fence, Moira's hodgepodge of campers and cages waited. I breathed in the cool autumn air and felt refreshed from doing something besides listening to gears grind in my head. A surge of defiance followed. I leapt onto the trunk of the rudely parked blue sedan and strode over its roof, splitting Pippo's Mercedes in half with a line of dusty footprints.

Knowing the man's temper all too well, Marilena squealed. "That's going to piss him off."

"Who cares?" I jumped off the hood, head high and arms raised in a full circus-queen salute to my one-woman audience. "The blood of baby animals paid for this car. I'd tell him to his face that I did it."

"You just might have to."

I followed Marilena's gaze back to the restaurant's doors. Pippo marched out, his dark stare fixed on his sullied car.

He quickened his pace. "Who did this?"

Bolstered by the half liter of house wine we'd had with dinner, I raised my chin and chirped, "I did."

"You little shit. You need to learn respect."

"For you?" Inches from his boiling eyes, I said, "A man who steals animals' lives flash by flash?"

Short breaths burst from the photographer. His arms clenched and unclenched. I watched him raise a widespread palm and figured he was about to deliver his rage across my face.

"What's this all about?" Giorgio's drawl flowed out of the darkened circus a moment before he did.

I didn't realize I was shaking until the photographer's arm eased back down.

"You tell your goddamned woman to keep her feet off my car." He swatted dirty prints off his hood with one hand and fished keys from his pocket with the other. "She cleans it tomorrow or there *will* be trouble." Pippo lunged into his car, spewing gravel as he peeled away.

"Why, Giorgio—how chivalrous of you," I said. "Happened to be nearby?"

Giorgio shrugged and reached out, steadying my hand, suggesting a drink to calm my nerves. Smiling like the Cheshire Cat, Giorgio tugged me along as he backtracked into the circus. I followed him, leaving Marilena and good judgment in front of the restaurant's door.

In the darkness of his camper, I listened to wine gurgle from its bottle. Giorgio settled next to me and coiled a curl around one of his fingers. He said, "You like the way I play with your hair."

His breath on my neck. Warm hand caressing my shoulder.

He said, "You need someone to touch you."

I longed for one man's arms but found myself easing toward another's.

"You want me."

But I didn't want him. I wanted Stefano.

Giorgio bulldozed on top of me. "I know how to please you."

"This isn't pleasure." I squirmed under him. "You've never come close to pleasing me."

"Liar." He licked the side of my face.

"Never."

His erection shrank like an old balloon.

"What the hell do you expect?" Giorgio rolled away, slammed his fist against the wall. "I pulled a muscle in my thigh last night. Haven't slept well all week. Had to break up your stupid fight with Pippo. And the food here is *disgusting*."

Standing at the edge of his bed, Giorgio clutched his crotch and stared as if expecting an apology and a plea to resume, but his chiaroscuro antics would never again fool me into seeing him as more than a Machiavellian man.

"Who the hell did you sleep with before me?" he yelled. "Superman?"

"Enough, Giorgio. This—*we*—are over."

"*Nothing's* over." He shook his head as I fumbled with buttons and straightened my skirt. "In the last two months I've slept with seven women—*two* of them married." He watched me pull on my shoes. "You'll come back. They always come back."

In that moment, with his sneering face and threatening eyes, I saw Giorgio perfectly. I saw how he had exposed my needs, manipulated my loss, and burrowed his way into my life. And in that moment of clarity, with no contrived affair to hide behind, I could finally get down to the business of asking myself what the hell I was doing.

I ran to my trailer, to the only pieces of Stefano within my reach. Deep in my closet, under the leather tools that were too heavy for him to take and the sweaters that were too bulky, laid a shoebox of cassettes. I pulled out Dire Straits, and Mark Knopfler soon bared his heart to Juliet, asking her when she was going to realize it was just that the time was wrong.

Slumped on the floor, face buried in the fibers of Stefano's crimson sweater, I inhaled his scent. If only we'd tried to love each other somewhere besides the circus. What if it was just that the place was wrong? No. Blaming the circus made even less sense than blaming our parents. I sank deeper into his sweater, shrouded myself in darkness, descended into the quiet. The depth of quiet that makes the world seem still. Even makes a circus seem still. It is the stillness that I remember. And how clear everything became once the wheels in my head stopped.

I saw a flicker of color, a hint of an idea: *Stefano and I had created our own problems by attempting to separate the parts of the other we wanted from those we didn't, as if doing so ensured our emotional safety.*

I reached for the thought, prodding it with my finger, encouraging it to emerge: *Just as Stefano needed me to nurture him and feed him, his proof that I wouldn't leave him as others had, I needed to be the sole recipient of his attention, as if dedicating himself to anything else lessened his feelings for me.*

I took hold of the concept and drew it closer. Like a magician's scarf trick, colors flowed into the night—hues of understanding, rainbows of potential, brightening my world with a revelation: *Stefano's passion enflamed all areas of his life—his elephants, his food, his problems, his love. For two years, I'd both fanned and fought his fire, summoning it some places while smothering it in others. Success would have left me half a man.*

I wanted the whole man.

I wanted the warm, solid feeling of my hand in his. I wanted to listen to his breath while I fell asleep, to feel the length of him spooning against me while I basked in the warmth the closeness of our bodies created. I wanted Stefano's honesty, his honor, his love, and I would embrace the parts of him I had shunned just to have the rest. Tracing where he'd scrawled his name inside the closet door, I realized that I didn't love him in spite of his passion; I loved him because of it. Stefano wasn't perfect, and neither was I, but we were perfect for each other.

I want the whole man.

Hope sparkled within me. Faith that if I reached for Stefano, he would still be reaching for me.

Skimming through life isn't enough anymore.

With picks of my father's determination and shovels of my mother's endurance, I dug deep and found hope, faith, and courage. Buried treasure.

The defensive, stubborn girl eased her grip on the maturing woman in me. I still had that girl's strength, but less of her fear. Still had her adventurous spirit, but not her need to hide behind it.

Yes. I would declare my feelings to Stefano, tell him about Giorgio. And if I were pregnant, I would tell him that too.

Empowered by my mother, my father, and two Baileys in a curbside bar, I braved my way back to the perfumery I'd visited the week before, on the day we had arrived in *Spalato*. I remember how the woman's caring eyes had drawn me into her shop during my first stroll through the city. This time, I fiddled with tubes of gloss and mustered the strength to ask this near stranger for all the help she could give.

"Hello, American circus girl." The blonde's face brightened. "More lipstick already? Perhaps a new shade of blush?" She pulled a carton from under the counter. "We have some new colors fresh from—"

"No colors." *Shit-shit-shit-shit-shit-shit-shit,* echoed my mother's voice. "I've come to ask for help." *Shit-shit-shit-shit-shit-shit-shit,* echoed my own. "I might be in trouble."

She set the box down.

"I've missed two of my periods. Menstruation. Do you understand? I'm afraid I'm pregnant. I need help."

"Your husband, he does not want a baby?"

"He's not my husband."

"Sorry. I mean your friend."

"He's not my friend."

"I see. And you wish to—"

"I only need to know whether or not I'm pregnant."

"I understand. There is a doctor who makes a procedure." She said a word I did not understand. "It is a camera that sees inside of you."

"He can tell me for sure?"

"The camera does not lie. If there is a baby, he will see it. You will see it too." She touched my hand. "I can make the arrangements. Take you there."

A few mornings later, a balding man in a tired white coat called me into his office and motioned to the metal exam chair. I took a deep breath and concentrated on the emptiness of the dark-paneled walls surrounding me. With my stomach exposed and my future at stake, I held my breath and let the doctor pass his cold ultrasound wand over my belly.

He cleared his throat, looking uncomfortable as he swiveled his video screen toward me. Dark blobs wavered behind fuzzy gray and white lines.

"Oh God. What is all that stuff inside me?"

He spoke softly in Croatian. The woman from the perfumery translated, saying "Nothing is there."

"Nothing?" I studied the hazy masses. "Are you sure?"

The doctor took my hand and shook his head.

"Oh thank you." I squeezed his fingers, then reached out and squeezed his shoulders. "*Thank you.*"

He pulled back and spoke.

"What? What's he saying?"

"Your actions surprise him. He does not remember another patient who is happy when he gives her bad news, when she is not pregnant."

"Tell him this is good news. Very, very good news."

Relief. First in drops, then in waves. Swirling, rushing, magnificent waves heaving me closer to shore.

"Hey." I pulled the coiled phone cord through my fingers. "It's me."

"Kat'leen."

How I'd longed to hear him say my name.

"When you are coming back to Italy?"

"November 26—to Treviso. Still two weeks." *Forever.*

"Is okay if I come to see you?"

"I would like that."

"Tell them you take some days off. We go to Venice."

"Wait." *He must know, no matter the consequence.* "There was . . ." I clutched the phone to my face, pushed the hard black plastic into my temple until my eye watered. "Another . . ."

His breath rushed across the receiver. "Dieter or Giorgio?"

"How . . . Who . . ." Guilt buckled my knees as I waited for his outburst, but the yelling never came. "You knew."

"I saw them both in Rijeka, circling your camper like vultures. I smelled their *want* the entire time I was there." I listened to him breathing into the phone. "When you didn't call . . ."

"Giorgio."

Again I waited for his yelling to start, but Stefano remained quiet. I fought the urge to say that I wished it had never happened, but no words could take back what I'd done. And only by using Giorgio as some hideous viewing glass had I recognized what I'd forsaken in Stefano.

"I didn't want to hurt you, Stefano. I'm sorry."

"No. I'm sorry. I never should have left you. That night—if only—"

"Things happen for a reason. What if you'd never brought Rasta home and I had gone with you on the motorcycle to Milan? If things didn't get better, I would have left for America. Six thousand miles is a hell of a long way apart to work things out."

"Is what you want, Kat'leen? To work things out?"

"I . . . I don't know." *You* do *know.* "Yes."

CHAPTER FORTY

FULL CIRCLE

"I'm nervous, Marilena."

"About cleaning mussels?"

"About seeing Stefano."

"I'm teasing, Kathleen." She pulled a mussel from the tub of water it soaked in. "You see this?" She pointed to a tuft of green protruding from the shell. "You don't want it in your sauce. Pull it toward the mussel's point until it rips off."

I stared at the mountain of mussels. "I'm supposed to clean every one of these?"

Marilena dipped her arms elbow-deep and pulled out a handful. "They'd already be halfway done if you worked instead of whined." She shook the water from her hands and pulled two pots from a cupboard. "One for the pasta water," which she filled almost full, "and one to steam the *cozze*," which Marilena set on the counter. "Fill it up."

I lifted a mussel out of the tub and inspected it. "It's not even seaweed, is it? More like hair—which is kind of disgusting, don't you think?"

"If mussels don't disgust you when they're on your plate, they shouldn't disgust you in the kitchen."

"Okay, okay." I pulled green tendrils while Marilena minced garlic. "Stefano's going to ask me why I went with Giorgio. I don't have an answer . . . except that I needed to get away. Perhaps I knew better than to leave physically, so I left mentally—by hooking up with his exact opposite."

Marilena lit the fire under the pasta water and added a handful of rock salt. "Sometimes," she said, "walking away from something is the only way to see it clearly."

Her words reminded me of the time another woman had told me the same thing. I rolled around in my past for a few minutes and then said, "Life is just a big circle, Marilena. Years ago, I lived in a Volkswagen bus in San Francisco. This band I'd been following was between their summer and fall tour, so I stayed in the city doing temporary office jobs. One day on my way to work, this man runs a red light and bashes into my van. When I'd awakened that morning, I had a perfect traveling nest that enabled me to live the way I wanted. Half an hour later, nothing. I had to ask an aunt that I barely knew if I could move in with her." I tossed the last of the mussels into the pot. "They're clean. Now what?"

"Heat the pot over a low flame."

"Should I add oil or something?"

"It's their water we're after. Hold the lid on and shake them around like popcorn. Keep the pot moving and the flame low." Marilena tossed garlic into a frying pan she'd doused with oil. "Their water is where your sauce's flavor comes from. We don't want it evaporating."

I clutched the pan with hot pads and continued my story

over the clatter of shells. "So without my van, my home, life as I knew it ended. My Aunt Marilyn and I became close over the next few months, and one day I told her how lost I felt. You know what she told me? That I was lucky—because I was far enough removed from the life I'd been living before the accident that I could see it clearly enough to determine whether it was really where I wanted to be. If it still was, then great, she said, take the insurance money, buy a new van, and get back on the road. But if I figured out it wasn't, I ought to create something new. By changing the aspects of my life that were wrong, I'd bring strength to the aspects of my life that were right."

"Your aunt knew what she was talking about—are you shaking that pot, Kathleen?"

"I'm shaking, I'm shaking."

"Look inside. Are they opening yet? Is there any water?"

Salty steam billowed when I lifted the lid. "One opened. Two. Three. What do I do?"

"Spoon them out as they open. If you leave them in too long, you might as well be making pasta with chewing gum." She set a serving bowl beside me.

I pulled mussel after mussel out of the pot, their black shells spread wide like smiling faces with fat orange tongues of soft mussel meat. Along with the meat, I saw things I didn't want in my mouth. "What do we do about the guts?"

"It comes complete, Kathleen. We eat everything inside the shell. You're not burning that water, are you?"

"I'm not burning the water, Marilena."

The bowl filled with open mussels as the pot emptied until only two remained.

"Never eat shellfish that stays shut." Marilena tossed the two mussels and placed the pan with the garlic on her camper-sized cook stove. "Now strain your water into a glass through a single layer of paper towel."

We bent our heads down to watch sand and shell settle on the makeshift sieve while mussel juice filtered through the paper towel. "So?" Marilena asked. "What did you do about your van?"

"I bought myself a new van with the insurance check, fixed it up, and continued following the Grateful Dead—except that the second time around was even better. Rather than living a life I'd happened into, I chose to be there." Looking at the glass of cloudy water before us, I said, "This is our sauce?"

"Almost." She poured the mussel water into the pan of garlic and oil. The burst of steam spread the aroma of the sea. "If you wanted a tomato sauce, you'd sauté chopped tomatoes with the garlic and oil before adding the mussel water," she explained. "But you wouldn't add the liquid the tomatoes come in because—"

"Because we'd have the mussel water instead."

We both smiled.

"While this reduces, discard half the shells, but leave some for color. Wait until the last minute to toss it all together so the mussels don't overcook, and we'll have *cozze in bianco,* cooked to perfection."

Soon, spaghetti embraced the mussels in our bowls. Each time I made an effort to turn a pile of raw ingredients into a hearty meal, both process and product fascinated me more and more. I savored each bite, recognizing the individual nuances of parsley and garlic and sea. I'd eaten this dish dozens of times, but it had never tasted so good.

"So it's all a big circle," I said, washing dishes beside Marilena after Carmine had left for the bar. "I've been so many places mentally and physically since that thing with my van, learned so many things, yet here I am, three years later, in almost the same spot."

Seashells tinkled into the trash as Marilena scraped a bowl. "And what are you going to do this time?"

"I want Stefano. I want him more than anything I've ever wanted." I rinsed soap off the pasta pot and passed it into her waiting hands. "But it will never be the same."

"It's not supposed to be," Marilena dried the enameled dish and returned it to its place in her cupboard. "You're not the same. He won't be either. How can what's between you be the same?"

From across the *piazza* in Treviso, Stefano watched me drive a circus van onto the lot. Puffs of steamy breath rose from his lips, one after another, faster and faster, as if he were a locomotive building speed. I chugged to a halt next to him. Through glass, we held each other's gaze.

I rolled down the window.

My breath caught in my throat when he caressed my cheek. We stayed there, frozen in the moment of our first touch. In his eyes, I saw nervous hope. Could he see the same in mine?

I reached for his fingers. Stefano closed his eyes and inhaled, holding his breath as I pressed his hand against my face.

"Cold hands," I said.

"Italy is freezing lately. Yugoslavia too?"

"Not so bad. A lot of rain . . ." How handsome he looked with his cheeks flushed from autumn's chill. "Milan is good?"

Stefano shrugged. "I work for a moving company. The hours are long, but at least the job doesn't follow me home. My mother says *ciao.*"

"Thanks . . . You see your parents much?"

"Sundays for lunch," he said, reaching for the cigarettes in his pocket. "Wednesdays for dinner, when I'm home early enough from work."

"Wow. Twice a week instead of twice a year."

"We still fight." Stefano flicked his lighter and inhaled a mouthful of smoke. "I guess is a start," he said, smiling and looking down in a way that made him look sheepish.

"And your gramma?"

"Fine." He stared at my face. "You've lost more weight."

I nodded. "Too much. I'm working on gaining some back."

Stefano looked in the back of the van. "Rasta?"

"Marilena's keeping him while we're in Venice."

"Good. Good." He studied three yellow and blue trucks as they trundled into the lot. "The *elefanti* are okay?"

"Seem to be. I don't see them much."

"Giuseppe?"

"Same as always."

Stefano tossed his cigarette and flattened it into the asphalt. "I'm going to find him when we come back. To apologize. I ran out on him too." He fumbled with the change in his pocket. "I don't miss the circus, Kat'leen. It helped me when I needed it, but I don't need it anymore." Stefano pulled on the door latch and reached for my hand. "All I want from here is you."

Twenty minutes later in Mestre, we boarded a train to cross the water to Venice. Rails tick-tocked beneath the train, counting down the seconds until we would be alone. In the empty space between our seats, Stefano's fingers found mine. Though he held onto me with the strength of an elephant keeper, his skin no longer felt as rough.

He slipped a small package between our hands. "For your birthday."

Layers of ribbon and tissue unveiled a necklace. Irregular black beads suspended a triangular pendant of tarnished silver. "How unusual." I ran my finger over hand-stamped markings and down the single strand of beads that hung from the point of the triangle. "It's beautiful. Thank you."

"Is Tuareg. Nomads. The man who sold it says is old," Stefano explained. "All the beads are made by hand. The thread is weak—has been broken and tied in knots. A few may be missing, but the beads are still perfect. They just need to be restrung. The pendant," he said as his finger traveled down my collar bone to rest between my breasts, "is meant to sit right here."

His touch rocked my body. I leaned into him as he clasped the beads around my neck. The necklace seemed to cling to my bare skin. I held Stefano's hand against my chest and let his warmth wash through me as Venice, the eternal symbol of perseverance, emerged from the fog.

Pink paint. A gilded mirror. The same lopsided chandelier. My palm slid easily over the smooth wooden dresser that had knocked against the wall when we'd made midnight love on top of it. At the window, I looked down at the Cannaregio Canal and recalled the early-morning fish market ruckus from our last visit. *So long ago.*

Turning around, I said, "It's the same room."

"I wanted everything perfect."

"It doesn't have to be perfect, Stefano. It only has to be real."

He dropped our bags next to the door and came to me, took my face in his hands.

Lips so close, we shared the same breath. A timid kiss. Hesitant hands reaching for bodies they knew so well. His scent. His embrace. Home.

Buttons, zippers, skin. We plunged into each other, made frantic love. Love for the past, as if raw force could wipe away the months we'd spent apart. Then, exhausted, we held each other's bared bodies while our lungs caught up with our frenzy. As our breathing slowed, our thoughts were no longer of the past.

Stefano whispered in my ear, "Can you love me again?"

"I never stopped." My tears fell on his chest. I smoothed the drops across his skin, blended them with his sweat, spread them through his curls. "I want all of you. Everything you have been, everything you are, everything you will be."

I want the whole man.

Stefano wiped my cheek with his finger.

I said, "But that only works if I give you all of me. I always thought that meant I would lose myself. Not anymore. You know who I am. You've seen my best and my worst, and you're still here. I believe in you, Stefano. I believe in us."

The second time we made love, we made slow love, deliberate love. Love for our future. We lingered over each touch, savored each taste, prolonged each pleasure. Understanding that our future would be as entwined as our bodies were at that moment, I anchored myself to Stefano, to the breath, the life, the love that coaxed my own into being.

I'd been running for years—trapped, as a friend once said, by the very wind in my hair. That relentless running had brought me to the one place I wanted to stay: with Stefano. Because if I didn't, I would spend my life searching for what I have found in him: Permanence. A kindred soul. Proof that I am both capable and worthy of love.

The day I arrived at the circus in Spain, I carried only a backpack. When I left Circo Moira Orfei in 1991, two years of my life overflowed from the bags and boxes Stefano and I squeezed into an Italian-sized station wagon. Pots, pans, and photographs. Jewelry, scarves, and the black woolen vest I'd bought in Rome. Hand-painted pasta bowls. My Easy Bake oven. Blankets from Greece. A pink stuffed elephant ballerina; a dog-eared, tear-stained journal; and a leather notebook filled with Marilena's recipes. Useless or treasured, these were belongings I would not leave behind. Nor would I leave behind a single memory, a single experience, or the lessons I learned from them.

As much as I had tried to blame the circus for dividing Stefano and me, it's just as likely that our marriage to Moira is what held two opposites together, and I must credit her and her circus for teaching me that life is more than a linear sequence of people and places. I will never say that my circus years were all good, but I will say that good came of them. I may not remember how to ride an elephant, but I will remember how to open my heart to love. I may never again fly through the ring on an ostrich, but I will refuse to allow the weight of my own fears to hold me captive. I may never dive into another shark tank, but I will dive wholeheartedly into the untamed emotions of an authentic life.

Car packed and goodbyes said, Stefano took my hand and set his gaze on the elephant tent. The moment he crossed the threshold, all seven elephants turned their heads. Their rumble started low, like distant thunder. Soon, a deafening roar trembled the air and filled the tent. Little Shiva, head bobbing and ears flapping, punctuated the chorus with porpoise squeals. Humbled by their affection, Stefano lowered his head. I wondered if the elephants understood he would never return. Elephants may never forget, but I believe they forgive, and surely these elephants forgave Stefano for breaking the chains that bound him to them.

True to the legacy of the Hindu deity Ganesha, they helped both of us remove the obstacles in our lives. My debt to these symbols of patience, strength, wisdom, and dignity could never be repaid, for it was here in the elephant tent that I learned my most important lessons. Simplicity. Truth. Respect. Love. These were the ideals I wanted to live by, and these were the things Stefano had to offer. Neither his elephants nor I would ever forget.

Hand in hand, we returned to the car. Rasta jumped in, climbed over the seats, and wedged himself into a perfect Rasta-sized hole between two boxes. I slipped in after him and patted my pocketful of bills—my full retainer, given to me by Walter the night before. Because I had enough balls to be honest with him, he'd said. Answered truthfully when asked my intentions after seeing Stefano in Venice. I refused to run under the cover of night, choosing instead to leave the circus on my own terms, head high and heart full.

Stefano slid into the driver's seat and squeezed my hand. "Ready?"

I nodded. "For anything and everything."

My circus adventure was ending, but the greatest journey of my life had just begun. Glancing back at the sea of yellow and blue, I thought about how Italians use the same greeting for both goodbye and hello and whispered, "*Ciao*, *ciao*."

EPILOGUE

A RECIPE FOR LIFE

Oregon, two decades later

I hear his motorcycle approach and look up from my work. The dogs are already at the gate, yapping and turning in circles. Lunchtime. Stefano will be hungry; he is always hungry. His hunger still makes him *nervoso*, especially if a meal is not yet in the works. It's as if he fears food will never come again. I sigh and smile. I love him, all of him, even the great hunger that can agitate his normally sweet demeanor until it verges on craziness.

He revs the Guzzi's engine just before shutting it off. His footsteps pound across wooden deck boards as I arrive in the kitchen. To ease his anxiety, I swing open the pantry just as the front door opens to a rush of cold autumn air, scampering canine feet, and the swish of riding boots across the threshold.

Stefano doles cookies to our three dogs, Noodle, Squeak,

and Sweet Ding. Rasta is here only in spirit. He lived to the ripe old age of seventeen, fraternizing with chickens and horses rather than ostriches and tigers, and is buried in the shade of a nearby tree.

"Ciao, amore." Three strides into the room and Stefano is nestling his chilled fingers into my curls and kissing me with lips that haven't touched a cigarette for fifteen years. His hazel eyes light on mine for only a moment before he turns to slice a crust off the freshly baked loaf of bread on the counter. "Food?" he asks, moving toward the refrigerator. His rummaging produces a chunk of spicy salami. The cutting board and knife are already in my hands when he turns around. He winks and begins to peel the meat.

"It's going to freeze soon," I say, watching our cat Jake wind around Stefano's legs. Across the room, another cat, Elwood, curls beside the fire burning in the wood stove. Stefano stops his work to reach down and stroke Jake's tail. "I thought I'd pick the last of the tomatoes and make a sauce," I continue. "A quick sauce." Quartering the San Marzanos and draining their juices means they won't have to cook so long, which will not only placate his urgency, but also capture any fresh taste of summer that remains on the vines.

Stefano nods as he offers me the first slice off the salami, my favorite part because it is firmer and chewier, and I savor the wedge of spicy meat he places in my mouth.

"The sauce sounds perfect," he says. "Is it ready yet?"

I step outside and walk toward the garden, away from the stand of Douglas firs shading this old motel where my mother once lived. Her new home is just ten minutes away, in a house on a hill, where her husband showers her with the love and companionship she deserves. My widowed grandmother lives in a cottage next to our home. Stefano adores her, adores how she lessens the void his own grandmother's passing left some years back. It is good to be surrounded by family, just as it is good to be in close contact with Stefano's parents.

As Stefano matured and gained his footing, their past disagreements lost traction, and the intangible barriers that kept them at odds turned to dust. These days, Stefano worries if he doesn't speak to his mother by phone once a week. We have made the pilgrimage back to the land of pasta and polenta a dozen times, and Angela has made nearly as many journeys to America. Angelo has overcome his hectic coaching schedule and fear of flying to travel here twice. During his last visit, I remember the pride with which he witnessed his entrepreneurial son live his own version of the American dream — the successful import business he built from scratch, the home he helped renovate, the five acres of land he nurtured to park-like splendor. And I remember how Angelo's shoulders jerked as he swiped at goodbye tears in the airport. Public tears, from a man unaccustomed to displaying emotion. How proud he must be of the son who pulled himself out of the muck of his late teens and early twenties. Proud, perhaps, that while wading through a different kind of muck in the circus, Stefano found a soul mate that he was willing to lean on, to prop up, to walk beside. A wife to share life, liberty, and, as Stefano says, "the *purr-sweet* of happiness."

I pick a dozen richly hued tomatoes to fill my basket, and I appreciate the contrast of brilliant red and deep green as I lay a frond of basil on top. Returning to the house, I pause to bask in the warmth I feel as I step into the great room. Our home, which we have toiled to renovate over the past few years, fills me with contentment. I glance over the ceramic floor, 600 square feet of Italian tiles in this area alone, set with nine straight days of knee-bruising labor, and I appreciate how well they complement the plaster painted in colors reminiscent of the great marble halls of Milan. My eyes pause on the sturdy cabinetry, crafted with our own hands, and come to rest on our bountiful kitchen where Stefano already has a pasta pot on the stove and is slivering a clove of garlic. I inhale the aromas of a happy life and know that this is a place I will never need to escape.

AUTHOR'S NOTE

GIVING BACK

A portion of the author's revenue from book sales will be donated to Elephant Nature Park in Chiang Mai, Thailand, and the Elephant Sanctuary in Hohenwald, Tennessee. If you're interested in helping these magnificent animals, you can find small and large ways to donate by visiting LoveInTheElephantTent.com or KathleenCremonesi.com.

Elephant Nature Park is the vision of Sangduen "Lek" Chailert, a tiny woman with a gigantic heart. On her 250-acre reserve, she has saved dozens of elephants, many leftovers from banned logging operations. Using a combination of volunteer labor, personal funds, and international donations, Elephant Nature Park offers sanctuary, advocates for elephants' rights and welfare, and educates both Thai people and the rest of the world on the Asian elephants' fight for survival. Seventeen years after leaving Circo Moira Orfei, while traveling in Thailand, Stefano and I stumbled upon this magical place and were once again surrounded by elephants.

Virtually every elephant at the park has a horrific past. Some were methamphetamine addicts, drugged so they could work 24 hours a day; one's foot was blown off by a landmine; another was blinded by an owner who pelted one eye with rocks and shot the other out with an arrow. Others were so mistreated, they arrived bodies broken and riddled with infection.

Italy is 5,000 miles from Thailand, but the mentality of keeping a wild animal in chains and forcing it to perform for anyone's enjoyment is not so distant. I believe that the circus holds a place in modern society, and I honor its influence on my life as I cannot imagine another likely scenario in which I would have crossed paths with my soul mate. But I feel very strongly that no exotic animal or caged, domestic animal should be a part of the spectacle. During our years in the circus, Stefano and I never witnessed the level of abuse most of Lek's rescues have suffered. But some circuses do abuse animals. Every circus owner will argue that their menagerie is not mistreated. Even when that is true, it is wrong to shackle animals for entertainment or profit. Circus owners may argue that their elephants are content with their lives. No.

Hell no.

Perhaps captive elephants accept their fate, but I believe it is only because they understand that their destiny is out of their control.

Stefano and I jumped at the opportunity to spend the remaining five days of our vacation at Elephant Nature Park, sleeping in a bamboo hut and donating our labor to feed and bathe elephants, repair fences, bag manure, and clean mud holes. Between tasks, we informed day visitors of the park's mission and encouraged them to learn more by introducing them to the animals. Observing the elephants interacting freely with their family groups is heartwarming, and watching the four babies tussle with each other in the mud pit can be pure belly-laughing joy. Despite the scars, limps, and other blatant reminders of the elephants' histories, it is clear that they are finally living in peace.

Working toward the success of this sanctuary was both a humbling and empowering experience for Stefano and me, and we continue to support the park. For over twenty years, elephants have bound our hearts and fueled our dreams. In a very small way, we are finally giving something back.

ACKNOWLEDGMENTS

Some books take a long time to write, and some take even longer, especially when the author ran away with a circus in lieu of college. And no matter how long they take, manuscripts often wouldn't reach the finish line without a community of supporters offering patience, encouragement, and straight-up critiques along the way.

Mom, I cannot imagine a more generous or supportive person. You've helped my dreams take flight since before I could walk and have steadfastly had my back since before you could hold me in your arms. I am grateful every day for your friendship, love, and presence in my life.

To my father and the rest of my family, American and Italian, I appreciate your willingness to let me spill bits and pieces of our lives onto these pages. And thank you to Tonya Alanez, the best friend a girl could ask for during her formative years. Your unflinching curiosity and tenacity set my own into high gear and helped open the doors of my future.

Allison Picard, a woman of many wise and wonderful words, you always believed in this story, even when I didn't. Thank you for keeping the faith that these memories would one day become a book. Danuta Pfeiffer and Jacquie Manning, thank you for your endless time, encouragement, generosity, laughter, tears, and honesty along the way. And for at least trying to teach me the difference between an adverb and an adjective. I cannot imagine a more perfect writing group — and if there is, their wine definitely isn't as good.

I'm grateful for all the past writing group members, colleagues, friends, and extended family who trudged through early versions and encouraged me to keep at it, especially: Kelly Wilson, Nome May, Tamara Embrey, Cai Emmons, Angela Rinaldi, Marilyn Harryman, Zoe Hood, Mabel Armstrong, Michael Harryman, and the ever-encouraging Anne Summers. Cary English, your passion for life and love lives on in these pages.

Eric Myers, my faithful agent, thank you for your stamina and commitment to go the distance. Your enthusiasm has been indispensable. Willamette Writers, your top-notch conferences helped bring these words from the storage room to the bookstore. Jack David and the rest of the team at ECW Press, thank you for taking a chance on my story — especially Emily Schultz, my editor, whose gentle hand and strong support eased me through the final steps.

Bryan Batt and Melissa Hart, thank you for your generosity to read and review an advance copy.

And last, but certainly not least, to my husband, whose love has never waned. You are my best friend. Without you, there wouldn't be a story to tell. Thank you for having a heart large enough to offer refuge to wild animals and a wild girl.

To everyone above, and to all those I may have missed here but who know who they are, *grazie mille*. I appreciate your contributions to this work. You are all elephants in my life.

Published by ECW Press
665 Gerrard Street East
Toronto, Ontario M4M 1Y2
416-694-3348 / info@ecwpress.com

To the best of her abilities, the author has related experiences, places, people, and organizations from her memories of them. In order to protect the privacy of others, she has, in some instances, changed the names of certain people and details of events and places.

LIBRARY AND ARCHIVES CANADA CATALOGUING IN PUBLICATION

Cremonesi, Kathleen, author
Love in the elephant tent : how running away with the circus brought me home / Kathleen Cremonesi.

Issued in print and electronic formats.
ISBN 978-1-77041-252-1 (BOUND)
978-1-77090-730-0 (PDF)
978-1-77090-731-7 (EPUB)

1. Cremonesi, Kathleen. 2. Women circus performers—Mediterranean Region—Biography. 3. Women circus performers—United States—Biography.

I. TITLE.

GV1811.C74A3 2015 791.3092
C2014-907594-4 C2014-907595-2

Cover design: Michel Vrana
Cover images: tent © Valentino Sani / Arcangel Images, elephant © Tribalium / Shutterstock
Case image: © kvasay / vectorstock
Author photo: Jamie Hooper
Interior images courtesy of Kathleen and Stefano Cremonesi, except where otherwise credited.

PRINTING: FRIESENS 5 4 3 2 1
PRINTED AND BOUND IN CANADA

Mechanics' Institute Library
3 1750 03409 3107